W9-BNW-857

FUNDING
HIGHER EDUCATION

The Praeger Special Studies
Series in Comparative Education

General Editor: Philip G. Altbach

ACADEMIC POWER: Patterns of Authority in Seven National
Systems of Higher Education
  John H. Van de Graaff
  Burton R. Clark
  Dorotea Furth
  Dietrich Goldschmidt
  Donald F. Wheeler

ADAPTATION AND EDUCATION IN JAPAN
  Nobuo K. Shimahara

CHANGES IN THE JAPANESE UNIVERSITY:
A Comparative Perspective
  edited by
  William K. Cummings
  Ikuo Amano
  Kazuyuki Kitamura

COMPARATIVE PERSPECTIVES ON THE ACADEMIC
PROFESSION
  edited by
  Philip G. Altbach

FUNDING HIGHER EDUCATION: A Six-Nation Analysis
  edited by
  Lyman A. Glenny

US AND UK EDUCATIONAL POLICY: A Decade of Reform
  Edgar Litt
  Michael Parkinson

Published in cooperation with the
Center for Comparative Education,
State University of New York, Buffalo

FUNDING HIGHER EDUCATION
A Six-Nation Analysis

Edited by

Lyman A. Glenny

Foreword by Ladislav Cerych

Contributors:

Rossetos Fakiolas, Aldo Gandiglio, Pierre Goldberg,
Jan-Erik Lane, and Alberto Moncada

PRAEGER

PRAEGER SPECIAL STUDIES • PRAEGER SCIENTIFIC

Library of Congress Cataloging in Publication Data

Main entry under title:

Funding higher education.

   (Praeger special studies series in comparative
education)
   Bibliography: p.
   1. Education, Higher--France--Finance.
2. Education, Higher--Greece--Finance. 3. Education,
Higher--Italy--Finance. 4. Education, Higher--Spain--
Finance. 5. Education, Higher--Sweden--Finance.
I. Glenny, Lyman A. II. Fakiolas, Rossetos.
LB2342.2.F8F86   379'.1214   79-4557
ISBN 0-03-049616-0

PRAEGER PUBLISHERS
PRAEGER SPECIAL STUDIES
383 Madison Avenue, New York, N.Y. 10017, U.S.A.

Published in the United States of America in 1979
by Praeger Publishers,
A Division of Holt, Rinehart and Winston, CBS, Inc.

9   038   987654321

© 1979 by Praeger Publishers

Printed in the United States of America

This book is dedicated to

my mentors

Frank Bourgin

Richard G. Browne

T. R. McConnell

Kirk Porter

and my wife

Helen

FOREWORD
Ladislav Cerych

The relevance of comparative studies in education no longer
needs to be justified. It may be asked, however, whether a topic as
specific as the one at hand, that is, the problems of financing and
budget procedures in higher education, can be usefully explored by
comparing the experiences in countries as different from each other
as Greece and the United States, or Sweden and Spain. The present
volume, I believe, provides an affirmative answer to that question.
It also illustrates a particular relevance of comparative studies,
which is not always fully recognized.

It can be argued that this relevance, and thus the specific reasons justifying comparative studies in higher education, fall under
three categories (Cerych 1974): (1) borrowing ("learning from the experience of others"); (2) creating pressure for change and innovation;
and (3) gaining a better understanding of one's own system by using
the comparative method as an analytical tool.

"Borrowing" has undoubtedly been the main rationale for comparative education since its early stages of development (Noah and
Eckstein 1969). Even today, most international meetings and comparative studies undertaken probably have the same purpose in mind:
to find out about how things are done elsewhere; to learn from the
achievements and failures of others.

A less widely acknowledged, but far from negligible, motive behind comparative studies is the belief that they can have an impact on
policy making. Showing that a specific country is lacking considerably
in its enrollment ratios, its expenditure on higher education, or the
participation of its low-income groups in education compared to other
nations has often put strong pressure on policy makers to offer more
facilities and appropriate larger resources. Formally, this influence
will seldom be recognized, and certainly some countries are more
open to it than others. But, in general, such an impact of comparative studies (intended or unintended) cannot be denied.

However, in the particular case of financing and budget procedures in higher education, the third rationale for comparative studies
seems to me the most significant. By showing that identical or similar procedures have led to very different results in different countries,
or that similar outcomes (both positive and negative) in various countries have been produced by widely different procedures, it is possible
to point to deeper factors that influence the success and failure of particular methods of financing or decision making.

The comparative method thus becomes, first, an instrument that allows us to ask the right questions, and thereby, second, to orient our search for the real forces that determine the results of specific policies. An example will illustrate this point: The British University Grants Committee (UGC) has often been considered an almost universally appropriate model for reconciling a necessary degree of central control against institutional autonomy in the distribution of public funds to different universities within a country. Yet, probably very few, if any, of the "UGC models" succeeded when they were imported into other countries. In other words, the "borrowing rationale" of comparative studies did not justify itself. But a closer look at why they did not succeed can be much more rewarding. Obviously, some preconditions were not or could not be fulfilled: the existence or absence of certain social attitudes and behaviors, specific pressure groups, historical traditions, and the size of the educational system—all of these and many other elements made the UGC pattern a relative success in one case and a relative failure in others.

By comparing a number of national experiences concerning the financing and budgeting procedures used in higher education, the author and editor of this volume have, I believe, presented one of the very few tools we have for identifying a certain number of strategic parameters and for testing their behavior under different stresses, different socioeconomic and educational configurations, before taking costly policy measures. In a more general way, this volume also throws some new light on the really basic forces that hasten or retard innovation and on the mechanisms that determine, beyond purely national circumstances, the behavior and the problems of almost any higher education system in the social, cultural, and economic context of the last quarter of the twentieth century.

ACKNOWLEDGMENTS

I am grateful to the Ford Foundation for providing the financial support that made this comparative study possible. Members of the Foundation staff were unfailingly generous in giving moral and intellectual support as well.

We, as a group of authors, are especially grateful for the help of the dozens of government officials who graciously gave time for interviews, furnished pertinent documents, and provided us with insights into the fund allocation processes for higher education in their nations. The list of these officials is too long to be presented here, but our thanks go out to all of them. Our study could not have been conducted without their generous cooperation.

I personally want to thank Professors T. R. McConnell and Leland Medsker of the University of California, Berkeley, and Richard Millard and John Folger of the Education Commission of the States, and Donald Smith, Vice President of the University of Wisconsin System, for reading the analytical chapters and providing provocative and critical comment on the early drafts. I should also like to thank our two translators, Katherine Freschi of Mill Valley, California, and Philip T. Cockle of Mercoire, France; our manuscript editor, Gene Tanke of Berkeley; and the typists who provided the several drafts, Mildred Boman and Norma L. Needham.

I am appreciative of the fine work and excellent cooperation given by the authors of the five European case studies. Theirs was a true labor of professional dedication, and their work reflects the excellent judgment of those persons who helped me in their selection. I am grateful to each of them personally.

CONTENTS

LIST OF TABLES

LIST OF FIGURES

1
INTRODUCTION
Lyman A. Glenny

Comparisons may be odious, but in our everyday lives and in the public arena they serve many useful purposes: they can reveal objectives to be achieved, modes of operation, practices for survival, and means for solving problems that are new to us. This book considers the allocation of funds for higher education in 5 European nations and 17 of the states of the United States, comparing the different administrative practices followed and the political issues that affect the outcome of those practices.

In order to prepare the reader for the European case studies (Chapters 2 through 6) and the analyses that follow (Chapters 7 and 8), we shall begin in this chapter by discussing some of the dimensions of conducting such a comparative study, and by offering some information that should be helpful in drawing meaningful interpretations. First, we will describe the more detailed objectives and methods used in preparing this book, and then we will discuss pertinent differences and similarities between the United States and European nations. This is followed by a section that presents information concerning the size, scope, and operational features of the higher education systems in the various states and nations. Finally, we will discuss some of the principles that have been developed in democratic societies to govern the allocation of public funds to institutions of higher education.

OBJECTIVES OF THE STUDY

The need for comparative studies of the practices and technologies for allocating funds to higher education institutions has been demonstrated many times in recent years. Many institutions have focused on the subject in special conferences or have made it a part of their concern with other more academic issues.* International scholars, wherever they may meet, generally get around to discussing financial and budgetary problems of their own countries. Given the widespread economic and demographic stabilization taking place in the Western world after a period of vast expansion in higher education, pressure has arisen in most industrialized nations for higher education institutions to be more accountable, more efficient, and more productive in the use of public funds. Politicians want curricular reform and programs for lifelong learning but appear unwilling to approve substantial increases in the monies allotted for higher education. In some nations actual reductions in enrollment in the colleges and universities seem imminent, and in other nations funds fall short of enrollment increases—the extreme case being Italy.

While every national higher education system confronts problems of curricular reform, not all simultaneously face serious retrenchment of resources. Some developing nations, and others in transition from agricultural to industrial economies, find themselves in much the same condition as the industrialized nations during the 1960s, that is, beset with rapid expansion of enrollments, insufficient space, and greatly increased budgets. For both types of countries, a major disability in considering policies and their possible outcomes is the lack of knowledge of how other societies have dealt with them. Even within the United States, where a great deal of homogeneity could be assumed to exist among the states, one state seldom has much knowledge about what other states are doing to solve almost identical problems. The increasing amount of comparative information furnished by the Education Commission of the States, by regional associations, by national associations of various types of colleges and universities, by the Chronicle of Higher Education, and by research centers such as the one at the University of California, Berkeley, apparently fails to reach the majority of policy makers who need it.

Even when comparative information is at hand, it is often ignored or played down by politicians and their staffs, who assume their own state to be unique, requiring different solutions to problems for which other states have already devised workable solutions. Nations tend to act in the same way. For example, the higher education institutions in the United States are legally controlled by the individual states. During the past five years, many states encountered fi-

---

*Examples are the Organization for Economic and Cultural Development (OECD), the Center for Education Research and Innovation (CERI), International Council for Educational Development (ICED), the European Cultural Foundation, the Council of Europe, and the United Nations Education, Science, and Cultural Organization (UNESCO).

nancial crises that directly and negatively affected the welfare of their colleges and universities. Yet the problems they faced and the solutions they adopted appear to be unknown to other nations, which have just recently faced, or are now facing, similar circumstances (Bowen and Glenny 1976).

The goal of this study is to help fill that void by comparing pertinent information and practices in the United States and five European countries, with the objective of providing a document mutually helpful to lay persons, educational planners, and policy makers and their staffs around the world.

The design of this book is drawn from a comprehensive three-year study of budget practices, processes, procedures, organizations, staffing, and technologies used in 17 states of the United States, conducted by the Center for Research and Development in Higher Education from 1973 to 1977. The resulting six volumes of research findings (Glenny et al. 1975; Glenny 1976; Meisinger 1976; Purves and Glenny 1976; Bowen and Glenny 1976; Schmidtlein and Glenny 1977), with some adaptations, provided the descriptive framework for this study.

More specifically, this book examines critically a limited num-budgetary equity among institutions, and to appropriate recognition of differences in quality and quantity. It attempts to provide comparative information on the following subjects:

1. The formal policies, formulas, and guidelines for allocating public funds among the different types of colleges, institutions, and universities considered a part of higher education;
2. The central agencies, ministries, and other offices that review, recommend, or make decisions on the allocation of funds;
3. The methods by which such agencies differentiate allocations among types of programs, levels of students, and, when possible, the criteria used to reflect qualitative differences in programs and institutions; and
4. The major educational and social issues that impinge directly on either the budget process or budget outcomes.

In seeking information on these objectives we have dealt primarily with government agencies above the campus or institutional level, rather than with governing boards and officers of colleges and universities. Many departures from this approach will be found because much of the money going to disciplines, chairs, or departments within institutions in the European countries bypasses the institution as an administrative unit. Rather, funds from the central state agencies go directly to professors or to internal units, without considering any institutional position on the subject.

Further, we assumed in the U.S. research that within the total amounts of money traditionally available for higher education it is the staff members of the several budget review agencies who really determine most of the specific incremental amounts to be awarded to programs and institutions. The politicians primarily confirm the professional decisions and seldom make more than minor, politically oriented adjustments. (Two of the seventeen states, however, provided notable exceptions to this assumption.) In Europe, where firmly established bureaucracies prevail, we expected to discover similar practices; but, as the reader will find, exceptions were found there, too. Nevertheless, we focus on the practices of bureaucrats rather than on the decisions of politicians. We particularly sought to obtain information on allocation methods, analytic techniques, and the extent of detail required regarding campus enrollments, programs, costs, and operations. The European case studies are primarily descriptive, whereas the comparative chapters, which introduce data from the United States (see Appendix B), analyze broader social and economic issues affecting budget practices.

Some of the questions addressed throughout the book are as follows: What relationship exists between the actual number of students, unit costs, and student-faculty ratios and the amounts of money allocated to institutions or programs? What devices are used for allocation, and why? If equity among institutions is a goal in making appropriations, how is it to be achieved, and by whom? What criteria are used to support various levels of quality? What role do political negotiations, rather than bureaucratic formulas or allocation guidelines, play in the decision-making process?

Beyond these fairly technical matters, we have selected a few issues that seem universally pertinent to budget practice and to the amounts that a nation must appropriate for higher education; we have analyzed these issues from the perspective of a policy maker who wishes to know which foreign practices appear to be good or workable and which appear to be bad or likely to produce weakness or malfunctioning in the society.

From the answers to these questions and the analyses of these issues, we hope to identify some ideas, practices, structures, and policy alternatives that will prove beneficial to persons struggling with problems of resource allocation.

PROBLEMS IN CONDUCTING COMPARATIVE STUDIES

Any attempt to make comparisons among several nations (or even between two) calls for meticulous care in choosing what is to be compared and the methodology to be used in making analyses. For many years, sociologists have theorized, written, and advised us on the pitfalls confronting the comparative scholar. Ladislav Cerych of the European Cultural Foundation has recently contributed some special knowledge about what to expect when making comparisons in education (ICED 1974), and Burton Clark reinforces some of these admonitions in an article in Change magazine (October 1976).

Both authors agree that the outcomes of comparative research can be useful simply because they offer descriptive comparison in like categories or taxonomies; however, neither of them considers such description to be as useful as detecting trends among the nations compared or providing correlations between data and the analysis of complex relationships. Cerych indicates that certain key variables could determine the shape of many relationships, such as those between an effective higher education system and the degree of centralization, administrative control, student unrest, institutional autonomy, and innovative capacity.

We examine such complexities as budgeting processes, the organizations and the people involved, and the autonomy of various agencies; we also deal with faculty power centers, tenure, enrollment constraints, and centralization versus decentralization. These and other matters cannot be analyzed systematically country by country; in some, the subject is not an issue, whereas in others the social-educational issues seem almost identical, but the resolution of them brings entirely different results. Hence, while we provide a description of budgetary processes for higher education in each country, we focus our analyses on issues that often have dichotomous characteristics or substantial variances, which lend themselves to fruitful comparative methods.

The problem-solving approach as a methodology for comparative research receives high priority from Cerych and other sociologists, who see it as a core about which to rally internal typologies and taxonomies in order to provide common analytical data bases. Problems related to access, transfer, degree equivalency, student financial aid, and autonomy and centralization would be illustrative of this approach. On this point, we have perhaps been less fortunate than others using the comparative approach. For use in analyzing the issues, we sought to validate and find trends in the data bases themselves; but our luck and perspicacity in this endeavor fell short of the ideal, primarily because of the inadequacy of the European national data systems, but also because some systems are not available in published form. In lucky moments data not previously published became available, but often we were stymied by the simple lack of collection, aggregation, and distribution of information by the nation states.

Each of the five chapters that focuses on a European nation has been written by a scholar native to that country, following a common outline of subject areas. All of these scholars (two political scientists, two economists, and one sociologist) have previously studied and written on government and higher education in their countries. In turn, I visited each of the five countries and, with the help of each local scholar, personally interviewed the principal persons, of whatever rank, who would know the most about the subjects of focus. By conducting these interviews and reading the papers of my colleagues in each country, I attempted to overcome the deficiencies attributed to research that relies on a single person to conduct a fairly superficial survey and analysis of a number of countries.

Documentary materials also became available, some in English and some in the native languages, of which rough translations were made. Discrepancies in my perceptions were discussed with each local scholar while I was still in his country. In addition, both of the "issue" chapters (7 and 8) were reviewed in each of the five countries by the scholar of contact there and at times by some other native official or scholar.

Finally, in dealing with the subject of planning, which leads and in some ways guides the annual budgets and even the longer-term budgets prepared in some countries, I have taken due cognizance of three contemporary models of planning: social demand, manpower, and cost-benefit. (For additional details on methodology, see Appendix A.)

COMPARING EUROPEAN COUNTRIES WITH STATES IN THE UNITED STATES

Most Americans themselves remain uninformed about the vast range of organization, practice, and tradition in the different states of the union.

U.S. Practices

Superficially, government organizations appear quite similar: each state has a legislature (known by a number of different names); each legislature has two houses (except Nebraska, which is unicameral); each state has a governor; each governor is looked upon as the "chief executive" of the state; and each governor has a staff. Moreover, each state usually has at least the two major political parties on its ballot for electing legislators and a governor, and, after a specific period of residence in the state (usually one or two years), one can automatically (after registration) vote in the elections for these political officers. All states now have civil service (merit) systems to choose permanent staff for the various agencies of government. States elect not only the governor; many also elect other officials—such as the state superintendent of public instruction, the attorney general, the secretary of state, the comptroller, and even the chiefs of the health, welfare, and highway departments. But most is not all, and, even where the similarities appear identical to the untrained eye, the actual differences may be large and the consequences deriving from them very great.

For example, the states have "strong" and "weak" governors. Strong governors are those who have power to appoint officials who in other states are elected; who control formulation of the executive budget, which includes funding recommendations for all state services; who have the item or item-reduction veto power; and who have four-year rather than two-year terms of office. They can achieve their goals much more easily than the weak governors, who may have only a small part of these powers. The strong governors, such as those in California, Illinois, New York, and Wisconsin, could almost be considered equivalent to European premiers or prime ministers. They construct the budget and the legislative program, and they usually win in struggles with the legislature over differences in policy objectives. A weak governor, on the contrary, may have no more influence, or even less influence, than the speaker of the lower house or the chairman of the state senate, or the chairman of the house appropriation committee. It is not an either-or proposition. The range of strengths of governors, as carefully developed by J. A. Schlesinger (1965), shows the weakest governor on a 20-point range at 7 points (Texas) and the strongest governors at 20 points (Hawaii, Illinois, and New York).

Both Alan Schick (1971) and Ira Sharkansky (1968, 1970) have shown in detail the pronounced differences in states—differences in mores, organizational forms, traditions, historical accidents, and strong leaders at opportune times. Schick, among others, has conducted comparisons of state budgeting practices at different times. His analyses pinpoint the range of difference in activities relating to budget practice and budget innovation. In higher education, the differences in organizational form, coordination, and control are sufficiently great that some scholars, attempting to classify them for analytical purposes, find themselves almost in the position of placing each state in a separate class.

Two conclusions may be drawn here. One is that the states individually have the capacity to develop entirely different structures and processes for higher education to a greater degree than is common for most other state services. This result relates to the second conclusion, which is that the U.S. government under the federal Constitution has no direct power or control over education—neither elementary nor secondary or higher. It is a power "reserved" to the states.

Nonetheless, the national government through a system of grants-in-aid to the state governments has been able to add conditions or "strings" that require the states to comply with a particular national law and its supporting administrative regulations before receiving a grant. This system of "subventions" allows national influence on, or control of, many subject areas, most of which are not specifically mentioned in the Constitution. The federal government, when giving large sums for specific purposes to higher education, usually does so by categorical grants to individual colleges and universities, effectively circumventing the state governments in order to deal with these state subdivisions directly. (The federal government has a rather long history of such circumvention of state government by dealing directly with cities and counties, which are also legal subunits of the states, on airports, slum clearance, city streets, sewage, and so on.)

Although the federal government has applied its general laws relating to fair labor standards, affirmative action for minorities and women, and certain safety and record-keeping requirements (commented on below), it has not developed a coherent national policy for higher education, nor does it seem to have either the intent to do this or the organizational machinery to carry out such an intent if it were to be legally manifested. A national policy or plan for higher education has never taken a stronger form than when it provided the initial subventions to the states, which established the system of land-grant institutions and, later, when it gave money grants to universities and colleges for programs and research purposes related to national priorities. Historical evidence would indicate little federal attempt to control educational policy as such in colleges and universities. Recent grants for teaching services and research purposes have followed a similar pattern. Once an institutional plan—or, in a few cases, a federally required state plan—has been approved by the federal granting agency, little or no control beyond that agreed to in the plan is exercised over the use to which the monies are put. The federal agencies collectively do not form a national ministry or department. On the contrary, the hodgepodge of granting agencies may disagree in their specific objectives, and they often diverge out of sheer ignorance of the many activities of the other agencies. Attempts by the federal government to computerize research projects by subject in order to prevent unnecessary duplication notably fails because of the individual emphases or design characteristics of each project, however much they may be said to deal with the same subject area. It may safely be said that there is no overall federal policy in relation

to higher and postsecondary education; and no serious attempts by
the president or the Congress have been made to form a coherent
policy out of the diverse individual ones.

The federal authorities do, however, require an immense
amount of accounting and reporting on the grants given to assure that
affirmative action, safety, and minimum wage standards are met.
Some university leaders and their associations have asserted that the
costs to the institution of such onerous reporting requirements ex-
ceed by far the need for validating university actions. The Sloan
Foundation, in 1976, began a three-year study of the interventions of
the federal government into the operational and academic affairs of
higher education. Regulations relating to the protection of human
subjects in research and discussions on the possible regulation of
certain genetic research have led the foundation and concerned university researchers to reexamine the federal role to determine to
what extent its historical nonintervention policy is threatened by recent laws and regulations.

One consequence of the federal government's leaving control of
the substance of higher education to the states has been a plethora of
"experiments" in organization and process by the states. Our findings in the budget study showed that no two of the seventeen states
studied had similar decision processes or even similar organizations
for budget review; and the range of sophistication in their uses of
modern budget technologies went from a naive back-of-the-envelope
type of data system and financial control by one or a few persons to
an array of technological uses that provided data, information, simu-
lations, and analyses through the use of specialized teams of staff
members at various points in the decision process. Some states had
elaborate costing techniques, others had none; some attempted a
modified form of program budgeting, but many still used objects-of-
expenditure and functional types; some had no specialists devoted
solely to reviewing higher education budgets, while others had eight
or ten persons and sometimes that many in each of several different
state agencies.

European Practices

Europe, with its long tradition of national boundaries and its
different cultures and languages, would seem to offer the ideal setting for finding diverse patterns of development in the budgeting of
higher education. The absence of private or proprietary education in
some nations would seem to heighten this possibility. Also, the grave
problems following World War II in the attempt to establish closer
European cooperation—and, later, a "European community"—to

counter or balance the economic and political power of the Russians, Arabs, Japanese, and Americans are a clear indication of the distinctive national interests and parochial objectives of the individual countries. The history of Western Europe would almost force those of us on the American side of the Atlantic to believe in the individuality of each country and, therefore, to assume the great differences exist in the organization and the financing of the higher education system in each of them.

But the historical picture also reveals forces that have created similarities in outlook, practice, and organization—even in the underlying assumptions over who should be allowed higher education, and why. Then, too, the oldest European universities, some of which date back 600 to 800 years, have in many ways transcended the political tides that have defined national boundaries and forcibly brought about "national" homogeneity and conformity. These venerable institutions view their setting with a cosmopolitan aloofness, maintaining their own mores, traditions, and practices with considerable disregard for the surrounding nation or even the city in which they are located. As we shall see, in some countries the ancient traditions survive with little change, untouched by modern politics or management practices.

Also, historical attempts to create a common European governance or legal structure, notably by Charlemagne and later by Napoleon, and more recent attempts at cooperation by much of Western Europe on common markets, inflation, and rationales for dealing with unemployment, tariffs, energy, and other matters have all encouraged a good deal of intensive communication among the nation states, which may result in a more common perspective on government and higher education organization than might be expected from a superficial look at European history. A colleague at the Berkeley Center* wrote to me while this study was in progress: "You may find more similarities among the European countries than you did among the states in the United States." Whether we did or not, his prediction may soon turn out to be valid, for UNESCO, CERI, NMHE, the Institute of Education of the European Cultural Foundation, and other organizations have been formed to increase, among other things, communication between researchers and leaders of higher education in Europe.

Cumulatively, all of these emerging forces have made an impact, bringing increasing similarity among the nation states in their control and financing of colleges and universities. And in almost every nation, the common problem in relation to higher education is to

---

*Center for Research and Development in Higher Education at the University of California, Berkeley.

overcome not the national bias or cultural norms but, rather, the distinctive norms of the university communities themselves. The traditional universities look very much alike from one country to another and receive funds from their governments and other sources in much the same ways for teaching and research. The modern European states, in their effort to seek common solutions to problems, have tried to force the older universities to go against their traditions and deal with the immediate political problems of access, mass higher education, campus expansion, new universities, or new types of postsecondary institutions. These developments have forced the nations to look for ways to allocate resources equitably among the old and the new universities, and among old and new modes of education, while at the same time encouraging greater efficiency through decentralization and decision making at the local level, within guidelines that are applicable to all institutions, old and new.

The European problems relating to greater access, equal opportunity, campus construction, and new institutions have been familiar to U.S. political and educational leaders for at least 20 years. Both Western Europe and the United States now show trends leading to surpluses in the number of college and university graduates looking for traditional kinds of employment. From the economic perspective, the issues facing public officials appear to be very similar. The official attitudes of government leaders have converged to slow down funding during this period of depression, high inflation, lower attendance rates, and disaffection with higher education because of manpower surpluses and uncertainty about the role that higher institutions can or should play in the modern state. Indeed, official perspectives within the states of Europe are very similar to those within the United States. The outstanding problems are how to treat institutions and students equitably, and yet be able to reduce the state funding per student, contribute sufficiently to research without "pampering" the professors or harming the economy, improve the quality of instruction at the undergraduate level, and shift the educational emphasis toward job-oriented programs. Only a few Western nations (including Greece and Spain, in this study) have not yet reached this point, but current conditions are bound to lead them to a confrontation with these same problems.

COMPARATIVE BACKGROUND INFORMATION

Since the objectives of this study were limited to those that could be achieved in a relatively short period of time, and with limited resources, several dimensions of comparative studies by international organizations, especially UNESCO and OECD, are omitted—not for

lack of relevance but for lack of time to provide additional analyses
after becoming familiar with the many reservations each nation inter-
jects in providing what is ostensibly "common" data. Indeed, even
in dealing with the five nations involved in this study, many problems
have risen over the comparability of the data and information gathered
by the authors of the case studies.

Data on State-/or National-Funding Efforts

Many studies look at comparative figures for national GNP and
the proportion allocated to higher education as its share of national
income. Such data indicate the priority that higher education holds
in relation to other services of the nation states. For example, in a
related study at the Berkeley Center, substantial shifts were found in
the United States in the percentage of state income going to colleges
and universities, with more than one-third of the states providing a
smaller share in 1977 than in 1973, some dropping their share by 5
percentage points while others, not formerly providing as much or as
high quality education, actually increasing their shares (Ruyle and
Glenny 1978). A somewhat similar pattern of changing priorities has
occurred in some of the European countries. Sweden, for example,
increased the percentage of the GNP for higher education from 0. 044
in 1966 to 0. 073 in 1973, but by 1975 it had dropped back to 0. 070.
In Greece the proportion of government current revenue for higher
education rose from 1. 77 percent to 2. 31 percent in 1973 and then
was reduced to 2. 12 percent in 1975. In France, higher education
received 0. 055 percent of the GNP in 1968, which dropped to 0. 041
percent in 1975. The percentage of state or national revenue of GNP
for higher education is an important indicator of its priority in the
spectrum of public services, and it impinges on the technical budget process by responding to the prevailing social attitudes of support, indifference, or animosity toward colleges and universities.
These attitudes affect final outcomes of the budget process and, even
to some extent, the technology used in building a state's higher education budget.

Demographic Considerations

One characteristic of four of the five European countries, and
of the United States as a whole, is the drop in the number of live births,
a factor that will have a great impact on future college and university
enrollments in several of the countries. It will be felt most within
the United States, where the number of live births declined steadily

TABLE 1.1

Annual Number of Live Births, 1968–76
(in thousands)

Year	France	Greece	Italy	Spain	Sweden	United States
1968	832.8	160[a]	53.1	665	113.1	3,502
1969	839.5	154	53.5	664	107.6	3,600
1970	847.7	145	53.8	661	110.2	3,731[a]
1971	878.6[a]	141	54.2	670	114.5[a]	3,556
1972	865.1	141	54.6	670	112.3	3,258
1973	854.9	138	55.1	666	109.7	3,137
1974	799.2	144	55.6	678[a]	109.9	3,160
1975	740.0 (est.)	142	56.0	661	103.6	3,149
1976	n.a.	n.a.	56.3[a]	662	98.2	3,165
Change[b]	-138.6	-18	0.0	-16	-16.3	-566

n.a.: data not available
[a]Highest year.
[b]Difference between highest year and 1975 or 1976.

Source: Data for France, Greece, Italy, Spain, and Sweden furnished to the editor by the authors of the respective case studies; for the United States from the U.S. Public Health Service.

13

from the peak year 1958 to 1976. As Table 1.1 indicates, the difference between the year in which the most babies were born and 1975 or 1976 shows a reduction of 138,600 births in just a five-year period in France, an 18,000 reduction in Greece, and about 16,000 less for both Spain and Sweden. Only Italy has maintained a rather stable number of births over the past ten years. Since the drop in the United States occurred earlier and more severely than in the other nations, a watchful eye on the consequences for institutional enrollments by type of institution and for the financing level for higher education may provide a preview of what will be happening on a smaller scale in the European nations.

Projecting ahead for the United States, the number of young people between 18 and 22 years of age who will be available for college entry will begin to drop in 1979/80 and will continue to drop until the mid-1990s, or roughly 24 percent from 1980 to 1995. The rate at which these young people go to college will determine the degree to

TABLE 1.2

Total Population and Total Higher Education Enrollment, 1976
(in thousands)

	Percent Total Population	Total in Higher Education	Appropriation for Higher Education
France	52.8	811	Fr 6,102[a]
Greece	9.0[a]	102	Dr 2,181[a]
Italy	n.a.	731	L 55,000[b]
Spain	36.1	n.a.	Pts 19,800
Sweden	8.2[a]	130	Kr 1,995
California	21.2[a]	1,790	$1,599
Florida	8.3	364	$409
Michigan	9.1	481	$554
Texas	12.2	648	$903

n.a.: data not available
[a]1975.
[b]1971.

Source: Data for France, Greece, Italy, Spain, and Sweden furnished to the editor by the authors of the respective case studies; for the United States, from Ruyle and Glenny 1978.

which enrollments will rise or fall for the age group. That rate has
been slowly dropping in the United States: only 38.8 percent of the
age group now attend college, as against the high of 41.3 percent in
1969, according to the U.S. Census Bureau surveys. The rates of
attendance in all countries could move either up or down, depending
on public policy and social pressures on the young.

In order to provide a comparative base of U.S. states in Table
1.2, we have included California, Florida, Michigan, and Texas as
examples from the 17-state study, along with the 5 European nations.
Note the high numbers of students in college in comparison with the
total population in the states and the fact that some of the European
nations, such as France and Italy, seem to be catching up to the state
proportions.

Data on Attendance Rates

Studies often include data showing two percentages: of the total
population and of the total age group (usually 18 to 22 or 24 years),
the proportion of secondary school graduates who enter college. (See
Table 1.3 for the data furnished for the five European countries and
the United States on the percentage of the age group attending.) These
measures have been used frequently, sometimes separately and sometimes together. However, each can be misleading, especially if college and university practices are given as the reason for the particular result. The data may instead reflect public policy to keep the
actual number, and therefore the proportion, of any of these groups,
down to the legal number required to meet manpower production quotas; this is the case in the USSR, and there are increasing tendencies
in this direction in other Western countries such as Sweden, where
the new "planning frames" may limit entry into various disciplines or
professions. Just as important, the data may reflect more on the
practices of elementary and secondary schools than on those of the
higher institutions. If compulsory schooling ends at the age of 15 or
16, if secondary education is insufficient or inadequate, or if young
people are divided into those who enter technical training and those
permitted to receive preuniversity education, the fault may not lie
with higher institutions. At any rate, these ratios have little direct
effect on the technical budget process for universities, although they
may heavily influence the total amounts of public money available for
higher education.

TABLE 1.3

Higher Education Attendance Rates by Age Cohort, 1968–75

Year	France	Greece	Italy[a]	Spain	Sweden		United States[b]
1968	14.4[c]	n.a.	n.a.	10	9.5[d]	10.3[a]	39.7
1969	13.9	6.5	n.a.	11	9.5	9.5	41.3
1970	14.6	6.7	n.a.	12	9.5	9.7	39.1
1971	15.2	7.0	13.7	13	8.7	9.2	38.9
1972	16.1	6.6	n.a.	14	7.6	8.4	37.8
1973	17.5	7.1	16.4	15	7.2	7.9	36.6
1974	18.3	7.7	n.a.	16	7.0	7.5	36.6
1975	19.4	8.7	18.1	18	7.3	7.9	38.7
Change[e]	5.4	2.2	4.4[f]	8	-2.0	-2.4	-1.0

n.a.: data not available

[a] 20–24 years.

[b] 18–24 years (Bureau of Census, Current Population Reports Series P–20, No. 319 Table A–4, February 1978).

[c] 19–23 years.

[d] 20–21 years.

[e] Change between 1968 and 1975.

[f] 1971–75

Source: Data for France, Greece, Italy, Spain, and Sweden furnished to the editor by the authors of the respective case studies; for the United States from the U.S. Bureau of the Census.

Centralization and Autonomy

Budget allocations also have a direct bearing on the issues of autonomy and decentralization of higher education in the European nations. In France and Spain, the government now tries to avoid making the major decisions on who should get professorships or how appropriated resources should be transferred or reallocated within institutions, by shifting those decisions from the state ministries to the institutions themselves. Faculty members holding major departmental chairs may be strongly opposed to this shift, because, as we point out in Chapters 7 and 8, it gives the university administration decision powers that formerly rested with the chairs, or with the chairs in collaboration with the government. The government would like to decentralize responsibilities by giving them to the universities rather than to the traditional chairs. Who should have autonomy? The chairs? The majority of teaching faculty? The universities? The students? The state?

Influence of Process and
Organization on Funding Allocations

These interesting and important issues arise when nations are faced with an increasingly complex number of institutions, programs, and students, and the resulting problems have a direct bearing on funding allocations and, certainly, on the amount of control exercised by budget ministers and staffs after appropriations are made. The power centers consume resources to manage an organization, and may also greatly influence the formulation of the budget that goes to the government from the ministry, state department, or coordinating board. No study has been able to show a relationship between the amounts of money generated for higher education because of particular organizational forms of internal government or particular techniques practiced by the leaders of education institutions; instead, the controlling variables are related to general social and economic conditions and to the confidence higher officials have in the integrity and efficiency of the leadership of colleges and universities.

In the United States, research has shown little or no advantage in the amounts of money appropriated when there is a separate coordinating or governing agency for higher education as opposed to no such agency, or when higher education is consolidated with elementary and secondary education or administered separately. However, in the 17-state study, the amount of money appropriated per full-time-equivalent student proved to be less in states with coordinating boards than in states with consolidated governing boards (Glenny 1976). No research has supplied information on whether different organizational forms, persons, or centers that have autonomy in the area of higher education also have an impact on the technical formulation of budgets or their monetary outcomes.

These as well as other important variables are related to state budgeting and financing, but they must be considered in their proper contexts. They are important, even critical, in certain settings. They may determine the actual numbers of students in colleges and universities, the purposes for which money is spent, and which internal teaching centers or departments will receive favored treatment.

PRINCIPLES IN ALLOCATION OF PUBLIC FUNDS

Public funding of higher educational systems seldom avoids a great number of controversies during each budget cycle, and certain principles have evolved to smooth out the worst of them. Faculty members seemingly have an unending need for more money, and politicians, with justifiable fears, hesitate to increase taxes in order to generate anything like the sums requested. At the same time, the political leaders and their ministries must make difficult decisions about which institutions and programs should get what shares of the available funds. Politicians have special interests in meeting the desires, if not the actual needs, of their constituents. Higher educators also promote and protect special interests. Given this situation of limited resources and a clash of interests, reasonable persons, over time, have developed certain principles, which they believe ought to dominate the decision process of budgeting. These principles relate to the degree of equity believed to prevail in the allocation of the funds among institutions and programs, the degree of certainty of getting the minimum amounts needed for essential operations, the extent to which the amounts can be anticipated for planning purposes, and the due process that characterizes the procedures for arriving at the final sums.

Each of these principles may become an issue in any budget review and approval process, although seldom can all parties with vested interests in the budget outcomes be fully satisfied on each one. A discussion of each principle will reveal its strengths and the reasons for encouraging widespread agreement on its underlying assumptions.

Equity means "fair share" rather than "equal share" in budgeting. Fair share merely means that, given the conditions and circumstances of competing for funds, each party will get the share that enables his operation to continue at a level commensurate with established needs. In higher education this means that each publicly supported institution (representing the internal professional core responsible for teaching and research) should obtain funds proportional to its needs in relation to the needs of the other public institutions.

The difficulty in arriving at this just solution can usually be traced back to lack of agreement on the assumptions to be employed in making the allocation decisions. For example, if a new and growing state college that has not yet earned a reputation for high quality sees an older, well-established, and distinguished university receiving more money per student or per faculty member than it receives, the institutional leaders may question the assumption that established quality rather than promising development ought to be rewarded more. An even more difficult case may arise when two or more entirely different types of institutions are involved, for example, an institute of technology with a few related engineering programs and a university with many different specializations in the liberal arts and sciences at both undergraduate and graduate levels. How can fair shares then be determined? Again, it can be done only by prior agreement on the assumptions about the level of support required to maintain a balance of quality in programs between the two institutions—a difficult accomplishment at best. Nevertheless, equity of this kind has been achieved by certain formulas, which we shall discuss shortly.

While the usual basis for conflict lies in quality factors, factors relating to the expansion or development of new programs or chairs also create tensions between institutions that come to be expressed in budget allocations. Equity in situations of this type can be achieved only if prior agreement has been reached, or a public policy established, that sets the missions and functions of each institution and establishes a timetable that determines if operational goals have been achieved. For example, expansion may be made dependent on the number of new students in a program or the number of graduates produced. New programs may be made dependent on the efficiency level achieved in certain related programs (or all existing programs of the institution), or perhaps on the production of certain numbers of completers of a basic set of courses on which the new program depends. The assumptions for equity in cases of this kind would normally lie in the broad ongoing planning for the higher educational system.

Predictability about how much money the university, institute, or college will receive is another of the common budget goals. Here the objective allows an institution to make reasonably accurate estimates of its future governmental income primarily by using its previous budget and then using objective factors to generate the sums for either a larger or a smaller budget. (In theory, the estimate could also be made from a zero base.) Again, the factors built into a formula, or a set of them, could be based on a simple student-faculty ratio, or on the number of class or teaching hours of the faculties, or on more complicated factors, such as costs of various units per student, program, or credit hour. Prediction allows the institution to plan for change and to begin implementing such plans for the next year or budget cycle without having to wait until the allocations have been made, a time that may be very near the beginning of the next academic year, when only the most cursory, ad hoc planning can be done. To be fully effective beyond the mere generation of a sum of money, formulas must be related to the different missions and objectives of each institution or system of institutions, and to the support they give to a multifaceted but coordinated system of higher education.

Certainty of funding may be only an offshoot of predictability, but it has the characteristic of eliminating capricious or unexpected last-minute changes in budget policy that could substantially change the amounts to be granted to institutions, or it could create such conditions of uncertainty as to leave the major interested parties bewildered about what can or cannot be done, perhaps with a yet undetermined amount of money. Examples could be the sudden abandonment of a long-used formula, the last-minute interjection of zero-base rather than incremental-base practices, or the introduction of shares based on the number of particular types of students attracted to certain kinds of programs. Uncertainty would especially prevail if such changes failed to consider the distinctive missions or programs of each institution.

The term due process has its modern legal basis in English common law and means that the process and procedures by which decisions are reached are fair ones. The concept contains many elements, but, for budget-process, its primary characteristic is a fair and open hearing of evidence, which the persons seeking public funds wish to present to support their case. Hearings are expected at each higher level at which a budget receives review and possible modification. If new arguments or assumptions, a different basis for calculation, or other major changes are sought by a budget review agency, the pleaders for funds are to have time and opportunity to produce the fresh evidence they believe required to counter any inimical elements that may have arisen in the hearing. In the end, due process is a procedure on which "reasonable" persons may agree. In budgeting, it cannot contain the full legal meaning of endless challenge and counter-challenge in the courts. The budget must proceed through its steps with a good deal of regularity if the government is to act on it within the time preset for legislative action. Nevertheless, those who plead for money from their governments for higher education purposes, as well as those who hear, review, and made decisions, must have reached some form of consensus on fair proceedings (as well as on the broad purposes to be served, against which they will "measure" requested funds and programs), or they will slip into mutual mistrust, with resulting accusations of favoritism and arbitrariness.

The technical bases for reviewing budgets normally revolve around significant data aggregations relating to numbers of students, faculty members, student-credit hours, academic programs, unit costs, or other factors that may be used alone or in combinations to establish means for arriving at equitable allocations, which can also be counted upon by potential recipients prior to the actual appropriation.

These technical bases most often take the form of student-faculty ratios, either for the institution as a whole or discipline by discipline. In nations or states that enroll many part-time students or employ numerous part-time faculty members, these figures usually require conversion to a full-time equivalent (FTE) basis. If not thus equated, inequities among departments and disciplines, as well as among institutions, must inevitably result.

The student-credit-hour (SCH) basis, commonly used in the United States to denote the number of hours a student spends in classes, requires an accumulation of about 125 hours in order to obtain a baccalaureate degree. (The range is between 117 and 135 hours.) The credit-hour system permits transfers among institutions of earned hours, thus allowing students to avoid losing credit for work already accomplished. This assumes, without factual foundation, that knowledge gained by the student directly correlates with the number of hours he or she has spent before a teacher in a classroom. However invalid the assumption, the practice is widespread in the United States, and work loads for budget and management purposes may be expressed in each faculty member's teaching so many credit hours per term or per year. The number, for example, may be 250 per term for classes taught to students in the first 2 years of college, 175 in the second 2 years, and much lower figures for the master's and doctor's degree candidates. The overall average faculty load (used in lieu of the student-faculty ratio) is derived from the total hours taught at each level in each discipline, aggregated for the whole institution, and then divided by the total number of FTE faculty. The result is the average work-load figure. Many variations of this technique characterize practice by the different institutions and states of the United States.

Unit costs, derived in concept from industrial production measures to achieve specific objectives within a particular cost, are increasingly developed and used as the basis for budgeting higher education. The simplest and most unsophisticated method of arriving at such a cost is to divide the total institutional budget or state appropriation by the total number of students (FTE or head count) enrolled in the fall term. This rough approximation of per student cost, historically used by legislators to establish a rough equity among institutions, has given way to far more sophisticated derivations of cost. Generally, the direct costs of a credit hour in each course are determined, indirect teaching support costs are then apportioned to each of the credit hours in each course, and allocations of overhead costs to the credit hours are made by apportioning them among the schools, departments, and disciplines—either on the relative proportion of credit hours or FTE students, or on the direct and indirect costs accumulated at the departmental level. The variants in costing processes are far too numerous even to mention here, and definitional problems have never been entirely overcome; although the National Center for Higher Education Management Systems at Boulder, Colorado, has provided great help in this area.

These technical bases for measures have laid the groundwork for the development of formulas that can generate the major proportion of the instructional budget for each college and university. By providing weightings for class and degree levels, quality components, and exceptional cases (such as a new university just getting under way, or an older institution losing enrollment rapidly), the formulas become quite complex—the playthings of management systems people and computer specialists. Additional formulas may be developed for libraries; for the maintenance of buildings, grounds, and utilities; and, in cases where research is not included in the teaching budget (as is normal in the United States but not in Europe), a separate formula for research may be constructed.

Nevertheless, in working out the unit-cost system through the participation by staff from each institution, the assumptions built into formulas are known, and presumably agreed to, with the result that an institution in making its estimates of students in each course or program for the coming year may also estimate with fair accuracy the amount of funding it will receive from the government.

Formulas tend to provide the desired element of predictability, but because of political actions they may fall short of the desirable goal of certainty. If the state does not have sufficient income to cover all costs generated by the formulas, then the state must either raise taxes to do so or reduce the proportion of the formulas it will fund from 100 percent to something less than that. Such changes can be accomplished, however, within a due-process framework. (In the United States, most states cannot legally borrow money for use in operations, so budgets must balance for each budget cycle.)

As nations and states move into these technologically advanced systems of budgeting, as many of them are, the greatest problem confronting them is deciding which and how many data elements to collect, aggregate, analyze, and make general use of at the higher levels where budget review takes place. The costs of collecting all data that could conceivably be needed for any contingency requires Crocean levels of funding. The general rule usually adopted requires only the collection of such data as can be used directly in validating or supporting the formulas or in contributing directly to the solution of fore-seeable problems. However, even an amount of data considered mea-ger by technicians will be expensive to collect initially and to maintain on a routine basis. Hence, the size and complexity of the institutions and of the system as a whole must be considered, and considered very carefully, or the costs of providing data and the formulas built on such bases will outweigh their advantages. Simple systems do not require expensive unit-costing information systems and formula constructions, as complex ones may. What will be considered sufficient will depend on the degree of achievement of the elements previously discussed: equity, predictability, and certainty, along with due process. Recent-ly, institutions and states have placed high on their priority lists an-other element, accountability, which may require more data, more analyses, and more reporting than necessary to achieve the other four characteristics. Accountability has increasingly become the primary goal of governments in both the United States and other nations.

In discussing equity, accountability, and due process, one can-not lose sight of the elements that provide the framework within which the budget process, the technological bases, and the measurements for efficiency and accountability find their logical places. That ele-ment is planning. We previously cited the need for fixing the social and economic parameters within which the higher education system would need to operate if equity among different types of institutions were one of the goals of the budget process. That planning framework, when agreed to or made binding on the budget review authorities, tends to reduce capricious action and provides more certainty about what will be expanded, what will be contracted, and what the missions are of the different types of institutions. If kept in mind, not as a blue-print but as a set of guidelines, such a framework allows short-range budget decisions to be made within existing funding constraints with-out undue risk of appearing capricious in relation to the specific wel-fare of higher institutions, their staffs, and students. With the kind of participative planning that has become politically de rigueur in most Western countries today, such frameworks can protect both those who plead for money and those who have the power to grant it.

In reading the national case studies that follow and the subse-quent international comparisons and analyses of the budgeting issues encountered in the study, the elements that appear important or es-sential to good budget practice might be kept in mind. The case study authors were given no special instructions to consider or deal with any particular elements of equity, predictability, certainty, due process, or planning. One's own conclusion must be drawn from the descrip-tive reports of the budget process and the data provided for each na-tion. Most of the authors have provided some sociological, political, and economic comments, which aid in the analysis of the process.

The following five chapters present a description of the practices, organizations, and political machinery used to determine funding allocations in France, Greece, Italy, Spain, and Sweden. Pertinent descriptive materials for individual states of the United States are drawn from Appendix B and embedded in the two analytical chapters that follow the five national case studies. Chapters 7 and 8 deal with some of the major issues that directly affect the amount of resources and the way they are allocated. Most of these issues now cut across the national boundaries of all these countries, or will do so in the immediate future. The several methods of resolving these issues, and the impact of such resolutions on the organization, operation, and quality of the higher education units, may provide the basis for some nations to learn vicariously what might help or hurt them in their own attempts to develop and maintain a vigorous system of universities, colleges, and institutes.

2
THE UNIVERSITY SYSTEM
IN FRANCE
Pierre Goldberg

Before discussing the allocation of resources in the French
system of higher education, we shall outline some of the characteristic features of that system, which should help explain the facts that
are to be presented later.

ORGANIZATION OF THE SYSTEM

This analysis deals only with universities. French universities,
which are by far the most important part of French postsecondary education, have developed in many different ways, especially in the last
ten years or so. But first we shall offer a brief review of all postsecondary education.

Postsecondary Education

There is extreme diversity within the French postsecondary educational system. The system itself includes:

1. The universities themselves, which are the oldest as well
as the largest institutions in France (772,000 students enrolled in
1975/76).
2. The écoles, which include engineering schools, schools of
industrial management, the Ecoles Normales Supérieures (originally
concerned with preparing students for work in higher education and
research), the Ecole Nationale d'Administration (leading to the most
responsible posts in public service), the Ecole Nationale de la Mag-
istrature, and so forth. In 1975/76 these schools catered to a total

of 108,000 students, including those enrolled in special classes preparing for their competitive entrance examinations. This is the most renowned sector of postsecondary education because its role is to train the administrative, scientific, technical, and even political elites of French society, including a growing proportion of university teaching staff.

3. "Short" technical educational facilities, including the Sections de Techniciens Supérieurs, which are part of the secondary educational system and therefore the Ministry of Education, and the University Institutes of Technology, a more recent innovation (1966), which is affiliated with the universities. These two types of institutions, which provide two-year courses leading to specific professional diplomas, enrolled 90,000 students in 1975/76.

4. Various vocational schools, whose aims make them closely related to the "short" technical training courses. Under this heading we include the Ecoles Normales, colleges that train the permanent teachers of state primary schools. In 1975/76, 47,000 students were enrolled.

There are at the present time nearly 1,017,000 students enrolled in postsecondary schools in France. However, when we allow for duplicate enrollments, which exist particularly between the elite écoles and the universities, and between the private and public sectors, the total comes down to 980,000-990,000 students, of whom 85,600 are foreign. The admission rate to postsecondary institutions is thus about 21 percent.*

The full extent of the problem of allocating resources is brought out not so much by the situation in a given year as by the evolution of total student numbers and options over a number of years.

Table 2.1 shows that the number of students has greatly increased, with the full extent of the phenomenon that has been brought out by the admission rate of the 19- to 23-year-old group: within the space of a few years it has progressed from 7.7 percent to 19.8 per-

---

*The admission rate is defined as the relation between the number of French individuals who continue their studies after the Baccalauréat and the population of the 19- to 23-year-old group on January 1 of the year in question. The discrepancies between the figures we have just quoted and the statistics most frequently published can be explained by the fact that a certain number of engineering schools, as well as the University Institutes of Technology, are legally attached to the universities, although in many cases there is no real contact because their role in postsecondary education is quite different. This is why we have chosen to count them separately.

TABLE 2.1

New Entrants and Total Enrollments and Their Relationships, 1967/68-1976/77

Year	Enroll-ments	Population of 19- to 23-Year Old Age Group	Relationship (percent)	New Entrants	Population of 18- to 20-Year Old Age Group	Relationship (percent)
1967/68	504,540	3,191,500	15.8	115,997	865,482	13.4
1968/69	586,026	4,058,700	14.4	148,163	868,800	17.0
1969/70	602,712	4,325,500	13.9	127,636	860,500	14.8
1970/71	635,350	4,360,800	14.6	144,139	854,300	16.9
1971/72	662,457	4,360,000	15.2	154,402	842,730	18.3
1972/73	699,160	4,334,600	16.1	160,102	840,270	19.1
1973/74	745,242	4,260,000	17.5	179,143	833,500	21.5
1974/75	772,067	4,222,500	18.3	186,648	832,500	22.4
1975/76	811,258	4,177,500	19.4	198,571	830,000	24.9
1976/77	821,591	4,160,000	19.8	195,167	833,500	23.4

Source: Service des Etudes Informatique et Statistiques (SEIS) 1977.

TABLE 2.2

Distribution of University Enrollments, 1967/68–1976/77
(in percent)

	1967/68	1969/70	1971/72	1973/74	1974/75	1975/76	1976/77
Law and economics	22.4	22.4	22.3	23.1	24.0	23.9	23.6
Arts and humanities	33.6	34.3	35.0	31.9	31.5	31.3	30.8
Sciences	22.8	19.8	17.4	16.8	16.3	16.1	15.9
Medicine and odontology	16.7	17.3	17.3	18.9	18.7	19.2	20.2
Pharmacy	3.5	3.4	3.4	3.8	4.1	4.1	4.1
Institutes of technology	1.0	2.8	4.6	5.5	5.4	5.4	5.4

Source: Service des Etudes Informantiques et Statistiques (SEIS) 1977.

cent, showing clearly that demographic growth is not the only cause of the increase. Since 1968, and especially since 1970, the admission rate of new entrants has been several points higher than that of the general enrollment rate.

This general upward trend conceals marked differences among fields of study (Table 2.2). Medicine, pharmacy, law, and economics are tending to grow, although the latter two are now showing signs of leveling off. Arts and humanities are decreasing in relative terms, and the sciences are decreasing in absolute terms. Finally, the low number of students in University Institutes of Technology clearly illustrates the problems of developing technical and technological education in France. It is at this level that we can gauge the importance of questions concerning the allocation of resources and, above all, their redistribution.

We conclude this brief survey by referring to two structural features of higher education in France, namely the dominant role of Paris and the Paris region (Table 2.3), and the scale (especially regarding universities) of the public sector, which accounts for 93 percent of postsecondary students and nearly 99 percent of university students.

TABLE 2.3

Distribution of University Enrollments and New Entrants

	1973/74	Percent	1976/77	Percent
Enrollments				
France	745,242	100.0	821,591	100.0
Paris	248,374	33.3	289,429	35.2
Provinces	496,868	66.7	532,162	64.8
New Entrants				
France	179,143	100.0	195,167	100.0
Paris	52,141	29.1	66,589	34.2
Provinces	127,002	70.9	128,578	65.8

Source: Service des Etudes Informatiques et Statistiques (SEIS) 1977.

University Structure

The Loi d'Orientation for higher education, passed by the French Parliament in 1968, introduced many changes in the administration and institutional organization of universities.

Each university, which now groups together a certain number of the former faculties devoted to a single branch of study, is headed by a president elected by the University Council from among teachers of professorial rank. The council itself is made up of representatives from each category of people involved in the university: teachers of all levels; students; administrative, technical maintenance, and service staff; and outside persons chosen for their professional or scientific competence.

The University Council has complete control over teaching matters (although it must obey the national regulations governing the award of national degrees and diplomas), over the appointment of teachers (although selection procedures inherited from pre-1968 practices leave the major initiative in the hands of consultative committees made up exclusively of teachers), and in financial and disciplinary matters.

A Scientific Council, whose members are teachers or researchers, is competent in dealing with all questions of research policy, its organization, and the distribution of financial resources.

Each university is divided into a number of teaching and research units (UERs), headed by a director elected by the UER council. This division is organized either along disciplinary lines (each UER comprising courses centered around a dominant field of study, such as law, the arts, humanities, science, economics, or medicine) or according to level (first, second, or third cycle—each cycle covering two years of instruction). The possibility of a hybrid organization, intermingling fields of study and level, which is particularly suitable for the development of multidisciplinary studies, has hardly been explored.

Financially, the UERs are governed by a decree to the effect that it is the university that receives the allocations of various kinds furnished by the state and then proceeds to distribute these resources among the UERs, according to criteria and procedures over which the university has full control.

However, certain UERs who benefit from special grants also receive allocations directly from the state and are free to employ them as they see fit, within the regulations specific to their case. These UERs, who are quite independent of the university with which they are affiliated, are generally teaching establishments with a closely defined vocation. They include the University Institutes of Technology (IUTs), engineering schools, institutes for political science, and so forth.

Control and Administration of the University System

Between 1958 and 1974, primary, secondary, and higher education were all supervised by a single authority, the Ministry of Education. The position of scientific research was much less stable because it depended, simultaneously or in succession, on the prime minister, the Ministry of Education, and the Ministry of Industry. Within the Ministry of Education, the universities came under the General Directorate of Higher Education and Research.

This administrative organization, however, was extremely unwieldy and difficult to manage. When, in 1974, Valery Giscard d'Estaing was elected president of the republic and a new government was formed, the opportunity was taken to create an independent ministry, the Secretariat of State for the Universities, whose organization is outlined in Figure 2.1.*

Three consultative bodies advise the Secretariat of State for the Universities (until 1974 they reported to the minister of Education): the National Council for Higher Education and Research (CNESER); the Conference of University Presidents (CPU); and the Consultative Committee of the Universities (CCU). The CNESER and the CPU were formed in 1968, but the CCU is much older.

The CNESER is roughly the equivalent at the national level of the University Councils. Two-thirds of the members are elected representatives of students, teachers, and administrative staff; the other third are ministerial appointees—members of Parliament, trade unionists, or individuals chosen for their competence in the fields of education and research. This council must be consulted by the minister of Higher Education on all questions concerning higher education or research, but it can only give its advice, which the minister is not obliged to follow. In reality, the cumbersome size of CNESER (90 members), its lack of representation (owing to very low participation in university elections, particularly among students), and the completely discretionary manner in which the nonelected members are chosen have all contributed to its gradual decline in influence since 1970, —to the benefit of the Conference of University Presidents (CPU).

The CPU, on the other hand, was not written into the 1968 law for the organization of higher education. It began as an informal group in 1970 and was officially recognized in 1971. It includes all university presidents, who meet in plenary sessions or specialized

---

*There are two types of Secretariat of State in France: those attached to certain ministries, which have little scope for independent initiative; and the independent Secretariats of State, which are rather like small ministries. This distinction corresponds to a clear difference in political weight.

FIGURE 2.1

Organization of French Higher Education

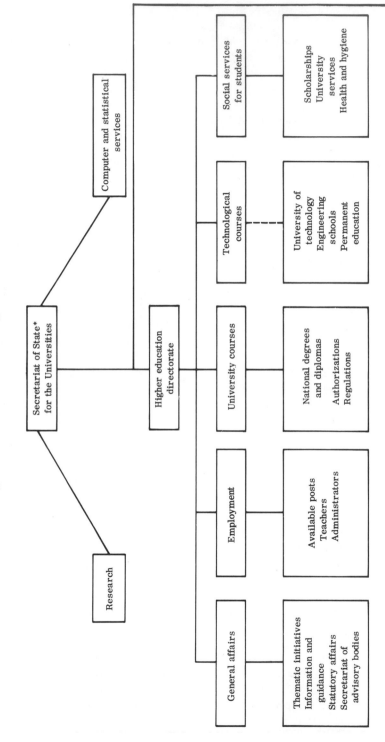

32

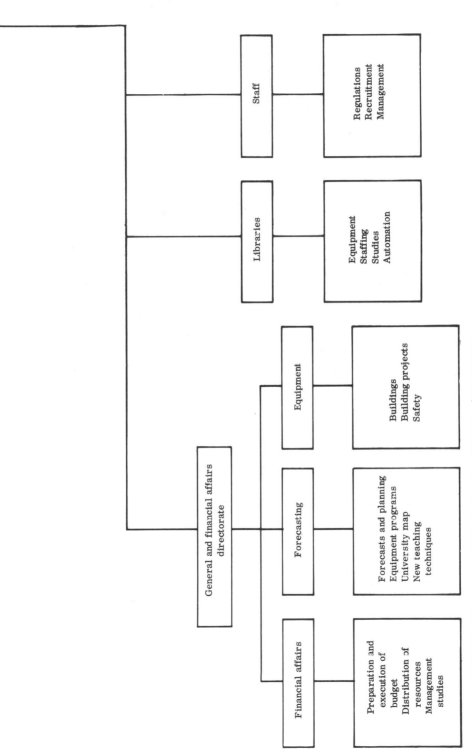

*As of 1978 this office was given full ministry status (Ministry of Universities).

Source: Compiled by the author.

33

committees (research, pedagogy, funds and resources, international relations), and it has only an advisory role. But the quality of its members, their unquestionable representativeness, and the fact that they have real responsibilities in their own universities make it impossible for the minister or government departments to ignore its points of view. As a result, the CPU is gradually displacing the CNESER in dealings with public authorities.

The Consultative Committee of the Universities (CCU) was set up prior to the 1968 law. It is comprised exclusively of teachers, either elected or appointed by the minister of Higher Education, and its task is to submit the names of teachers in each of the four grades of higher education (professor, assistant professor, lecturer, and junior lecturer) and for each major field of study, for appointment by the minister. This means that its findings, based essentially on the research and scientific competence of each candidate, govern each teacher's career.

At the regional level, the minister of Education and the secretary of state for the universities are represented by a rector in each of the 26 academies into which France is divided. According to French administrative practice, the rectorats are merely government agencies with very little power of initiation, and, indeed, almost none in matters of higher education. However, in 1977 the growing number of universities and university centers and the increasing diversity of their material situations, led the incumbent secretary of state for the universities (A. Saunier-Seite, herself a former rector) to try to give more importance to this administrative level.

Research administration organization presents a special situation in France. The public authorities have very extensive responsibilities in scientific and technical research, but these have long been scattered. In practice, each ministry of the government supervises one or several national research centers whose activities come within their field. The most important ministries and research centers are:

1. The Secretariat of State for the Universities: responsible for all university laboratories and research centers, and the National Center for Scientific Research (CNRS)—the CNRS is both a research center with its own research teams and an instrument of the government's scientific policy because it can finance selected university research teams; its connection with the Secretariat of State for the Universities is largely a formality;

2. The Ministry of Industry: the Commissariat for Atomic Energy (CEA), the National Center for Space Studies (CNES), and the National Center for the Exploitation of the Oceans (CNEXO);

3. The Ministry of Agriculture: the National Institute of Agricultural Research (INRA);

4. The Ministry of Health: the National Institute of Health and Medical Research (INSERM); and

5. The Ministry of Posts and Telecommunications: the National Telecommunications Research Center (CNET).

In 1958 a General Delegation for Scientific and Technical Research (DGRST), responsible directly to the prime minister, was set up to coordinate research activities undertaken by the public authorities and to rationalize medium- and long-term options in scientific policy. Aside from helping to draw up and coordinate scientific policies, this administrative body also supervises their implementation.

All budgetary resources devoted to research in the ministerial departments are set out in detail in the "research provision" included in the draft Finance Law submitted to Parliament each year for a vote. One of the essential tasks of the DGRST is to prepare this provision and, in particular, to carry out the arbitration involved.

Clearly, the Secretariat of State for the Universities plays a small part in the conception of national scientific research policies. The task of carrying them out falls essentially to the DGRST as far as financial resources are concerned, and to the CNRS regarding their scientific content.

Financing of the Universities

The system by which universities are financed can be viewed as a one-way process: all initiation falls onto the Ministry of Finance; the universities and their secretary of state are little more than passive recipients. The 1968 law was aimed at giving universities a certain amount of financial autonomy, but it still exists largely in name only. As Table 2.4 shows, nearly 90 percent of total university resources in 1975 came from the Secretariat of State for the Universities.

The financing process has two distinct phases: (1) the preparation of the budget and the vote on it by Parliament; and (2) the allocation of these resources by the Secretariat of State for the Universities to the various establishments under its control.

Drafting and Voting of the Budget

In budget matters it is the government, and especially the Ministry of Finance, that monopolizes the preparation of the draft Finance Law every year. During this phase the Secretariat of State for the Universities, like most of the so-called "social" ministries, has almost no influence. Unwanted at the technical level, it is also suspected by the Ministry of Finance officials of being a mouthpiece for

TABLE 2.4

Structure of Total Resources Available to Universities, 1975

Nature of Resources	Percent
Secretariat of State	88.9
Staffing	63.2
State employees	59.6
Supplementary teaching	3.6
Operational overheads	16.5
General overheads	12.8
Research overheads	3.7
Equipment	9.2
Teaching	7.2
Research	2.0
Other grants	2.2
Other ministries	0.8
Local and other authorities	1.4
Other resources	8.9
University dues	1.7
Research contracts	2.2
Other sources	5.0

Source: A. Bienaymé, "Le Financement des Universités," La Documentation Française, Paris, 1975.

higher-education interest groups rather than the champion of the state's superior interest. Furthermore, the actual drafting of the budget is done in a rather mechanical way, leaving no room for broad policy options.

In working out the resources for general overheads, for example, the budget for the year n is obtained by simply updating the budget for the year n - 1:

1. Staffing costs are reviewed in the light of estimated salary increases, which are quite easy to forecast. They arise partly from changes in the sliding salary scales brought about by promotions, which are based essentially on seniority, and partly from increases in the value of an index point. This too is easy to forecast because it follows the general price index according to rules laid down in agreements between the government and government employee unions.

2. Expenditure on overheads per se is brought up to date by means of estimates based on increases in the various price indexes developed by the National Institute of Statistics and Economic Studies (INSEE).

For capital investment the Ministry of Finance fixes the approximate size of the provision and then negotiates the final sum and purpose with the secretary of state for the universities.

As very few new posts have been created since 1970, and as investments have declined considerably since 1969 (see Table 2.2), the Secretariat's influence has been greatly reduced and is limited to the final arbitration stages of the budget; these are the only decisions that can reflect the choices in the field of university policy made by the public authorities.

The only remark we shall make concerning these choices is that they appear to stem from the desire for a healthier financial situation and from an evident concern to slow down or even halt the growth of the higher education budget.

Distributing Resources to the Universities

The allocation of resources, which will be examined in detail in the next section, reflects a relationship between the secretary of state and the universities similar to that between the Ministry of Finance and the Secretariat of State for the Universities—the government body controlling the funds has all the power.

This is a recent development, of course. In the early 1960s the expansion of higher education was felt by France, as it was by all Western countries, to be vital for maintaining and upholding industrial growth. At that time the universities were run by the high priests of a new religion (the growth of knowledge), which deserved large and beautiful temples (universities). The minister of Education was simply a shadowy dispenser of small funds.

That period now belongs to the past. The minister of Finance, followed by the minister of Education and the secretary of state for the universities, has regained the initiative. A perfect illustration of the new situation is the development of studies on how universities operate and what criteria should govern the allocation of funds.

ALLOCATION OF OPERATING RESOURCES
FROM 1967 TO 1977

Before describing methods for allocating resources, a few terms concerning the nature and destination of university resources will be discussed.

The resources used to finance university activities are extremely fragmented, and each grant is kept separate from all others. This occurs largely for historical reasons and because of the bureaucratic nature of French university administration. University resources are examined according to purpose and destination (see Table 2.5).

TABLE 2.5

Universities and University Centers: The Structure of the National Budget, 1975

	Thousands of Francs	Percent
Staff	3,169,268	71.0
State employees	2,988,613	67.0
Supplementary teaching	180,655	4.0
Operation	828,292	18.6
General overheads	641,862	14.4
Research overheads	186,430	4.2
Equipment	465,500	10.4
Teaching	361,500	8.1
Research	104,000	2.3
Total	4,463,060	100.0

Source: A. Bienaymé, "Le Financement des Universités," La Documentation Française, Paris 1975.

Distinctions according to Purpose

A clear distinction exists between a provision for overhead and a provision for teaching.

Provision for Overhead

This covers the upkeep, heating, and lighting of university buildings, as well as the cost of operating various facilities, such as laboratories and workshops. This provision is used to pay for water, energy (electricity, gas, fuel oil), maintenance (odd jobs, painting, cleaning), and minor needs such as paper, small pieces of furniture, and so on. It can also serve to pay for nonpermanent administrative or maintenance staff.

Provision for Teaching

This includes salaries of the teaching staff, on the one hand, and supplementary teaching hours, on the other. University teaching posts are strictly controlled by the government, both through the official code for permanent civil servants and with respect to salaries and the creation of new posts. The creation of a teaching post in a university means that the state has agreed to pay the person appointed out of the state budget. Having become a state employee, this person is governed by the Civil Service Code. Consequently, the university has no control whatsoever over its teaching staff.

At present there are three distinct categories of posts, each with different professional obligations:

1. Professors or full lecturers, who are required to give three hours of instruction per week, either as a lecture or a graduate seminar (in theory, the university year is 25 weeks);
2. Assistant lecturers; and
3. Junior lecturers (both categories of lecturers are required to teach six hours per week, for the most part in the form of supervised study or workshops).

Provision for Supplementary Teaching Hours

This money is used to pay, at a fixed hourly rate, for instruction carried out by teachers in addition to their normal duties or for courses provided by individuals from outside the university. Since the provision for the number of teaching positions is clearly inadequate, a large number of universities have had to recruit teachers without tenure who provide courses at the lowest level and who are paid solely in terms of supplementary hours.

Provision for Nonteaching Staff

This covers administrators, technical staff, maintenance, and service personnel (ATOS). As in the case of permanent teachers, these posts are created by the state and the salaries are paid from the national budget. However, faced with the inadequate state provision for this kind of post, the universities have often been obliged to recruit extra staff whose salaries are paid from the budget for overheads.

Distinctions according to Destination

The resources provided for teaching activities are separate from those provided for research. They are allocated in a different way, communicated separately to each university, and distributed within each university by different procedures. We should also bear in mind that university libraries are governed by a special service of the Secretariat of State for the Universities, receive their grants directly, and administer them according to special rules and methods.

Allocation Factors

This study begins by outlining how the methods used for the allocation of resources evolved between 1967 and 1975. There are two reasons for using this time span. First, there is little source material for the years prior to 1967 and, second, the year 1975 saw the introduction of a markedly different approach. The latter part of this section will look more closely at this new approach and examine the new allocation methods it brought into being.

To begin with, the fact that resources are extremely diverse in nature and allocated in different ways makes it necessary to separate questions concerning the provision for general overheads from those of teaching.

Provision for General Overheads

The methods of allocating resources employed from 1967 through 1974 began to be questioned for a number of reasons.

Chronologically, the first reason was the appearance and development of new fields of study or new training programs, which included economics (1963), management (1970), and masters courses in science and technical studies (1970). These "intruders" upset the traditional field of study categories.

Next, the growth rate of the higher education budget was reduced, with the result that provincial universities began to challenge the logic of their different treatment from universities in Paris.

Finally, in 1974, increased oil prices and accelerating inflation, with their effect on grants toward maintenance and heating, brought many universities to challenge the realism of the traditional allocation based on floor area.

A certain number of reports by inspectors of the administration also drew attention to disparities among particular universities that were difficult to justify.

This general dissatisfaction led the central authorities to commission a thorough study of university overheads and their various elements in January 1974. This study was carried out by a body known as GARACES (Group d'Analyse et de Recherche sur l'Activité et les Coûts des Enseignements Supérieurs). By 1975 it had succeeded in defining new methods for dividing up the general overheads grant among universities.

The GARACES study revealed a heretofore unknown fact, which might seem paradoxical: the causes of most disparities in overheads among universities are due to factors related to the structure of the universities—physical premises, non-built-up areas, teaching and administrative staff. The number of students was only of marginal importance. More specifically, university overheads are proportional to the surface area of main and ancillary buildings, to the teacher-student ratio, and to the administrative- and service personnel-to-teacher ratio.

The paradox is only apparent. The number of students has its effect, but only in the long term; a steady increase, for example, can make it necessary to add new buildings or staff. But these new buildings and staff, which generate increased overheads, are very constrictive, that is, once in place, they are unaffected by temporary fluctuations in student numbers. In the case of France, they even appear to be little affected by marked trends toward a smaller student body, as in scientific courses, for example.

The revelation of these important facts led the central authorities to envisage new ways of allocating resources for general overheads. The methods used in 1976 and 1977 resulted from the GARACES study. It prompted the secretary of state for the universities to develop a new allocation technique capable of responding to three requirements: (1) the need for a closer understanding of true costs so that grants, within the limits of available resources, could be adjusted; (2) the need to reduce the least excusable disparities, particularly those between Paris and the provinces; and (3) the need for an instrument that would be sufficiently flexible and precise to reallocate certain resources in line with certain policies. One of the first steps in this direction was to help universities specializing in law and economics to achieve a better balance with those specializing in the sciences.

This new allocation technique is based on two cost bases. The first basis consists of the costs related to premises and ancillary buildings. An examination of the cost of maintaining buildings and non-built-up areas led the central administration to fix the basic rate at Fr 47 (about U. S. $2) per square meter of floor area and Fr 40 per square meter for undeveloped areas. This figure resulted from a study of the costs borne by all universities and also corresponds to the individual average most frequently encountered. It does not correspond to true maintenance costs, which are sometimes heavier, particularly for universities with very high buildings or prestige buildings that are very expensive to maintain.

The second basis consists of costs linked to teaching. These costs concern both teaching staff and the supporting administrative and technical staff. The GARACES study, having revealed a relation between overheads and the staffing ratio, and between teaching and nonteaching staff, decided to base allocations on the standard staffing ratio of each university. (The method used is described in the Note on the Calculation of Standard Staffing Ratios near the end of this chapter.)

Each university is thus classed according to three factors: the surface area of the premises and outlying areas, a standard teacher ratio, and a standard staffing ratio for administrative, technical, and service personnel. The first of these is used to calculate the fixed grant per square meter for built-up and non-built-up areas. The other two factors enable the number of "units of account" for each university to be calculated. Once this is done, the general total for all universities is divided into the national budgetary allowance. In this way the exact value of a "unit of account," and thus the grant of each institution, is obtained.

Briefly, the value (in French francs) of the allocation for overheads in a given university (i) is found by applying this formula:

$$\text{Function}_i = \underbrace{(47 \times FA^i) + (0.40 \times NB^i)}_{\text{allocation "surface area"}} + \underbrace{4335 \ (N_{ST}^i \times \theta) + N_T^i \times \theta_{AS}^i)}_{\text{allocation "staffing"}}$$

FA: Floor area	N_T^i: Number of teachers
NB: Non-built-up area	θ_T^i: Standard teacher ratio
N_{ST}^i: Number of students	θ_{AS}^i: Staffing ratio for administrative, technical, and service personnel
N_T^i: Number of teachers	

It is still a delicate task to offer a judgment on this new approach to allocations. But the methods chosen to fix the "standard" staffing ratios are likely to have at least two partly contradictory effects. The introduction of a standard rate for each group of universities will clearly contribute to homogeneity among universities in the same group. On the other hand, the division of all universities into a number of groups based on size and the main subjects taught will help maintain and even reinforce existing disparities among universities in different groups. For example, in the case of groups containing universities from both Paris and the provinces, it has been possible to reduce disparities. On the other hand, there is absolutely no change in the treatment of the various fields of study; these have simply been maintained without modification, and there has been no attempt at new explanation or justification.

Resources for Teaching

We have already seen how the resources for teaching fall into two categories: teaching staff and supplementary teaching hours. These two categories give rise to two distinctly different methods of allocation for teaching staff and supplementary teaching hours.

Teaching Staff

Up until 1971, new teaching posts were created as the need arose. They depended on the outcome of negotiations among the central authorities and the heads of institutions, faculty deans, and university presidents.

Previously, the rapid increase in student numbers had created pressing needs for new staff, which led the public authorities to adopt a policy of systematically creating new posts. This relative well-being facilitated the development of many informal procedures wherein the only criterion more or less respected was student numbers. The well-known lack of strict regulations regarding attribution enabled the most influential universities to enjoy clear advantages over the national average. In this situation the universities of Paris (large in size, some long-established and eminent, geographically and sociologically close to the centers of public decision) were the best placed. The advantages they acquired during this period, and gradually established as their due, help explain their relatively comfortable material situation in comparison to provincial universities.

After 1971, however, fewer new posts were created. A bleaker future made disparities harder to accept, and the need to reduce them called for more rigorous criteria and stricter procedures for fund allocation. In each of the six basic fields of study an average national staffing ratio was calculated based on the relation between the number of enrolled students and the number of teachers. A guideline, or "theoretical staffing ratio," was then defined for each institution, equal to the national average and weighted according to student numbers. The creation of new posts could now be concentrated on universities whose real ratio was the furthest from the theoretical level. The final phase consisted of negotiations concerning the subject and level of the new posts.

These criteria are still in use today, and the same approach has now been extended to administrative, technical, and service personnel.

Supplementary Teaching Hours

The provision for funding supplementary teaching was in a plight similar to that for regular teaching staff. The criteria for allocation had long been extremely vague, and the customary procedure left almost everything to negotiation. The only framework for these negotiations was respect for the number of students and for the provision that the allowance would not be reduced from one year to the next. Only a massive increase in the number of permanent teaching posts could help bring down the amount of this allocation.

This situation changed little until 1975, when a reduced budget obliged the central administration to review all allocations and procedures for their attribution. A preliminary study was once again commissioned to GARACES, which proposed an allocation procedure based on the observed gap between the staffing potential of each establishment (the number of teaching posts times the service obligation in hours) and the teaching needs (calculated from the number of students and from course requirements as laid down by the official texts governing the award of national degrees and diplomas). The result of applying these criteria was, in 1976, to reduce by more than 30 percent the allocation for supplementary teaching hours in the universities.

CONCLUSIONS AND FUTURE PROSPECTS

The foregoing description of allocation methods has brought out a number of fairly permanent features: fragmented resources and procedures, a year-by-year approach, and exclusive reliance on quantitative criteria.

We must now look at the consequences. Do such methods encourage the development of university autonomy, officially introduced by the 1968 law for higher education? Or do they instead tend to reinforce the traditional French tendency toward centralized administration? How far do they enable policy-making institutions, such as the university and the central administration, to control their own development and that of the university system as a whole?

Failure to Develop Real Autonomy
in University Management

It has already been stressed that universities are extremely dependent on the state, which provides over 90 percent of all their resources. This dependence is increased by the manner in which these resources are distributed.

At the university level, the resources for general, pedagogical, or scientific activities are split up into a multitude of categories. This is sometimes because of the legal status of certain resources (such as those for teaching or administrative staff), or budgetary rules (such as the distinction between general overheads and supplementary teaching hours). The result, as far as management is concerned, is a set of water-tight compartments, which makes an overall approach impossible. Any attempt to achieve coherence or efficiency is therefore gravely handicapped and can only succeed by secretly bending the law.

Just as the resources are split up, the corresponding criteria and procedures governing their allocation are also kept quite separate. Allocation determinations must be made by the different departments of the central administration, which slows down the decision-making process, so that efficient short-term management is made next to impossible.

Finally, the strict adherence to the annual rhythm of the budget and the fact that the Secretariat of State for the Universities is very dependent upon the Ministry of Finance discourage all attempts at controlled planning.

Failure to Enhance Central Control
of University Activities

Present practices are the first obstacle to central control. In theory, the implementation of new allocation methods for general overheads ought to have led to a redistribution of existing resources, essentially benefiting provincial universities. However, this potential redistribution was greatly undermined by maintaining a budgetary practice introduced in 1970, which stated that no university should see its provision for overheads, expressed in current francs, reduced from one year to the next. This "stop-valve" presented no problem when budgets were growing; in fact, it merely recognized a long-established feature of previous budgets as accepted practice. Before 1970 no university had ever had its provision for overheads reduced in current francs.

To maintain this practice at a time of budget stagnation, however, imposes very powerful constraints: redistribution can only operate within the narrow limits of the budget growth rate in real terms, on the one hand, and the inflation rate, on the other. In any case, one result was to greatly reduce the effect of the new allocation methods worked out by GARACES. Of 66 universities in metropolitan France, 7 of the 13 universities in Paris took advantage of the "stop-valve" provision, whereas only one provincial university did so.

But behind practice lie methods. From this point of view, one fact appears to be of central importance. These methods have developed inconsistently, when seen in terms of the resources to which they are applied. The studies carried out by GARACES, as has been seen, revealed that operating costs are hardly affected, in the short term, by variations in the flow of students, as they arise essentially from "structural" factors: physical premises, major items of equipment, administrative staff, and teachers. But, in the long term, the evolution of these structures, and hence of running costs, correlates with trends in student numbers. Universities are only built, equipped, and provided with teachers if the social demand for university education appears likely to continue.

Considering all of these different aspects as a whole, we are obliged to conclude that the central authority—the Secretariat of State for the Universities—is relatively powerless. Although the procedures for allocating resources for general overheads and for supplementary teaching hours are based on fairly sophisticated and precise criteria, the procedures for making decisions affecting the structure of universities are either very crude (as in the case of staffing) or nonexistent (as in the case of buildings and equipment). This lack of refinement and sophistication of the allocation procedures affecting structure stand in almost inverse proportion to their influence on the medium- and long-term prospects of the system, and in particular to their influence on future running costs.

Therefore, when one considers only formal procedures, it must be concluded that the state secretariat does not have full control over the future development of resources for teaching purposes, or over the consequent rise in overheads.

Central Administration:
Contradictions between Role and Practice

The central authority takes shelter behind the policy of university autonomy, proclaimed by the 1968 law, claiming to be "neutral"

and "objective" and justifying its interventions as being for management, technical, or legal reasons exclusively. The immediate result
of this attitude is that its allocation procedures rely almost solely on
quantitative criteria. Only then, it is claimed, can "fair" distribution,
which both the universities and central administration demand, be
guaranteed.

The notions of goal, program, and choice therefore have no place
in discussions on resources. Such discussions are exclusively concerned with whether or not the criteria employed for distribution are
"equitable".

Following the logic of this attitude, the central authorities refuse to impose, or even suggest, standards that conflict too much
with the existing method of allocating the various resources. As we
have already emphasized, in considering the procedures employed
since 1975 for allocating funds for overheads, old "norms" tend to be
perpetuated, even though the most unjustifiable disparities have been
reduced.

Logically, autonomy also implies that the central authorities
should allocate resources among the universities but should allow
them to be responsible for internal redistribution. The hypothesis
implied in this power sharing is that the universities are homogeneous
centers of power, capable of making choices and imposing them on
their constituent parts. In fact, this is rarely the case. The universities, as reconstituted by the 1968 reform, are often merely formal
juxtapositions of completely independent UERs (teaching and research
units) developed from former "faculties" that specialized in a single
field of study. These former faculties have held on to all the power—
in terms of prestige as well as resources—they had built up prior to
1968, and they are able to lay down the law to the more recent or less
influential UERs.

The allocation of resources within the universities thus follows
a completely different pattern from that at the national level, and we
might well ask to what extent these two approaches complement or
contradict each other. But the most striking thing is that the central
administration has no knowledge at all about this internal distribution.
For example, it is at present unable to assess the impact, at the UER
level, of the modified allocation procedures introduced at the national
level in 1975. This alone is enough to make us wonder about the real
objectives of the modification in question. Was it not essentially to
satisfy the administration's own internal requirements?

New Outlooks

To end our account on this note, however, would leave it incomplete, and would be unjust to an administration that makes daily efforts to improve its decision-making procedures. In fact, the procedures for allocating resources are still in the throes of change (as should be gathered from our account) and there are increased attempts to break the deadlock.

These initiatives can be classed into two major groups: (1) attempts to perfect existing procedures by recourse to quantitative criteria and (2) attempts to supplement existing procedures by introducing the idea of program.

Development of the Quantitative Approach

All of the efforts to expand the use of quantitative criteria aim at constructing an abstract basic unit, "the teaching module," which relates type of course, number of students, teaching staff needed, buildings used, necessary equipment, and technical and administrative personnel.

This standard model, once developed, can serve as the basic reference for all resource allocation; only decisions to set up new universities or to introduce new types of courses would remain subject to more political procedures. The assessment of potential demand for education, however, independent of the existence of facilities that satisfy this demand, is still a controversial issue.

With this module the authorities who allocate resources make their calculations for: the construction or extension of buildings, occasioned by a possible growth in student numbers and the demand for education; funds for equipment; the creation of new teaching and administrative posts for the new influx of students; funds for supplementary teaching, indispensable for the flexible organization of courses; and, finally, funds for overhead costs, which depend essentially on the "structural" aspect of the module—physical premises, equipment, and staff.

In France the first attempt in this direction began in 1966/67, when the University Institutes of Technology (IUTs) were created. Standardized plans were drawn up for these establishments to cover the pedagogical needs of each of the 17 departmental categories and to accommodate 300 students over a 2-year course of study. For each year, a standard staffing ratio was worked out: from 9 to 15 teachers for every 150 students, depending on whether the courses were considered to be at the secondary or tertiary level. The annual allocation for overheads was calculated according to the floor area of the buildings, the number of students, and the category to which a department belonged.

It turned out, however, to be far more difficult than expected to put these measures into practice. The IUTs never managed to attract the number of students hoped for. When they were first created in 1966, it was planned that they would have 168,000 students by 1972/

73, but as of 1978 they have hardly reached 44,000. Buildings and equipment that were planned far ahead are still not fully utilized.

The gap between the available facilities and public demand has caused many financial difficulties, for which the Secretariat of State for the Universities is now trying to find a solution. In spite of this setback, but profiting from the experience gained, the GARACES has undertaken a series of studies aimed at extending the "teaching module" approach to all universities. However, the work is not yet far enough advanced for us to give an account of it at this time.

Research Programs

The methods used for allocating resources for research appear to have benefited from the special status of research. According to the "research provision" of the budget, research is completely unaffected by the traditional administrative practice of dividing its funds into separate disciplinary categories, a situation probably reflecting the close attention public authorities have shown in recent years.

Before 1973, resource allocations were based on quantitative criteria alone. The provision for research overheads in each university was set in proportion to the number of titular professors and senior lecturers in residence; this method of calculation reflected perfectly the assumption that each teacher is also a researcher and divides his activities between research and teaching.

Later, the methods of calculation became more refined. Since 1973, a "basic" allocation and a "program" allocation have been established. The basic allocation consists of two parts: an allocation per research worker, teacher or nonteacher, and one proportionate to the most recent physical plant investments.

The allocation per research worker is modulated according to field study (it varies from Fr 900 for the arts up to Fr 5,050 for the sciences) and the type of research, which is measured in each discipline by two indicators: (1) the relation between the number of third-cycle theses and doctorat d'etat theses successfully defended each year and the number of researchers employed at the university; and (2) the relation between the number of researchers on teams associated with the CNRS and the total number of university research workers in their field of study.*

------

*The CNRS (the National Center for Scientific Research), aside from carrying out research in its own centers, has a policy of promoting selected projects. It awards supplementary funds to certain research teams, which it chooses on the basis of the research project itself and the scientific findings the research team can offer.

The allocation proportionate to investments is equal to: (1) 5 percent of the value of fixed investments over the six previous years and (2) 10 percent of the value of investments in equipment over the same period, excluding those in computer science, which are funded separately.

The program allocation, the major innovation in this procedure, is designed to support research programs for periods of over one year, (a step encouraged by the Secretariat of State for the Universities). This allocation is granted after an examination of scientific policy statements drawn up by the Scientific Council of each university to cover the next three years and, of course, based on the results of research programs previously selected for this procedure.

In this program-based allocation, the authorities have found a new instrument for furthering scientific policy, in addition to the Three-year Equipment Program, which determines university allocations to cover heavy research equipment.

NOTE ON THE CALCULATION OF
STANDARD STAFFING RATIOS

The Standard Teacher Ratio

When the GARACES made its inquiry into university overhead costs, each of the six basic fields of study corresponding to the specialization of teachers (law and economics, arts and humanities, sciences, medicine, pharmacy, and odontology) were examined separately within each university. For each university, and for each of these fields, the number of students was compared to the number of teachers. A teacher ratio was thus obtained for each field of study and each university.

These ratios were then mutually compared within each field of study and indicated that, in a given field of study, universities of comparable size (number of students) had similar teacher ratios.

All universities were then classified into "families" that grouped together, by field, those of comparable size. In this way 15 families, spread over the six basic fields of study, were identified. Each had its own standard teacher ratio, reflecting the average staffing ratio within that family. Each family was thus characterized by a distribution of observed staffing ratios.

As each university belonged to as many families as it had basic fields of study, it became possible to calculate their individual standard teaching ratios. The ratio is obtained by simply taking the average, weighted according to student numbers, of the standard ratios of each family to which a given university belongs. It is this ratio that now serves as a base when the allocation for the pedagogical staff is calculated.

The Standard Nonteaching Staff Ratio

A similar method was adopted for calculating the standard ATOS ratios. The essential difference between it and the previous method is how the various families are classified. Although size remains one of the two criteria employed, the other factor, fields of study, was replaced by structural complexity. Thus, universities were classified into the following groups: those with one basic field of study; two basic fields of study; three basic fields of study; more than three basic fields of study; and university centers, small universities, and local nonuniversity institutions.

Each of these families then had a standard ATOS ratio, which made it possible to calculate the standard ratio for each establishment. This is the ratio currently used to calculate the allocation for administrative, technical, maintenance, and service staff.

3
HIGHER EDUCATION FINANCING IN GREECE
Rossetos Fakiolas

INSTITUTIONAL STRUCTURE

The structure of the higher educational system, students enrollment, and goals of decentralization are governed by the allocation processes for higher education financing in Greece.

During the academic year 1976/77, five universities functioned in Greece—one each in Athens, Thessaloniki, Patras, and Ioannina, and one in the province of Thrace. Three additional universities are scheduled to open during 1977/78 in the cities of Iraklion and Rethimnon on the island of Crete.

The universities of Athens and Thessaloniki offer the major disciplines, whereas a limited number of subjects are presently taught at Patras, Ioannina, and Thrace. The University of Crete will open with faculties of medicine, physics-mathematics, and philosophy.

In addition to the universities there are seven independent postsecondary schools, six in Athens and one in Thessaloniki. The Technical University (known as the Polytechnic) and the Schools of Fine Arts, Industrial Studies, Economics and Commercial Studies, Political Sciences, and Agricultural Studies are in Athens. There is another School of Industrial Studies in Thessaloniki.

The author acknowledges the information supplied by the high officials of the Ministry of Education, K. Skoutaris, P. Voudoukis, I. Ioannou, and Pan. Moukios, as well as comments on an early draft made by Professor Emeritus S. Gedeon, Professors G. Pantelidis, Th. Georgacopoulos, and C. Drakatos.

Several other postsecondary educational institutions exist below the university level. These include the Pedagogical Academies for primary school teachers, the Academies for high school teachers, the School for Domestic Sciences, approximately 12 technical and vocational schools, and several others. About 20,000 students are now enrolled in these schools, which offer 2- to 4-year courses. None of these schools have the autonomy of an institute of higher education (IHE); teachers are appointed directly by the Ministry of Education, rather than being elected by the existing faculty. This area of postsecondary education is expected to expand rapidly, in order to relieve the enrollment pressure on universities and the schools equivalent to them.

There are also three cadet schools for army, navy, and air force officers, which function under the auspices of the Ministry of National Defense.

Enrollment and Staff

Between 1955 and 1976, the number of students enrolled in IHEs increased from 21,000 to over 100,000, and the number of teachers rose from 777 to 6,233 (Table 3.1). Two-thirds of the total student population in 1974/75 was enrolled at the universities of Athens and Thessaloniki; only 6 percent of the total was enrolled at each of the three new universities of Patras, Ioannina, and Thrace. The regional distribution of the student population has become more representative since then, but it will take many years for the new universities to expand to a more efficient size.

The student-teacher ratio was about 17 to 1 during the academic year 1976/77 (taking into account all members of the teaching staff). The number of "organic" positions—those that are approved by the Ministry of Education and that can be filled by graduates of the IHEs— was 8,877 during the same period and provides an even more satisfactory student-teacher ratio. However, as shown in Table 3.2, assistants comprised more than half of the teaching personnel, and of those only 163 held Ph.D. degrees. According to the regulations of the Ministry of Education, only Ph.D. holders can be assigned teaching responsibilities; the rest can only help professors in tutorial exercises. Slightly more than one-fourth of the teaching personnel hold Ph.D. degrees. If only those persons are considered qualified for teaching responsibilities, the student-teacher ratio in the Greek IHEs is then about 70 to 1—considerably higher than in most developed countries.

During the last three years, about 16,000 freshmen have enrolled annually. Applicants for the entrance examinations have averaged 60,000 to 80,000 annually. Therefore, only one in four or

TABLE 3.1

Number of Students and Teachers in Institutions of Higher Education, 1955-76

Academic Year	Number of Students	Teaching Personnel
1955	16,866	582
1965	54,261	903
1970	72,269	3,162
1971	70,161	3,420
1972	76,035	4,305
1973	80,041	4,752
1974[a]	92,920	5,466
1976[b]	102,000	6,233

[a]Unpublished data supplied by the National Statistical Service of Greece.
[b]Provisional data supplied by the Ministry of Education.

Sources: National Statistical Service of Greece, Statistical Yearbooks of Greece (1955/75); and Ministry of Education.

five examinees is allowed to enroll in the first year. Those who finish high school every year amount to about 50,000, of the total 18-year-old population of about 140,000. A considerable number of those who are not accepted into an IHE study abroad. From 1972 through 1976, about 6,000 high school graduates enrolled annually in foreign universities.

The number of new enrollments is determined every year by the Ministry of Education after consultation with the IHEs. The IHEs submit a detailed list of existing teaching facilities and faculties to the ministry, and states the number of students they can accommodate. As a rule, however, the number of new students stipulated for each IHE by the Ministry of Education is considerably higher than the number given by the institution.

TABLE 3.2

Number of Persons Employed by IHEs, December 1976

	Number
Authorized chairs and other positions	
Teaching staff	
Regular chairs	744
Independent chairs[a]	104
Tenured assistant professors	207
Tutors	1,843
Special teachers[b]	144
Assistants	4,683
Laboratory supervisors	1,152
Total	8,877
Administrative staff	
Regular staff	2,705
Employed on a contract basis	1,320
Total	4,025
Employed	
Teaching staff	
Tenured professors	496
Tenured professors holding independent chairs	66
Nontenured professors	61
Tenured assistant professors	106
Ighigitai[c]	151
Instructors	62
Research associates	17
Tutors[d]	1,004
Special teachers	102
Assistants[e]	3,244
Laboratory supervisors	924
Total	6,233
Administrative staff	
Regular staff	1,842
Employed on a contract basis	811
Total	2,653

[a]These are equivalent to regular chairs, but professors who hold them do not participate in elections of new professors.

[b]These are mostly aliens or Greek linguists who teach foreign languages.

[c]Postdoctoral degree holders with teaching responsibilities.

[d]About 600 of these hold Ph.D. degrees.

[e]Of these, 163 hold Ph.D. degrees.

Source: Ministry of Education, unpublished data.

TABLE 3.3

Revenues of the IHEs, 1975

(in millions of drachmas)

Institution	State Budget Allocations	Owned Property	Business Activities and Legacies	Other Sources (loans, et cetera)	Total
Athens University	661.3	29.000	8.700	358.200	1,057
Thessaloniki University	938.2	6.000	2.000	14.600	962
Ioannina University	114.5	0.836	0.534	n.a.	116
Patras University	218.1	0.134	n.a.	n.a.	218
University of Thrace	129.0	n.a.	n.a.	0.163	129
Athens Polytechnic	352.5	n.a.	97.300	n.a.	450
Athens School of Economics	54.3	0.516	0.914	0.901	56
Pantios School of Political Sciences	66.3	2.100	0.563	n.a.	69
Piraeus School of Industrial Studies	44.3	n.a.	0.850	n.a.	44
Thessaloniki School of Industrial Studies	51.0	n.a.	0.145	1.300	52
Athens Agricultural School	122.8	4.600	0.801	n.a.	128
School of Fine Arts	21.3	n.a.	0.126	n.a.	21
Total	2,723.6	43.286	111.268	375.164	3,302

n.a.: data not available

Source: National Statistical Service of Greece, unpublished data.

REVENUE SOURCES AND THE
STRUCTURE OF EXPENSES

State education at all levels is completely free. No tuition,
registration, or other fee is charged to the students. All basic textbooks are also free of charge. The revenues of the IHEs come primarily from state budget allocations. Only small sums accrue from
owned assets (such as real estate rents, dividends from shares and
bonds), business activities (such as publication of books and certification fees), and individual donations.

During the five-year period 1969-73, 92 percent of all current
expenses came from budget allocations; 6 percent came from property owned by the IHE and 1.7 percent from other sources. Of the
total revenue from owned property, 72.4 percent went to the University of Athens and about 20 percent to the University of Thessaloniki,
the Athens Polytechnic, and the Athens Agricultural School (Table
3.3). As a result, revenue from owned property and business activities amounted to only a small percentage of total expenses (around
2 percent) for all IHEs except the University of Athens. The four new
universities have no revenue from sources other than the state budget.

An annual survey on the financing of all kinds of education (public and private at all levels) was started in 1973 by the National Statistical Service of Greece (NSSG). The survey was based on a questionnaire sent to all educational and training institutions near the end
of every academic year. Detailed data on revenues and expenses
have been collected and processed for 1973, 1974, and 1975.

The sources of IHE revenue and the amount from each source
for 1975 are shown in Table 3.3. The difference between revenues
and expenses consists of cash balances and unused budgeted funds that
are left intact for use in the following year.

Current Expenses

The financial needs of the IHEs are for current expenses and
investment in fixed capital.

Current expenses are primarily for the salaries of the regular
staff, as well as rents, office and laboratory materials, fuel, library
books, and maintenance work. Most of these expenses are fixed because the majority of the teaching and administrative personnel are
tenured civil servants. Expenses for the remaining items are also
difficult to eliminate or even curtail. If these expenses are not included directly in the state budget, they become priority items in the
expenses covered by regular state grants given to the IHEs. This issue will be discussed in more detail.

Another current expense is for the wages and salaries of extra personnel or persons employed by the IHEs on a contract basis. These persons are not civil servants; their pay comes out of special items provided for in the budget for current expenses. The salaries of temporary lecturers and the majority of laboratory technicians belong to this category. These categories of expenses are not so rigid and, within limits, can vary from year to year. Nevertheless, detailed provisions for these expenses are made in the budgets of the IHEs.

Investment needs are for school buildings, equipment, the purchase of land, and capital repairs or renovation of buildings to suit educational purposes.

Budget Preparation

The different kinds of financial needs, and the fact that about 92 percent of all expenses are covered from state budget allocations, have led to various institutional arrangements for the financing of the IHEs. Each IHE prepares a detailed budget every year (some institutions prepare two per year). Each category of expense is stated separately and is met by specific sources of revenues. Even the money that comes from the state budget is administered in different ways, with specific arrangements made for every category of expense, and is controlled by different sections of the civil service.

All large universities and other schools have business sections with fully manned technical services in which economists, accountants, engineers, and lawyers are employed. Their primary duties are to translate faculty requests for current operations, as well as expansion, modernization, or organizational reforms, into financial terms and to prepare the budgets and supervise their implementation. The technical services are chiefly concerned with matters of design and construction work, including the cost accounting of all projects. Both the economic and the technical services are in close contact with the corresponding departments of the Ministry of Education.

FACTORS AFFECTING FINANCIAL NEED
AND EFFICIENCY OF OPERATION

The complexities of estimating economic need and the efficiency of operation in universities and other institutions of higher education are well-known. In the first place, it is difficult to calculate some of the basic components of educational expenses, such as the earnings forgone by students and the earnings some teachers make from additional jobs. In addition, the quality of the product—the educational

level and sophistication of the graduates—is not easy to evaluate.
Even if approximations were possible, the degree of maturity and all-
around stature of a graduate cannot be credited entirely to the IHE
from which he or she has graduated. The set of values with which the
students are confronted, that is, the entire social, economic, and
family environment, as well as the selection systems, which may or
may not allow those with the best intellect and attitude to reach college, plays an important role in this respect. A third factor to consider is the contribution of the IHEs to research and the social effects
of the university research effort. By its very nature, this effort and
the results from it do not lend themselves easily to statistical mea-
surement and evaluation.

In Greece there are entrance examinations for the IHEs, and
only one in five candidates is allowed to enroll because the number of
first-year enrollments for every IHE is fixed in advance by the government. The high standards set for the entrance examinations would
mean that only first-quality applicants are allowed to register. The
educational system would seem to be efficient by definition, because
of the high quality of the student input.

However, this may not be true because of two factors: (1) the
content of the examination itself and the preparation of the student for
it and (2) a large number of high school graduates prepare for foreign
universities and do not take part in the examination at all. An indication of this is the number of schools that prepare high school graduates for universities abroad. For example, some of the best high
schools in the country, such as the Athens College and the Moraitis
School, offer formal courses for the General Certificate of Education,
which is a necessary qualification for acceptance at a British university. Many other private colleges concentrate on preparing students
for Italian, British, U.S., and, recently, Romanian universities.

Another factor to be taken into account is the great number of
flourishing private tutorial colleges for students of the IHEs. With
the exception of a small number of schools and faculties in which lecture attendance is obligatory, few students attend the lectures. Usually students attend a few lectures at the beginning of the academic
year and then drift away to private tutorial colleges where, at a more
convenient time and in a more relaxed environment, they attend the
same lectures delivered by the university teachers. Some graduates
have never attended a lecture at the institution from which they graduated because they had full-time jobs or could not find places in the
classrooms when they tried to enter. Lectures may be delivered to a
maximum of 1,000 students, many of whom may be standing. In addition, the ability to impart knowledge skillfully has been used very
rarely as a criterion for the appointment of teachers.

This situation is improving gradually with the government decision to limit the number of students enrolled in the large universities

and schools and to direct more students to the new universities. Also, new teaching positions have been created, and efforts are being made to fill them immediately. Yet the high student-teacher ratio in the main Greek IHEs has been the most depressing aspect of higher education. It is primarily the result of the heavy student concentration in Athens and Salonica, and of the many difficulties encountered in the appointment of teachers. Financial restraints and shortages of qualified teachers are relatively minor difficulties.

The continental chair system, which is followed in Greece, gives professors prerogatives that serve to hinder modernization and efficiency in the IHEs. Accusations of favoritism and nepotism in appointments, as well as reluctance of established professors to share teaching and administrative responsibilities with new scholars are frequent.

To conclude, the strict system of entrance examinations, the operation of numerous private tutorial colleges for the coaching of both the candidates for IHEs and enrolled students, and the practices of the academic staff are not helping to achieve high academic or economic efficiency in the Greek IHEs.

On the other hand, teaching positions at the IHEs, especially professorships, carry high social prestige, great political influence, and salaries equal to those of cabinet ministers. These are incentives for top-level people to join the teaching staff and achieve high levels of efficiency in the institutions that they control. In addition, there is strong competition between schools and faculties for state funds, which one would expect to help eliminate inefficient practices. It should be noted that a great number of professors are also members of Parliament, bank governors, directors of social insurance organizations, or special ambassadors. Hence, change in the existing system is confronted with formidable obstacles. One of them is certainly the fact that being a professor is only a part-time job for many active IHE teachers.

INSTITUTIONAL MECHANISMS
FOR STATE FINANCING

As mentioned earlier, the state budget is by far the most important source of financing IHE operations. This financing is done primarily through the Ministry of Education. Since state funds are for current expenses and fixed capital, two other ministries are involved—the Ministry of Finance for current expenses and the Ministry of Coordination for capital investment. At the Ministry of Education the link between these other two ministries is established through specialized business sections that function within the General Divisions.

Ministry of Education

The administrative structure of the Ministry of Education is comprised of five general divisions: three for higher, general, and technical vocational education, one for religious affairs, and one for planning, computations, and technical teaching aids.

The General Division of Higher Education consists of the three divisions and one independent section:

1. Organization and Statistics, responsible for the establishment, organization, functioning, and academic programs of each IHE;

2. Personnel, divided into three sections responsible for the main and auxiliary teaching staffs and the administrative staff of the IHEs;

3. Academic and Other Student Affairs, divided into three sections. One section is responsible for the entrance examinations; the second for student affairs; the third is a business section that receives the IHE budgets submitted for approval to the Ministry of Education, checks the IHE balance sheets, works out and proposes to higher authorities the distribution of state funds among the various IHEs, and looks into any other economic matter of the IHEs and research institutes that come under the purview of the General Division of Higher Education. This section also collaborates closely with the business sections of other general divisions in the ministry. The coordination of the work of all business sections in the ministry is achieved through the General Division of Planning, Computations, and Technical Teaching Aids.

The one independent section within the General Division of Higher Education is the Section of Interuniversity Relations. Its staff helps promote relations among the Greek IHEs and educational and research institutions abroad. It does this by arranging the participation of Greek university teachers in conferences abroad and exchange programs, and by preparing cultural agreements with other countries.

The General Division of Planning, Computations, and Technical Teaching Aids has the following five divisions:

1. Planning and Operational Analysis. This consists of five sections that are responsible for the planning of public investment in various kinds and levels of education and vocational training. The functions of these sections include the provision of operational analyses of the various investment projects and the collection and compilation of educational statistics related to financial and technical matters. One of these sections is charged with preparing and implementing

the General Budget of the Ministry of Education. Another collects and processes all information available to the Ministry of Education and other ministries about students at all educational levels. The staff of this section collaborates closely with the Center of Educational Research (whose functions are described below) in an effort to determine the needs of the nation in teaching personnel of all religious denominations and in the various categories of skilled labor. They also investigate ways and means of attaining the educational goals set forth in official policy statements.

2. Technical Services. This division is charged with the approval of feasibility studies and architectural designs of all educational buildings.

3. Technical Training Aids. This has three sections responsible for the provision and proper use of teaching aids in state schools.

4. Computations. This has five sections, charged with the analysis, programming, codification, and financial control of the various investment projects of the Ministry of Education.

5. Design, Construction Work, and Evaluation of Projects. This consists of three sections responsible for the time schedules of design and construction work and the implementation of contracts signed with various Greek and foreign organizations. They are also responsible for the implementation of the budgets of the Ministry of Education for current expenses and for investments. The sections of this division collaborate closely with the Central Division of Educational Projects of the Ministry of Coordination.

The Ministry of Education employs about 750 persons, more than half of them graduates of Greek and foreign universities.

The General Division of Higher Education has approximately 40 employees—about two-thirds of them are university graduates. The head of this division is always a tenured professor, and his deputy is usually a person with at least 25 years experience in administration and education.

The General Division of Planning and Computations has approximately 107 highly specialized employees, working primarily in the technical and economic aspects of education. This division comes into direct contact with the business sections of the IHEs.

Heads of divisions and sections are always university graduates in various disciplines. Graduates in economics, engineering, mathematics, and law predominate among those who work in the business and technical sections. Those who make suggestions to higher authorities on general educational matters are mainly graduates in humanities and have had much experience in educational affairs.

The Center for Educational Research (KEME), mentioned above, is an autonomous research institute under the auspices of the Ministry of Education and offers valuable assistance to all decision makers of that ministry. This is a new center (founded in 1974) that employs about 74 persons, of whom 46 have done postgraduate work abroad. Most of them also have many years of experience in teaching, research, or public administration.

This description indicates that a great number of divisions and sections of the Ministry of Education are responsible for the allocation of funds to the institutions of higher education. It also shows that despite the autonomy enjoyed by the IHEs, higher education in Greece is under the strict control of the Ministry of Education. The basis of this control rests on the constitutional provision that higher education is a state monopoly, and on the fact that the relatively large sums of money allocated to the IHEs come from the state. One should not assume that state control is in itself inefficient. In Greece, historical developments and tradition have allowed the civil service to acquire considerable expertise in educational matters. Civil servants are capable of applying existing laws on educational matters and of administering large funds; they are in a position to offer valuable guidance to the IHEs with respect to the educational needs of the country and to help them assimilate new teaching methods and means of university organization without delay.

General Arrangements for State Financing

As mentioned above, some IHEs meet all their current financial needs through an annual grant from the state budget. Those in this category are the two schools of industrial studies and all the universities except those of Athens and Thessaloniki.

Other institutions get a state grant, but in addition, there are separate items in the state budget for the salaries of their administrative personnel, extra pay for the teaching staff, and other current expenses. Those in this category are the Schools of Economics, Political Sciences, Agricultural Studies, and Fine Arts. These institutions prepare two budgets every year. The first includes expenses covered by the grant and other sources and the second forms a part of the state budget.

The universities of Athens and Thessaloniki and the Athens Polytechnic get funds from three sources: a state grant, a special grant to cover lump sums given to retiring employees who do not qualify for a pension, and 0.5 percent of the value of all goods imported into the country. For the Athens Polytechnic, the state budget has items covering the salaries of its administrative personnel.

These differences in financing arrangements are the result of historical developments and do not express preferences for different institutions. Thus the new universities, which receive only a state grant, are not in a position inferior to the older ones, which, in addition to the grant, receive a sum based on the value of imports and have certain administrative expenses covered directly by the state budget. Even revenues from owned property are taken into account in determining the amount of state budget allocations to each IHE.

When part of a state grant is not spent, it is carried over into the following year, and the grant for the next year is reduced accordingly. If part of a credit item in the budget is not spent, it automatically becomes a surplus item in that year's budget and is held over for the next year.

Other Higher Education Income

Two additional categories of current expenses are provided for by the budget of the Ministry of Education but are not included in the budgets of the IHEs.

The first category is textbooks. According to law, every professor or lecturer must write a textbook on the subject he teaches, and every student is entitled to at least one textbook for each course in which he has registered. Professors and lecturers who have not written books suitable for their subjects recommend books written by others.

All books recommended have to be approved by a special committee of the Ministry of Education. They are then distributed by each institution to the students who are entitled to have them. The author is reimbursed in full for the cost of printing and manufacturing (which he pays), and is paid royalties on a sliding scale (royalty per copy decreases with the number of copies distributed). When a book recommended by a professor is by another author, or is a translation of a foreign text, a special committee of the Ministry of Education decides on a price at which all necessary copies must be purchased by the ministry.

The second kind of IHE expense that is borne directly by the Ministry of Education is the cost of meals provided to needy students at university facilities. Students in need are defined as those who come from farmers' families and those whose family income is below a certain minimum specified by the Ministry of Education. Every institution submits to the Ministry of Education a list of its students who qualify for free meals.* The ministry collects the lists and com-

---

*Similar lists are submitted by all schools of general and vocational education at the postsecondary level.

pares the number of students who qualify for meals with the sum included in its budget. The drachma cost-per-meal is then worked out, and each institution is given a sum proportional to the number of students included on the list. At present Dr 52 (about $1.40) are allowed for each student to have a free meal every school day during the academic year.

In the mid-1970s the quantitative ratio of current expenses to public investment in the state budget has been about five to one. For 1977 there were Dr 200 billion for current expenses and Dr 45 billion for public investments. These sums were slightly higher than those for 1976. The Greek GNP for 1976 was put at Dr 800 billion, and the forecast was for it to increase to Dr 920 billion in 1977 (the increase in real terms was forecast to be 5 percent).

As a rule, current expenses are met by revenues coming from regular taxation and other sources of public finance, whereas funds for public investments come mainly from domestic and foreign loans. Small portions of these funds also accrue from past public investments.

Ministries of Finance and Coordination

In the autumn of every year, a draft allocation of funds among ministries is prepared by the ministries of Finance and Coordination. This is done on the basis of need as presented by other ministries in their formal requests, taking into consideration the principles of government policy. This allocation is discussed at the ministerial level and various modifications are made. The amended proposals are incorporated into the state budget, which is presented annually by the minister of Finance to the House of Parliament in late November or early December.

Funds allocated for each ministry are earmarked and when the final budget is voted upon, every ministry knows exactly what funds are available for current expenses and public investments during the following year.

The state budget specifies in detail those funds for current expenses, just as it does for individual projects. In particular, project costs for new universities or schools, highways, or hospitals are always identified in the overall budget proposals. The same applies for some kinds of current expenses, such as the sums provided for salary increases or for the hiring of additional personnel.

Current expenses are controlled by the Ministry of Finance, but all public investment funds are controlled by the Ministry of Coordination. However, after each budget item has been specifically approved by the appropriate ministries, the sum is spent according to the procedure laid down for public expenditures supervised by the Budget Division of the Ministry of Finance.

GOVERNMENT-LEVEL BUDGET POLICY

For both operational needs and investment projects, the state budget is by far the most important source of financing for the IHEs. Therefore, policy decisions regarding allocations to the IHEs are made at the Cabinet level simultaneously with other decisions concerning salaries of civil servants and funds for public works, defense, medical care, and so on. These are mostly political decisions made by the prime minister and his Cabinet based on economic, social, and political considerations. As such, they are influenced by government policy principles, the validity of arguments put forward by interested groups, expressed attitudes of the electorate, and the ability of the state revenue department to collect the necessary funds without affecting incentives for higher economic efficiency.

Staff Influence

However, for various reasons, staff influence on these political decisions is heavy. There is great demand for public funds and the competition among claimants is keen; knowledgeable technocrats currently hold high positions in the civil service and, since the country is bent on economic development, their opinions cannot be ignored; the country is small in area and population, and therefore the margins for divergence in the allocation of development funds are narrow. Many of these decisions are based on technical considerations, such as those involving a more balanced regional distribution of educational activities, the optimal size of an educational institution, and the introduction of new subjects by the IHEs.

A few examples will help to clarify this issue. In the late 1950s there were only two universities in Greece, located in Athens and Thessaloniki. The remaining IHEs were also located in those two cities. There was an urgent need to establish more universities and to decentralize educational activities. These considerations led to a government decision to establish a new university in Patras, the third largest city in the country, and located at a distance from the two main urban centers. Following that decision, the necessary funds had to be provided for the purchase of land, construction work, and current expenses. Similar considerations led to the establishment of universities in Ioannina, Thrace, and Crete, and to the plan (not yet realized) to move the Agricultural School from Athens to Larissa, a rapidly growing city located in the midst of the agricultural area of Thessaly.

Decisions on financing may follow other decisions. For example, there is pressure from many quarters for measures that would encourage people to remain in smaller urban centers, especially in cities that are far away from Athens and Thessaloniki. This pressure has led to government decisions in favor of increasing student populations of universities located on the "periphery." Once this decision was made, the appropriate funds had to be allocated for the appointment of additional teachers and administrative staff, the expansion of university installations, and so on. The decisions to abolish registration and tuition fees, to give all students the necessary textbooks free of charge, and to subsidize student meals were also political ones and resulted in a sharp increase in state financing of IHEs during the 1970s.

In all of these cases, decisions at the highest level have been based on the need for expanding educational facilities at the university level, improving the regional distribution of these facilities, and on the policy of giving lower-income groups better opportunities for university education. Another criterion for allocating funds to higher education has been the need to modernize existing facilities. As a rule, a decision to modernize has important financial implications because it involves heavy construction work and the purchase of expensive equipment. In decisions of this kind the institutions themselves can often play an important role. If an IHE presents convincing arguments to the Ministry of Education and the Cabinet of Ministers, it stands a greater chance of receiving the requested funds.

An important characteristic of developments so far has been the continuous and rapid expansion of all types of state educational facilities, particularly those at the higher levels. Issues of consolidation and modernization are frequent but have not appeared to be pressing. The problems of recent overexpansion experienced by some universities abroad, with the resulting pressure for contraction, have not been experienced by any Greek university or school of higher education. Only isolated examples of overexpansion exist, as in some schools of religious study.

Procedural Steps in Financing

It will be useful here to describe seven major steps in public spending for higher education, with mention of the government agencies involved in the process of spending (Figure 3.1).

Step 1. Individual departments submit their financial requests to the University Senate.

Step 2. After all requests have been submitted, the University Senate (assisted by the University Office of Budgeting and Management and the Office of Administrative Affairs) designs the University budgets for current and capital expenditures.

FIGURE 3.1

Organization of Greek Higher Education Budgeting

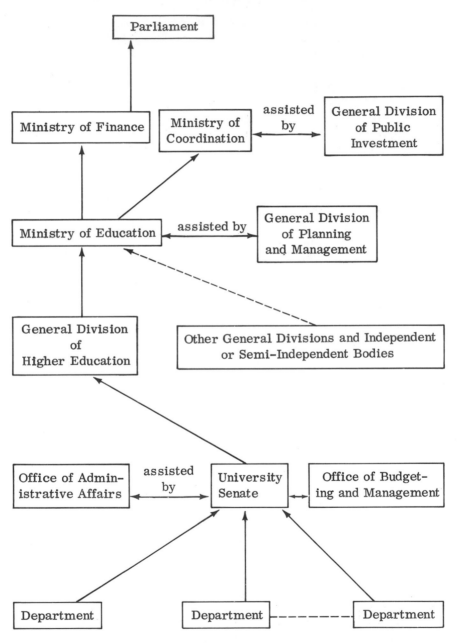

Source: Constructed by the author.

Step 3. University budgets are submitted to the Ministry of Education, more specifically, to the General Division of Higher Education.

Step 4. After all requests (those for current and capital expenditures for higher education, as well as those for general education, technical and vocational education, and so on) are in, the Ministry of Education (assisted by the General Division of Planning and Management) designs its budgets for current and capital expenditures and, like all other ministries, submits the first budget (for current expenditures) to the Ministry of Finance and the second budget (for capital expenditures) to the Ministry of Coordination.

Step 5. The Ministry of Finance designs and submits the General Government Budget for current expenditure to Parliament for approval; simultaneously, the Ministry of Coordination (assisted by the General Division of Public Investment) designs the final General Government Budget for capital expenditures.

Step 6. Parliament approves the General Government Budget for current expenditures.

Step 7. Spending for higher education takes place in accordance with previously approved expenditure items.

MAIN CRITERIA FOR THE
ALLOCATION OF CURRENT EXPENSES

One of the main criteria for the allocation of current expenses is the number of students registered at each school or faculty. Because the largest item of current expenses is salaries of teaching personnel and administrative staff, the number of teachers and other staff is important.

About ten years ago the Personnel Division of the Ministry of Education made a survey of necessary teaching posts, taking into consideration the different requirements among faculties for seniors, assistants, and laboratory supervisors. Data were fed into computers and the results obtained were compared with the answers received from questionnaires distributed to the senior teaching staffs of the IHEs. On the basis of this investigation regulations were issued concerning the number of chairs allowed by school and faculty, as well as the number of assistants and others to be allowed to each chair.

As shown in Table 3.2, teaching personnel provided for in the charters of all IHEs amounted to nearly 9,000 persons in 1976. In that year just over 100,000 students were registered. Consequently, the average student-teacher ratio approved and budgeted by the Ministry of Education was 12 to 1, which could be considered more than satisfactory.

However, as Table 3.2 also shows, only two-thirds of the teaching positions provided for were actually filled. In the past, it was fairly common for positions to remain vacant for a long time—a fact attributed to the actions of professors who had vested interests in these positions (because they taught in two chairs, their books were used by and sold to more students, relatives and friends were being prepared to occupy vacant chairs, and so on).

There are accusations that such situations still exist, but the Ministry of Education considers the incidence insignificant. There are strict legal procedures by which every school must advertise and fill within a certain time both newly created and established-but-vacant positions. If a position is not advertised within the time specified by law, the minister of Education is authorized to do so. The minister is also authorized to appoint a teacher to a position that has been vacant for a long time. In all these efforts the ministry is, in fact, exerting pressure on the institution to absorb budgeted credits from the item of current expenses.

It should be noted that some positions fall vacant because the subject has become obsolete while many others must be divided because of advances in specialization. Also, it usually takes more than one year to fill a vacant or newly established post, so that many positions listed as vacant for a specific year are in the process of being filled.

Given the satisfactory student-teacher ratio provided by existing positions, the financial authorities have the choice, in responding to the increasing demand for higher education, of raising standards or expanding the number of students (and therefore also the number of teachers and other administrative personnel). A third choice is to increase only the number of students in general and vocational postsecondary educational programs below the university level.

The second criterion considered in formulating the operating budget is the subject area of each faculty. Administrative experience in each institution and at the Ministry of Education has led to rules and formulas about the ratios of expenses for each kind of study. The ministry determines and publishes these ratios. Table 3.4, which shows the current expenses per student in every IHE during the period of 1969-73, indicates that the cost per student has been proportional to the subject taught. Thus for students in the Athens Polytechnic and the Agricultural School, where there is much laboratory work, this cost is far above the average, and for students in the political sciences, where only tutorials and teaching of large classes take place, it is considerably below the average. Because of low student-faculty ratios, the School of Fine Arts has the highest expenses per student.

The cost per student is considerably higher for the University of Thessaloniki than for the University of Athens because the former

TABLE 3.4

Annual Current Expenses per Student
(in drachmas of 1977 value)

Institution	1969	1971	1973	Average (1969–73)	Average Annual Percent Increase
University of Athens	7,210	9,034	14,498	10,176	19.6
Thessaloniki University	9,087	12,633	20,913	13,040	23.2
University of Ioannina	n.a.	18,698	30,441	24,303	27.7
Patras University	16,413	15,770	29,835	21,823	16.0
Athens Polytechnic	25,111	30,169	39,685	30,594	12.0
Graduate School of Economic and Commercial Sciences, Athens	3,131	4,331	7,166	4,540	23.0
Pantios School of Political Sciences, Athens	2,507	3,238	6,057	3,457	24.7
Graduate Agricultural School of Athens	18,256	29,169	42,004	30,360	23.2
Graduate School of Industrial Studies, Piraeus	2,682	3,846	5,948	4,068	22.0
Graduate School of Industrial Studies, Thessaloniki	4,611	8,092	7,786	7,022	14.0
School of Fine Arts, Athens	25,096	38,342	47,197	37,575	17.1
Total*	8,923	12,420	20,037	13,050	22.4

n.a.: data not available
*Weighted mean.

Source: Ministry of National Education and Religious Affairs, The Cost of Higher Education (Athens, 1976), p. 37.

trains both engineers and agronomists, for whom there are separate schools in Athens. The cost is also high in the new universities, mainly because the anticipated economies of scale have yet to be realized (basic teaching and administrative staff have been provided for only a few dozen students in some faculties).

Between 1969 and 1973 current expenses per student increased by 9.7 percent in real terms (or about 124 percent in nominal value at current prices). This is an indication of the efforts being made by the financial authorities to raise standards.

An addition criterion for the allocation of state funds is the amount of revenues produced by owned property. In fact, this amount is deducted from state budget grants to the IHEs. Thus the universities of Athens and Thessaloniki have the same number of students, but Athens has only 80 percent of the budget allocations of Thessaloniki because of the relatively large revenues received by Athens from its owned property.

Decentralization of higher education has been the third important criterion for the allocation of both capital investment funds and funds for current expenses. There have been pressures in the last 20 years to slow down and eventually halt further growth of the universities of Athens and Thessaloniki. Determining the optimal size of each school is a problem almost as important as decentralization. An optimal size is difficult to determine, but with the present standards of administrative and organizational experience in the country it is felt that 30,000 students is a large number to administer. The universities of Athens and Thessaloniki have exceeded this number, and there is heavy pressure to limit further growth.

Decentralization has many problems. Within about 15 years the number of universities has increased threefold, and nearly 10,000 students are now enrolled in the new universities. As a rule, the rapid expansion of educational faculties results in lower standards— at least temporarily. The critical issue in this respect is the fact that both teachers and students of the new "provincial" universities consider them second-choice institutions, and there is the risk that second-rate graduates will result. With respect to teachers, a large number of applicants for various teaching posts in the new universities would have few chances of being elected to posts in universities and schools in Athens and Thessaloniki. The same applies to the students. Even those who come from areas where the provincial universities are located put the universities of Athens and Thessaloniki as their first and second choices, respectively, on their applications.

INFORMATION AND DATA SYSTEMS

Because all of the IHEs are financed through the state budget, the Ministry of Education information system is rather elaborate.

Institutions, however, need not report the number of students, teachers, and administrative staff to the ministry because in most cases the numbers are known in advance as a result of allocation quotas. Every IHE prepares and submits regular annual budgets to the Ministry of Education, in which all expenses claimed must be accounted for by information on activities, employment of staff, and number of students.

In addition, the National Statistical Service of Greece (NSSG) has a senior member of its staff who is permanently located in the Ministry of Education. By law, all statistics collected by the various departments of the Ministry of Education are sent to the NSSG through this senior staff member, who organizes the collection of data and checks for adequacy, accuracy, and prompt processing. Furthermore, the NSSG conducts annual surveys on the revenues and expenses of education at all levels, as mentioned above.

Therefore, the number of students (by class level, program, and so on), faculty members (by rank and program), and administrative and academic staff are all known to the Ministry of Education. The same, of course, applies to the student-faculty ratios and the costs per student, course, or discipline.

All of this information is published regularly by the NSSG in its "Statistics of Education" series, and by the Ministry of Education in special issues such as The Cost of Education. This latest publication came out in 1976 with detailed statistics on the numbers of students, teachers, and administrative personnel, the sources of revenues, and the categories of expenses of the IHEs. It also contained statistics on Greek students enrolled in foreign universities, and estimates of the statistical service of the Ministry of Education relating to cost per student, analyzed by expense category (current and total). For most of those statistics there are also annual reports since 1968.

Various committees and working groups are appointed by the Ministry of Education to investigate issues within higher education, such as questions about the location of facilities, the appropriate proportion of students in various subjects, the optimal size of an educational institution, the degree specializations of study offered in each institution, and so on. Recently, a top-level committee was appointed to study higher education in the fields of economics and business administration, and another group of experts has been asked to trace graduates in their present careers and specific jobs, and to investigate the issue of the amount of earnings relative to the cost of their programs. All of these committees prepare reports containing valuable statistical information and comments on the situation in the IHEs.

4

GOVERNMENT ALLOCATION PRACTICES FOR ITALIAN HIGHER EDUCATION

Aldo Gandiglio

The Italian university, more than any other educational structure in the country, has met with crises in the past decade. Conceived of and structured as an elite institution that would serve the ruling classes, the university has been overwhelmed by the advent of education for the masses.

THE ITALIAN UNIVERSITY

The Italian university has not been able to accommodate growing enrollment into its traditional framework. Enrollments have increased fivefold over a 20-year period, from 136,000 in 1955 to 731,000 in 1977 (approximately 900,000 including students not engaged in course work). Nearly 90 percent of upperschool diploma holders continue their studies at the universities.

This enrollment growth has brought the universities perilously close to collapse. The number of departments (facolta) have grown from 186 in 1951 to 288 in 1975, and university sites have increased from 27 to 44 during the same time; but this expansion proved totally inefficient because the overcrowded institutions were not able to transfer excess students to the new ones. The University of Rome, for example, has more than 110,000 enrolled students, but it is surrounded by other university sites, each with less than 5,000 enrolled students.

In spite of the high enrollments, the Italian university system is still characterized by strong faculty selection and by significant numbers of students enrolled but not taking courses (see Table 4.1). The ratio is one nonactive enrolled student to four regular students. Twenty percent of enrolled students abandon their studies between the first and second year, less than half receive their degree (laurea),

TABLE 4.1

Students University Enrollment, Taking and Not Taking Classes

Schools	1973/74				1974/75				1975/76*			
	Schools	Students Taking Courses		Students Not Taking Courses	Schools	Students Taking Courses		Students Not Taking Courses	Schools	Students Taking Courses		Students Not Taking Courses
		Total	First-year Students			Total	First-year Students			Total	First-year Students	
Scientific schools	57	94,144	34,977	23,643	57	99,562	34,957	22,638	57	99,695	34,722	n.a.
Schools of medicine and surgery	27	124,200	29,131	12,911	27	137,748	29,261	13,233	27	152,920	32,744	n.a.
Technical schools	52	112,288	34,733	25,521	52	123,387	38,970	27,794	52	131,221	41,099	n.a.
Schools of law, economics, and social sciences	79	155,016	58,358	48,131	79	166,378	62,829	50,658	79	173,144	70,317	n.a.
Schools of teaching and letters	73	189,508	56,420	55,115	73	189,300	60,911	56,433	73	174,326	58,913	n.a.
Total	288	675,176	213,619	165,321	288	718,375	226,928	170,756	288	731,306	237,795	n.a.
Fine arts academies	18	6,824	3,139	n.a.	19	7,411	2,955	n.a.	19	9,148	3,622	n.a.

n.a.: data not available
*Provisional data.

Source: Central Institute of Statistics from the individual universities and institutes.

and less than 25 percent receive their degree in the prescribed manner.

Selectivity according to the student's social status is very widespread. In 1967, for instance, 192 out of 1,000 students from entre-
preneurial and professional families received their degrees, while
only 5 out of 1,000 students from working-class families received
their degrees. To counteract this strong selection process, various
right-to-study provisions have been adopted, but so far they have not
been effective. State intervention has primarily concentrated on study
allowances instead of on food and dormitory services.*

The situation reaches dramatic proportions when one considers
the vocational statistics—the number of university graduates is 65,000
per year, while a decreasing number of them can be absorbed into the
labor market. In fact, it is foreseeable in the very near future that
schools will use fewer graduates to fill teaching positions than they
did in the 1960s. In the last 25 years, of the 340,000 new jobs for
graduates, 305,000 were created in the field of higher education.
Since only a small demand for graduates exists in Italian industries,
strong competition will be created in the labor market for highly
qualified people.

The new social reality, which threatens the very function of the
university, now clashes with an institutional organization based largely
on the "unified text" of 1933. This form of organization came about
during the fascist era and reflects all of the social norms and legislative interventions that occurred after the Gentile Reform of 1923.
Moreover, the university has not been forced to change its role, objectives, and structure to the new reality of mass education.

Since the activities of the Search Committee of 1962, every legislature has introduced bills to reform the university. Even today,
such bills still bear the stigma of mere "buffer" legislation. In 1969,
however, the student movement, through the Emergency Provisions
for the University law, helped upperschool graduates gain access to
all university departments and made levels of study more flexible.
In 1973, with the Emergency Measures for the University law, the
legal status of instructors was modified and the structure of several
university branches was democratized.

---

*The annual study allowances—L 250,000 for residents in the
city of a university seat and L 500,000 for others—are too small to
help most students significantly and have in any case been restricted
to students in the first and second years of study. They have also,
because of social conditioning, tended to favor the middle classes
over the lower classes. Nevertheless, more than L 80 million have
been spent in recent years on this item, involving more than 200,000
students—over one-fourth of all enrollments.

STATE ORGANIZATIONS AND FINANCING POLICY

Parliament

The role of Parliament has grown notably in the last ten years. With the advent of coalition governments, and even governments without a parliamentary majority (as in 1977), the powers of Parliament have increased in relation to those of the prime minister and the Ministry of Public Instruction.

Policy for Higher Education

Since the late 1960s, nearly all the laws approved for the universities have been proposed either by the government or by individual deputies. Although nearly all of these laws have imposed additional financial burdens on the government, in no case has the financial impact of any of these laws been discussed in Parliament. On the other hand, the nature of the adopted provisions explains which pressure groups have exercised their influence in the decisions of Parliament.

Government bills are usually fully discussed by the political forces representing interest groups. The attitudes of the education units of the several parties represented in Parliament are of great importance. Usually, in coalition governments, the prime minister, before presenting a bill, will examine it will responsible members of the coalition parties and perhaps agree upon its passage before Parliamentary discussion. If this happens, the discussion in Parliament assumes less importance.

However, with legislation pertaining to the universities, such a priori agreements are seldom reached, and the opposition is thus able to introduce modifications. It is essentially the lack of agreement between the coalition parties that has impeded the approval of all the higher education reform bills in Parliament, including those aimed at forming a revised system of university financing and student assistance.

When a government measure concerns university personnel, such as issues of salary and work load, it almost certainly sanctions an agreement already made between the prime minister and the trade unions. This blocks the ability of Parliament to determine the content of a law; particularly thwarted are the left-wing parties that must heed the pressure of the trade unions. Since the activities of the trade unions have intensified in recent years, measures of this nature have multiplied. Consequently, the cost of university personnel has grown in a way that is neither organic nor controlled. These runaway costs also reflect the lack of a general conception of university problems on the part of governmental bodies. As a result, no strategic plan for reform has been formulated. In the last decade the bargaining power of many professional teaching organizations has also dissipated. Today, most of them have been completely replaced by trade unions or have become trade unions themselves.

When government measures for the opening of new universities are introduced, the power of the prime minister, and thus of Parliament, is reduced because any decision on new universities is likely to affect those already in operation, which were established through subsidies from both public and private local groups. These groups generally have guaranteed financing of a university for its first few years only, after which time they have pressed for a law that transforms the university from a private to a state-owned institution. In cases of this sort, the pressure is quite diffuse, coming from local administrators and legislators, professors, and students who could not receive their degrees unless the university is taken over by the state.

Certain laws introduced by individual legislators are concerned with specific problems of personnel. In fact, many proposals are from legislators who are also university professors. For example, many of them are professors of medicine, who constitute the most powerful pressure group in Italian academia. A law was able to be passed allowing professors and teaching assistants in the schools of medicine to receive larger stipends than their colleagues in other departments.

Politics of the Ministries

Before the 1972–76 economic crisis, Parliament, in addition to controlling expenditures, had tried to increase substantially the monetary base for university expansion. There had been so few budgetary laws passed before the crisis that only two deserve to be mentioned: (1) the plan for operational support, introduced and voted into law in 1966 (its effects were reflected in the budgets of 1966 and 1970) and (2) the law on all educational and university construction, voted on in 1967 and many times afterward, and which was financed and modified by successive laws. With these two measures, the expansion of budgetary appropriations was mechanically assured; the only thing remaining for Parliament to do was complain about the insufficiency of capital!

After 1970 the absence of a long-range plan led to the collapse of regulation of budget growth. Costs have thus climbed very rapidly. Only since 1974, with the growth of inflation, have proposals for accountability at the parliamentary level been considered. By that time, however, the most consistent portions of the budget concerning personnel costs had already been approved by Parliament and were therefore automatically determined by the work contracts. It has been difficult to negotiate any containment or reduction.

The Ministry of Public Instruction

In this ministry one must distinguish between the minister of Public Instruction and his personal staff and the Office of General Management for Higher Education. Both are important decision-making organs of the ministry. There are also advisory organs, the most important of which is the Senior Council on Public Instruction, a main section of which concerns itself exclusively with the university.

The Italian political system formally recognizes university autonomy—the sovereignty of university institutions in appropriate matters and the absence of hierarchical ties to the minister or ministry. This autonomy was effectively granted formerly when only some university expenses were assumed by the state budget, that is, when other sources for the university such as property taxes and fiscal revenues had a greater importance. The powers of the government grew along with the increasing importance of state funds, but since all public expenditures in Italy are regulated by the government, the growth of these powers took place within discrete areas already prescribed by law.

The minister and ministry are not always bound by detailed laws. Their maximum power lies in setting general procedures for implementing laws already approved by Parliament, or in sending out interpretive circulars or instructions to all the universities (see Figure 4.1). They have no discretionary powers over expense items determined by law (which are essentially expenses for personnel, scholarships, and so on). Ministerial authority is greater over expense items that require the distribution of lump sums to the universities, provided there are no quota laws.

Relationship with the Ministry of the Treasury

The relationship between the Ministry of Public Instruction and the Ministry of the Treasury also plays an important part in determining individual expense items, as well as total amounts. The Ministry of the Treasury has the power to establish the maximum limits of a predicted expenditure, and because it manages the disbursement of all public expenditures it also has the ability to slow down the rate of capital outlay by postponing actual payments until a future date, thus raising the level of surplus funds.

The Minister and His Staff

Of the minister of Public Instruction and the Office of the General Manager, the minister has the more important discretionary powers, because he must establish general policies and procedures for matters not subject to law. In theory, the minister can apply decision-making authority to expenditure matters by exercising his

FIGURE 4.1

Organization for Funding Higher Education in Italy

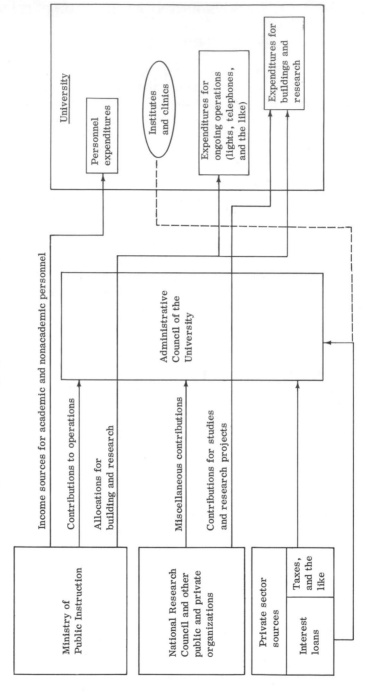

Source: Constructed by the author.

power to draw up plans and long-range programs. Nevertheless, in the last 30 years this has only been done once; subsequent attempts have remained at the planning stage.

Since 1968 a new minister of Public Instruction has been appointed by each new government, and only two of them have remained more than two years at the ministry. Nevertheless, even in the absence of long-range plans, the power of the minister may be arbitrarily applied.

Italian ministers do not customarily use expert technical advice in their decision making, but they do consult politically concerned parties to ensure consensus or at least neutrality on a given issue. We have already mentioned the influence of the trade unions in decisions regarding university personnel. Aside from listening to the unions, the minister regularly consults other groups on a precautionary basis. One of these, the Rector's Conference, a group of university chancellors with no legal power, is extremely influential with the minister. In fact, the social and professional prestige of certain science teachers, the power of scientific organizations, and the political ties between universities and political parties all apply pressure on the minister in ways outside the law. Nevertheless, as we shall see, it is precisely the heterogeneity of pressures that establishes criteria or rules that the minister must heed. Furthermore, in coalition governments the smaller parties have an undersecretary at the Ministry of Public Instruction who negotiates and argues the most relevant measures with the minister.

The Office of General Management

Just below the minister of Public Instruction and his personal staff is the Office of General Management for Higher Education, headed by the general manager (Direttore Generale), one of the most prestigious positions in the entire ministry. The welfare of higher education depends upon the effectively coordinated use of power by the minister of Public Instruction and the general manager. The former has great discretionary powers over operating functions, and the latter has the same over the implementation of new expenditure policies.

Even in matters regarding the attainment of previously prescribed standards of practice, the professional characteristics required from general management personnel basically fall in the legal-administrative category. Most employees have degrees in Jurisprudence and Letters. Only in the last few years, for purposes of data collection and organization of information, have persons with statistical and financial skills been employed. These new technical personnel do not have major responsibility or influence.

The most important professional skill required in General Management is knowing how to apply laws, regulations, and policy statements to specific cases. An understanding of university problems is not necessary. Officials at the middle and low levels rotate frequently, but those who hold important offices tend to serve long terms. The general manager, in fact, is practically unremovable. He would be replaced upon death, retirement, or promotion to another governmental body outside the ministry such as the Council of State (which is on an equal level with the administrative courts of the state).

General Management is divided into several offices, each of which must enforce specific groups of regulations concerning funds to be allocated or transferred to the universities.

The minister intervenes in ministry affairs to prevent violations of administrative regulations and laws, and often speeds the progress of certain requests through bureaucratic procedures at the urging of interest groups. General Management communicates with all of the pressure groups that cannot reach the minister.

FINANCING UNIVERSITY INSTRUCTION

Despite steady increases in public financing (especially through the Ministry of Public Instruction), university instruction has deteriorated in recent years, both in quality and in quantity. Although the number of regularly enrolled students increased from 205,000 in the academic year 1961/62 to 731,000 in 1975/76 (there were another 165,000 who were enrolled but did not take any classes in 1976), there has been no proportional increase in financing, no increase in construction, and little increase in the number of teachers. The student-faculty ratio has risen from 22 in 1961/62 to more than 32 in 1971/72. The mean standard of classroom space for Italian universities has gone from 50 cubic meters per student in 1968 to 32 cubic meters in 1973, whereas the optimal standard should be between 60 and 100 cubic meters per student. Current expenditure per student has risen from L 310,000 in 1961/62 to L 500,000 in 1971/72, but when deflation of the lira is taken into account the real expenditure per student has been decreased by 30 percent since 1962.*

_____

*Because of a delay in the release of the Annual Reports of the Universities, I have referred to the Economic Accounts of the Universities (published by the Central Institute of Statistics) for the academic year 1971/72; unfortunately, these lack data on the founding of several important university centers, such as Turin and Naples, in 1973.

Financing University Operations

Current expenditures in the university budget are financed through: (1) fiscal revenues; (2) investment income; (3) allocations from the state and from public and private organizations; and (4) proceeds from provided services.

Fiscal Revenues

These are the amounts that students pay to the university or the state for registration, graduation, libraries, discussion sections, laboratories, and building maintenance. These fees are authorized by law, but the type invoked and amount is determined by the administrative council at each university.

The importance of this item in university financing has been diminishing over the past 17 years. Despite increasing enrollments, proceeds fell from 30 percent of total current revenues (not including the "figurative" funds for faculty paid by the ministry) in 1961 to 21.5 percent in 1971, while the mean taxation per student dropped from L 63,000 to L 59,000. This decline indicates that politicians and some academic economists favored a reduced fee level, with payments based on financial ability, as a means of increasing access to the university for the lower classes, and ultimately as a means of promoting a more equal distribution of wealth. This practice has been criticized by those who forecast a continuing reduction in the public financing of the universities, which they believe could perpetuate the present social status of students.

Investment Income

These are revenues from university investments, such as interest on financial holdings (bonds, shares, and so on) and from donated real estate.

Also included under this heading are the "figurative" rents and formal budget entries that refer to the buildings utilized directly by a university. This item has always been rather modest and is usually less than 4 percent of the total current revenues.

Allocations from the State

The revenues derived from "outside" the university (namely, the direct and indirect contributions of the state) increased from 35 percent in 1961 to 43.2 percent in 1971. If the "figurative" allocations—the payment of faculty and staff employed directly by the state —are included, the percentage jumps from 59.7 percent to 70.9 percent.

The state contributes funds to the university in many ways, primarily through the Ministry of Public Instruction, which appropriated nearly L 320 million for university instruction in 1971.

University administrations only consider as allocations from the state those funds entered in special budget categories at the ministry: in particular, "contributions toward operation," transfers for "the acquisition of teaching and scientific equipment," and "expenses for scientific research." In 1971 the sum of these three items amounted to nearly L 55 million, almost 30 percent of the readily available income of the university; the remainder is "figurative" income from the state that is not included in the university budgets, such as the payment of academic and nonacademic personnel (entered into the budget of the minister of Public Instruction), and the sums that the ministry earmarks for the research and teacher training of recent graduates and student assistants.

Allocations from Public and Private Organizations

These funds include contributions from local organizations, banks, and commercial and industrial associations, and from public and private research groups. Local organizations, banks, and associations often form consortia to coordinate appropriations for the university. Public research organizations (such as the National Council of Research [CNR] and the National Institute of Nuclear Physics [INFN]) contribute directly to the functioning of the university by financing research, and indirectly through scholarships and various research centers within the universities.

The data from university budgets are very imprecise and contain no reference to university activities funded indirectly by public research organizations. For 1971/72, it can be estimated that only slightly over L 20 million were transferred from public organizations and L 6 million from private ones; this is a very small amount when one realizes that public research organizations are the chief source of funds for research and equipment.

Payments for Services Rendered

These include payments for hospital stays, examinations and analyses carried out in university medical clinics, and for studies commissioned at university institutes. In 1971/72 payments of this sort comprised almost one-third of all current university revenues.

University Costs

From the academic years of 1962 to 1972 the total costs of the universities grew notably, rising from about L 115 million to L 350 million.* The sharp increase of costs began in the late 1960s; whereas costs increased by 35 percent between 1962 and 1967, they more than doubled in the next 5 years.

An examination of the expenses incurred by the universities and those that have cut most heavily into general operations will be presented. One should bear in mind that expenses of the current budget are assigned to: (1) personnel costs; (2) acquisition of goods and services; and (3) current allocations.

Personnel Costs

The principal items here are stipends, salaries, and allowances for the rank and file personnel. This cost increased from 62.2 percent in 1961/62 to 72.5 percent in 1971/72 (Table 4.2).

The Ministry of Public Instruction pays all academic and non-academic staff personnel directly, whereas the university must pay temporary faculty personnel and nonacademic staff of the university clinics. Over the years, the responsibility for paying certain types of temporary and part-time personnel has shifted from the university to the Ministry of Public Instruction. This has permitted an indirect increase in the universities' liquid assets.

The percentage of expenditure for personnel employed by the universities rose from 21 percent in 1961 to about 25 percent of the total in 1968 and then leveled off (not including the personnel employed by the state). In 1971/72, however, the percentage jumped to 45 percent of the total; this was the result of increased personnel expenses at the university clinics, which quadrupled in three years, while the expenses of other personnel only doubled. Payments for state employees have thus continued to represent an increasingly higher percentage of the universities' current expenditures (from 40.9 percent in 1961 to 50.7 percent in 1971/72).

A similarly sharp increase has been experienced in the budget items of the Ministry of Public Instruction. In 1970, for instance, L 127 million were appropriated, 50 percent of the current expenditures earmarked by the minister for university instruction. In 1973, this amount was L 198 million, 54 percent of the total, and in 1977 the amount was estimated at L 375 million, or 58 percent of the total. (The 1977 figure includes 2,500 professional positions filled as a result of the latest competitive examination.) Most of this increase has been brought about by the rising number of personnel employed and not from salary increases, which have been quite modest in comparison with those of other sectors.

---

*It should be remembered that total university costs include the "figurative" expenditure for personnel (most faculty and staff) employed by the state.

TABLE 4.2

Educational and General Expenses, 1961–72, by Area
(in millions of lira)

	1961/62		1966/67		1971/72	
	Absolute Value	Percent	Absolute Value	Percent	Absolute Value	Percent
Personnel expenses	40.5	62.2	87.4	68.4	233.0	72.6
State employees	26.6	40.9	58.7	45.9	163.0	50.7
University employees	13.9	21.3	28.7	22.5	70.0	21.9
Expenses for goods and services	18.4	28.3	34.3	26.9	74.0	23.0
Transfers	6.2	9.5	6.0	4.7	14.0	4.4
Total current expenses	65.1	100.0	127.7	100.0	321.0	100.0

Source: Data supplied by the Ministry of Education.

It is difficult, however, to determine precisely the numbers and composition of university personnel, whether employed by the state or by the university. Academically, it can be said that the number of ranked professors has increased very slowly: from 1,782 in 1951, to 2,091 in 1961, to 4,368 in 1973. The relative scantiness of academic personnel combined with the increase in required teaching duties has encouraged the growth of other types of teaching personnel—particularly the teaching assistants, many of whom are volunteers. (In 1973, 14,000 of the 26,000 assistants were volunteers.) Assistantship duties are carried out by recent graduates with 2-year scholarships or 4-year contracts. In 1977 approximately 6,000 held scholarships and 6,500 had contracts.

Acquisition of Goods and Services

This category includes a long series of expenses that are allocated annually to guarantee the normal functioning of the university—property, rents, cleaning staff, utilities, telephones, and record keeping. It does not include nonrecurring items, such as equipment costs. This category accounts for nearly one-fourth of the current expenditures of the universities. And of these expenditures, the university clinic costs (hospitalizing patients and operating laboratories) account for about 50 percent.

Fees and Charges

These consist mainly of a percentage of state-imposed fees and additional charges (which make up the fiscal revenues), tax exemptions, and course fees for various student categories.

FINANCING RESEARCH

Rather than exercising direct administrative and managerial power, the Ministry of Scientific Research coordinates the educational contributions of other public organizations, including the National Council on Research (CNR) and the National Institute for Nuclear Physics (INFN). Since these organizations have their own budgets and can make their own decisions, their importance in research activity is substantially greater than that of the Ministry on Scientific Research.

These public organizations deserve mention primarily because they allocate resources directly to the universities, thereby assuring research funding and helping to keep university costs under control. In addition, the creation of research groups provides for the employment of many kinds of personnel. Nonteaching technical employees reinforce various important research projects, which is important productively and economically.

The interests of these public organizations account for the great concentration of resources in disciplines related to the natural and applied sciences—mathematics, physics, chemistry, and engineering—and tend to balance the smaller allocations destined for humanities, law, and medicine.

The National Council on Research

In the National Council on Research (CNR), policy decisions regarding research are largely influenced by university professors and by their discipline affiliations. In fact, the CNR president has almost always been chosen from among the university rectors (chancellors), after being nominated by members of the Administrative Council, which is also subject to the influence of the professors. In recent years, this professorial influence has been balanced somewhat by the growing influence of large corporations, both public and private, in various sectors of industry.

There is also formally sanctioned influence in the rules governing the composition of the CNR's advisory committees, which have the power to make judicial inquiry into decisions and regulate financing activities. Each of these committees works with the Administrative Council on a group of disciplines, suggests activities, and examines all proposed research projects. Elected committee members represent the various special interests concerned with research. The electoral mechanism, however, is such that the university professors are always in the majority in each of the groups of disciplines. The categories are made up largely of permanent university professors, associate professors, and researchers of the CNR and the Council on Public Administration. Thus, the university, through its professors, has the determining voice in research politics and policies in the CNR.

The CNR also cooperates in the financing of the university's research activities in three ways: (1) by direct participation; (2) by financing research projects; and (3) by allocating scholarship monies.

Direct Participation

The CNR conducts research directly through its own institutes, centers, and laboratories, many of which are located in the universities. At these facilities, the center director is often also the director of a university institute for a particular discipline. The costs of personnel and equipment in the center, with the exception of the salary of the director, are borne entirely by the CNR; the CNR owns all the equipment, but the personnel report to the university.

However, a new law on public employment (1976), for which supporting regulations are still being developed, has established that personnel paid by the CNR must have a regular and stable working relationship with that organization, and must dedicate themselves exclusively to research activities. This regulation halts the exchange of university personnel and personnel dependent on the CNR, and will probably increase the autonomy of the institutes, centers, and laboratories within the universities. This could mean that fewer research activities will be carried out in the universities, weakening university priorities in favor of teaching.

The Financing of Research Projects

Funds from the CNR also reach the university through the financing of research projects introduced by professors. The criteria that the advisory committees have traditionally used for the allocation of these funds can be described as principles for "keeping everybody happy"—resulting in the dispersion of funds without priorities.

However, the CNR recently has attempted to ensure that CNR-financed research activities respond to important social needs such as environmental protection, energy policy, and social welfare. If these were the CNR's stated objectives, it would be possible to establish a few national priorities and to deny financing to other projects of less social value. Also, in the last two or three years a step has been taken to control the quality of research by reserving a set amount of finances for "finalized" projects, which are examined directly by the advisory committees and thus approved not only by the CNR but by the Inter-Ministerial Committee for Economic Programs (CIPE).

Recent amendments to old practices have made the CNR better able to choose its financial involvements and have given it the duty of allocating projects and of managing and verifying research entrusted to various groups.

Awarding of Scholarships

Until 1973, young persons heading for university careers sought scholarships mainly from two sources—the universities themselves or the CNR. These scholarships paid the most and often subsidized study abroad, and CNR scholarships required fewer teaching assistantship duties.

Since 1973, scholarships granted by the universities have been issued in four-year assignments that have many characteristics of an employment contract; these offer support superior to that provided by

CNR scholarships. However, CNR scholarships have gained another advantage—the 1973 law on public employment (see section on Parliament) treats CNR scholarship recipients as CNR personnel. This new system constitutes additional separation between universities and research organizations. Nevertheless, the CNR scholarships are still used by individual university teachers, even those on the permanent staff, for study sojourns abroad and vacations.

The National Institute of Nuclear Physics

The National Institute of Nuclear Physics (INFN) works with university physics institutes in the same ways that the CNR works with the universities as a whole. The physics institutes are branches of the university created to promote a greater flexibility in the use of finances, because institute-financing procedures are not subject to the state's accounting laws, as are regular university procedures.

The study of physics has always been considered an elite discipline in Italy. The number of physics institutes is small, approximately 15. The necessity of sharing equipment, the intense exchange of findings, and the occasional integration of research groups have allowed the INFN to avoid the problems of finance dispersion characteristic of the CNR. The INFN is currently experiencing problems similar to those of the CNR as a result of the 1973 law on university and public employment.

INTERNAL ALLOCATION SYSTEM

Decisions on expenditures within the universities are made at three levels: the rector (chancellor) with the Administrative Council; the school or department (facoltà) and the institute; and the university chair (cattedra).

Organization

Before 1973, when the Urgent Provisions for the University law was enacted, the rector had the most power within a university. He was appointed only by full professors, who were very few in number and who in turn were regulated by the deans (members of the Academic Senate).

Before 1973, spending negotiations took place between the rector and the Academic Senate, although the Senate had no decision-making powers. The importance of the Senate resided in its power to nominate members of the university's Administrative Council, and in its position as representative of the rector's most important constituents, with whom he would not willingly seek conflict.

The Administrative Council, despite its broad powers, usually does no more than sanction decisions already made elsewhere or plans suggested by the rector. In addition, not all spending decisions pass through it; instead they can be referred directly to the rector as the administrative head of the university.

We must note in this regard the importance of the administrative director of a university. He is a civil servant with a particular sphere of power, nominated by the minister of Public Instruction from the ranks of the civil servants in that ministry. The administrative director may be particularly influential when the rector is new and inexperienced with procedures and controls or when the rector concerns himself primarily with scientific problems instead of administrative duties. If the rector is a strong and able manager, the administrative director's role will be limited to providing technical assistance for the management of administrative and technical offices.

With the 1973 law the Administrative Council became elective and has since been burdened with all the problems of the university; it now tends to regulate an increasing number of the rector's acts and decisions. In a few universities, the Administrative Council has assumed duties of initially suggesting expenses for programs, setting priorities, and studying the possibilities of formulating long-range budgets. The latter is a very recent phenomenon, which has yet to be evaluated.

The financial resources upon which the decision-making power of the rector and the Administrative Council focus are called operation allocations. The rector has power to negotiate, based on ministry criteria, with the minister of Public Instruction. It should be noted, however, that it would be difficult for the ministry to take part in establishing policy for any distribution of funds according to objective criteria; the difficulty stems from the scarcity of relevant data necessary to define a comprehensive financing plan. In fact, the data of the annual university statements are not comprehensively collected and organized, which is necessary in order for them to furnish useful information on real financial needs. According to a recent ministry publication, the indicators used in distributing funds (that is, the determination of enrolled students, giving more weight to the departments of sciences than to the departments of humanities) were not clearly established.

The Rector's Conference exerts collective pressure in an effort to avoid conflict among the various universities. While it has no direct power, the minister of Public Instruction must respect it in order to avoid criticism and adverse pressures on his operation. Often, a rector must assume the task of informing the minister about special funding needs in his university.

The differences in financial needs between large and small Italian universities should be noted here. The small ones are fortunate in the sense that the minimum state contribution satisfies a large part of their current financial requirements. For the large universities, state financing covers only a small fraction of those needs. Fund distribution on a national level assures a basic amount to all university chairs, derived from a variable quota based mainly on student enrollment; but this quota is never enough to cover the costs of the larger university chairs.

The operation allocations from the Ministry are supplemented by other incomes derived from registration fees, laboratory fees, proceeds from the provision of services (mainly those of the university clinics), profits from university holdings, and so on. The state contributions and a part of these other incomes are parceled out among the schools or departments on the recommendation of the rector and with the approval of the Administrative Council. Often this fund distribution is prepared by special committees that study the needs of the various schools and establish objective parameters whenever possible.

The first conflict that the Administrative Council must mediate is between the humanistic and the scientific departments. The humanistic disciplines have the greater number of registered students (although they have a lower percentage of students taking classes). The scientific disciplines almost always have greater space requirements and equipment expenses. These are the objective parameters, but they do not create any real differentiation among the disciplines. For this reason, it is often necessary to revert to stricter and coarser parameters. At the University of Rome, for example, one equal amount was established for all the humanistic disciplines and another higher but equal amount was established for all the scientific disciplines.

Allocations for Scientific Research and Equipment

Unlike operation allocations, which use funds controlled by the Administrative Council, allocations for scientific research and the acquisition of teaching and scientific equipment are made by the Ministry of Public Instruction and reach the university with predetermined assignments.

The process begins when the university's Administrative Council examines and coordinates the requests of its departments, institutes, and professors and sends these to the ministry. Often, to ensure financing, the requests are sent to other possible allocators, such as the CNR, banks, and so on.

After the Administrative Council sends a proposal to the ministry, negotiation for obtaining the funds takes place between the applicant (an institute or individual professor) and the ministry. The ministry creates a special committee, composed primarily of university professors appointed by the CNR or by the Senior Council of Public Instruction. This committee examines and proposes—in fact, decides—the fund distribution to be made for research expenses.

Since the amount allocated by the ministry does not always correspond to the requests, and thus does not fill the specific need (as is the case when the ministry allocation does not allow for the purchase of new equipment), the Administrative Council adds the required funds from other university sources in order to avoid withdrawal of the state allocation. Once the allocation is approved it is sent to the university, which acts only in dispensing the earmarked funds.

In a few universities, the Administrative Council has created funds to support certain research activities without depending on contributions of the ministry of the CNR. In other cases, universities have tried to make the research proposals of institutes or individuals where they are likely to obtain state funding.

Allocations for Personnel

The university has little authority in this area because most of its personnel are paid by the state. Its responsibility is limited to providing for part of the nonacademic and nonpermanent staff and the nonacademic personnel of the university clinics. The universities establish expenditures for these categories, according to their own policies.

State legislation does permit a "free university," which carries all personnel costs in its own budget. But there is only one free university, that of Trento. Benefiting from many funds derived from local organizations, it has a rather high number of permanent professors; and because it is free it can also pay higher salaries than the state and thus attracts high prestige university academicians.

Personnel policies regarding the number of academics hired and the type of requested discipline specialization develop essentially on the level of the university department or school. It is still the school or department that requests the Ministry of Public Instruction to announce a competitive examination to fill chairs or vacant positions. The ministry names a committee composed of five professors from the relevant disciplines; the committee nominates two or three candidates for each position and the department or school chooses the teachers after interviewing them.

Competition among the departments and the pressures directed at the Ministry of Public Instruction to create new positions can disturb the equilibrium among the various components in a university. In such an instance, it is the Academic Senate (composed of the rector and of the deans of the departments) that settles the arguments of the various departments.

As mentioned previously, the Ministry of Public Instruction has few decision-making powers in regard to personnel expenditures; it can veto some authorizations (although this rarely happens), or it can freeze the upper limit of national-level competitive positions. This procedure is different from the two-year scholarships and the four-year work contracts. For these, a national ceiling is established, and the awards are then divided among the various universities and finally among the various departments. Negotiation is almost nonexistent here.

A CONCLUDING STATEMENT

In terms of institutional organization of the universities, the sectors with the greatest powers are the Ministry of Public Instruction and the Administrative Councils of the individual universities. We have seen, however, that there are many legislative and political obstacles that limit their actions.

Yet another obstacle is the practice of "financing continuity." Once resources are allocated to meet an ongoing need, it becomes very difficult to divert them to other areas. Flexibility tends to be restricted to questions of how much to increase an existing allocation. In recent years, because of rising inflation, there has been some increase in decision-making flexibility on the allotment of expenditures, but it has been limited by the negotiation "games" occurring at lower levels.

It is possible to deduce a trend: in university spending, the senior decision-making body rarely implements its own spending policy, but more often acts as a clearinghouse for conflicts coming from lower levels. Thus in Italy we see the department councils responding to the institutes and individual teachers, the Administrative Council responding to the departments, institutes, and chairs, and the minister of Public Instruction responding to the universities, the departments, and often the institutes and chairs.

5

BUDGETING FOR
SPANISH HIGHER EDUCATION

Alberto Moncada

The organization and finance of Spanish universities have been deeply influenced by the Napoleonic centralized system of higher education, and after the Civil War of 1936-39 all education came under strict control by the state. The state designs or approves curricula for every degree and provides professional certification. The state creates each public university and approves the establishment of private ones. It also appoints academic authorities, teachers at every level, and administrative officials. The state owns most of the facilities and provides funds for institutions with fully earmarked grants.

ORGANIZATION AND SUPPORT

The rationale supporting state intervention in higher education is the outcome of a longstanding coalition between academics and governmental officials; it reflects ideological commitments to the Establishment, the vested interests of the professions, and the aspirations of a growing and politically oriented urban middle class that uses higher education to maintain its hold on public and private bureaucracies. Higher education in Spain has been neither an instrument for social mobility—only 5 percent of the student population comes from working-class homes—nor a platform for applied or useful research, since most industrial technology and "know-how" in Spain is imported from other Western countries.

The main concern of institutions of higher education is teaching at the undergraduate level, and their main outputs are teachers, members of the learned professions, and bureaucrats. The Spanish commitment to research is less than 1 percent of the national budget, and most research occurs outside educational institutions.

Organization of Postsecondary Education

Spanish postsecondary education is still mainly higher or university education. The reformers of 1970, instead of expanding or creating postsecondary fields of study or vocationally oriented programs, opted for an expansion of university responsibilities, putting under the university umbrella most of the formal full-time courses that a young Spanish person might follow after completing secondary education. One exception to university expansion is the state-controlled Higher Council for Scientific Research, where postgraduates and researchers may find jobs and receive grants. Another organization that finances other agencies as well as universities (although under the same governmental department) is the Ministry of Education and Science (MEC). The reformers of 1970, responding to the pressure of increasing student numbers, followed French precedent and established "first-cycle" institutions of higher education. These schools or colleges offer undergraduates three years of transferable or terminal study, and although they are not universities, they are under the academic (not financial) control of university authorities according to territorial demarcations.

Also outside university academic control are the art schools, where some 7,000 people take postsecondary courses in music, drama, and the fine arts. These schools receive guidelines and funds from the MEC. Twenty-two public universities and three private ones accommodate 510,000 students, or 18 percent of the 18- to 24-year age group. The Spanish version of the "open university" enrolls 27,500 students. Madrid, Barcelona, and Valencia have followed official guidelines to organize polytechnic universities in addition to conventional ones. Madrid and Barcelona together enroll more than 60 percent of the entire student population. In terms of fields of interest, the student population was divided as follows in 1975:

	Number		Number
Humanities	58,690	Sciences	50,746
Arts	5,361	Architecture	24,972
Law	36,157	Engineering	62,814
Social Sciences	34,314	Medicine	69,019
Teaching	44,560	Argiculture	11,432

Only 20 percent of the 20,820 university teachers have tenure and belong to the government civil service. The remaining 80 percent are appointed for one or two years and can be dismissed without any formal procedure. Appointments are based on proposals by individual universities and each one is approved by the MEC.

Budget Sources and Allocations

The Spanish fiscal budget covers governmental activities from January 1 to December 31. It is approved by the Parliament at the end of each year and includes all public incomes and expenditures for the year, although very often the government proposes and Parliament approves funds for extra activities that sometimes produce an increased treasury debt.

Funds are allocated to each department (ministry) in charge of a public service, and each handles them according to legal guidelines and controls set by the Finance Department. The Finance Department maintains at least one member of its own staff in every university, school, and other decision center of the nation in order to control financial expenditures.

Between 1964 and 1976, the government produced four-year development plans, which made an official commitment of capital expenditures for each period and invited the private sector to follow the same pattern of national priorities. These investments were geared to develop deprived sectors of the economy and to build up a stronger network of public services. The plans produced heated controversy and the system was finally abandoned in 1976, with the government going back to the one-year fiscal budget, not only for recurrent but also for capital expenditures.

Within the last 6 years, state funding allocations to education have more than doubled, mainly to finance compulsory schooling up to the age of 16 (one of the top priority goals of the reformers of 1970). Educational allocations in 1976 had first priority in the state budget and constituted 18 percent of the national budget.

Some other departments, such as the Labor Department, also have educational commitments, especially for vocational short-term programs at secondary and postsecondary levels; and the armed forces maintain huge training and remedial programs for their staff and recruits. The main item in the educational budget is the salary appropriation for teachers in the Spanish system of primary and secondary education.

Universities receive almost 100 percent of their income from state sources. Students pay almost a token fee, tuitions having been frozen at Pts 6,000 for the social sciences and humanities and Pts 9,000 for science, engineering, and medicine; and since October 1976 no more than 15 percent of a university budget may be obtained from student fees. The three existing private universities, founded on the basis of an agreement with the Catholic church and subject to state guidelines and control, can charge larger student fees and can also receive grants and loans from the government for capital investments and a limited amount for research; local government contributions have also been available to them.

TABLE 5.1

State Expenditures in Higher Education
(thousands of pesetas, current 1976)

Year	Capital Investments	Recurrent Expenditures	Salaries of Tenured Teachers[a]
1970	3,243.0	2,584.7	3,246
1971	4,084.3	3,024.4	3,398
1972	2,976.0	3,910.5	6,736[b]
1973	2,847.8	4,411.2	10,127[c]
1974	2,640.8	5,199.4	9,711[c]
1975	2,459.2	7,508.4	9,711

[a]The salaries of nontenured teachers are included in recurrent expenditures.
[b]The large increase is due to the incorporation in higher education of the three-year Technical Colleges and Teacher Training Schools.
[c]In 1973 the number of tenured teachers was greatly expanded, but starting in 1974, all teachers in Schools of Arts were paid and controlled by authorities other than those in higher education.

Source: Data compiled by the author from the Records of the Ministry of Education.

Table 5.1 gives an idea of the trend in state expenditures: in 1975 higher education received 14 percent of the Ministry of Education budget—about the same percentage as in 1973 and 1974. These figures are increased by other public expenditures such as state grants to students, research grants to teachers, and expenditures from local authorities for capital and recurrent expenditures of three-year colleges.

MINISTRIES AND AGENCIES INVOLVED

The operating budget of state universities is established every year by officials of the General Directorate of University Education and officials of the Directorate of Planning and Investment, both part of the MEC.

The officials of the Directorate of Planning and Investment have the main responsibility for formulating and reviewing all economic matters within the department. Officials at the Directorate of University Education, the Directorate of Research, and the Directorate of Protection of the Students have the operational responsibilities for the funds that each directorate receives; they also discuss with officials of the Directorate of Planning and Investment the economic targets of every program. The targets are the tools used by the minister to plan and made all economic decisions in two senses: they formulate the complete educational request and submit it to the Finance Department and then discuss it with Finance officials until an agreement is reached.

Research funds obtained from public monies go mainly to: the Higher Council of Scientific Research where in 1976 full-time researchers received Pts 2,785 thousand for recurrent expenditures and Pts 763,327 thousand for capital investments; and grants to individual universities. Full-time researchers are accountable to the Directorate of Research of the MEC. Universities receive research grants mainly because individual members of the faculty or ad hoc teams advance proposals that, if approved, mean a flow of money to pay some salaries and extra costs, as well as the capital costs incurred by the universities during the research. The MEC also funds programs to promote scholarship, to educate future researchers in Spain or abroad, and to train or retrain teachers. Most of these funds are administered by universities in functional budgets that are reviewed by the particular directorate of the MEC in charge of each program.

Spanish universities do not receive or administer funds for allocation to students. Spanish university students can apply for grants of various amounts and terms to the Directorate of Protection of Students in the MEC, which in 1976/77 had a budget of Pts 2.431 million. Academic performance and family income are the main criteria used in awarding grants. In the MEC budget and in the operational budgets of the universities there are allocations for the establishment and maintenance of university residence halls; the universities administer and control these funds and report their expenditure to the MEC.

Three-Year University Colleges

When three-year university colleges were introduced, a new arrangement allowed local authorities and interest groups to partici-pate in their establishment and maintenance. In areas where no uni-versity exists, authorized groups can establish three-year colleges if they can make the required financial commitments for capital in-vestments and recurrent expenditures. Such groups have usually been associations of concerned people from banks or credit institutions; local authorities have sometimes provided land or unused public build-ings. The college is academically accountable to the nearest univer-sity, which receives student fees and controls academic matters in the college. The college students have to pay higher fees than uni-versity students—partly to compensate for not having to travel to the university—and the state gives some help for the operational budget, usually in the form of a matching grant for teachers' salaries. Nearly 40 such colleges had been established by 1976. Without them the con-ventional universities would have been unable to cope with the increas-ing number of new candidates for higher education.

Agency Personnel

Senior officials at the MEC are usually academics. Only two ministers of education in the last 40 years have not been tenured uni-versity teachers. Heads of university and research directorates in the MEC are also usually members of academia interested in exer-cising political control of the educational establishment.

The administrative staff of the MEC consists of tenured civil servants, all with university degrees. In the National School of Pub-lic Administration, founded in the late 1950s to promote uniform stan-dards in the selection and training of public servants, some attention is given to educational administration. Most of the vacancies in the MEC administration are filled with people who have attended this school (entrance is by examination) for periods of three to six months. However, more than 50 percent of all existing bureaucrats in Spain work in nontenured jobs, without benefit of special training, because the need for a rapid expansion of services has been met by mass recruiting. Nontenured teachers in the universities have increased, in part, for the same reason.

A particular esprit de corps is developing among graduates of the School of Public Administration, who are basically indoctrinated with the principles of technocracy and rationality (which have often clashed with the realities of naked power in major political controversies). The Department of Finance appoints some of these graduates to the MEC on the basis of personal choice and availability of openings. Unless there is a strong personal conflict, civil servants in the MEC continue to work there until retirement. Most of them gain wide experience in the educational structure of Spain; some are deeply involved in trying to rationalize the higher education system, but the conservative educational persuasions of mainstream politics in Spain present them with formidable obstacles. Educational budgets have increased, but no parallel expansion of MEC personnel has followed, and this shortage of qualified people is keenly felt. Only 15 full-time officials in the MEC do all the planning, financing, and policy review for higher education.

GOVERNMENT BUDGETING POLICY

Fiscal budgets in Spain emerged in the late 1950s as instruments of governmental policy, mainly for two purposes: (1) to expand underdeveloped public services and (2) to correct the dynamics of an economic system based on a coalition of interests represented by local business oligarchies, politicians, foreign companies, and foreign nations, especially the United States. Economists and bureaucrats, equipped with Keynesian tools, tried to rationalize public investments and public services and, through development plans, also tried to establish guidelines for selecting national priorities. After 20 years of struggle, the structure of power and wealth of Spain has succeeded in killing most of the modernization proposals, especially fiscal reform and the expansion of public services. In education, this has meant that the government has remained committed to the maintenance of private proprietary schools, dominated by the Catholic church, which are given annual state grants and construction loans to maintain their enrollments, instead of to the creation of a network of free public schools at the primary and secondary levels. The MEC budget is used to support such arrangements, even though the high tuitions paid fall most heavily on working-class families. Despite this conservative policy, the aspirations of increasing numbers of students in secondary education have forced the state to expand public higher education, more by a brick-and-mortar policy than by improving working facilities, teachers' salaries, and opportunities for research. Political authorities have been made uneasy by the activities of university teachers and students, who have frequently complained in ways that are not convenient for maintenance of Spanish law and order according to the status quo, about the political reasons for poor conditions in higher education.

The system of allocations to higher education reflects this conflict (see Figure 5.1). Every year the Council of Ministers discusses the budget proposals submitted by the minister of Education in light of the economic situation in general and educational interests in particular. And although the educational budget is growing, the monies approved each year are mostly geared to building up badly needed facilities for primary and secondary education and to keeping the Catholic and proprietary schools afloat.

Moreover, as a recent survey on the relationship between education and employment has shown, neither business and industry nor public services require many university graduates. Because of the organization of labor in these areas and in the learned professions, only 10 percent of the regular jobs in Spain need people with higher degrees. In a sense, then, universities have become warehouses of the young, who, because of their family income, can afford to spend more time than the average out of the labor market, counting on their university credentials to obtain a higher-status position. Nevertheless, unemployment and underemployment among graduates is already common, especially in the humanities and social sciences, whose graduates mainly teach.

The Council of Ministers, when dealing with higher education, does not receive political and economic pressure from the establishment to foster university activities. On the contrary, most requests to do so come from foes of the establishment. And those who hold political power in Spain have learned during 40 years of dictatorship that answering popular or intellectual demands is not the best way to stay in power.

Each autumn, before its approval by the Council of Ministers, the budget for higher education and research is discussed by the minister of Education and the minister of Finance. The discussions, concerned mainly with the rate of increase over the current budget, constitute a struggle between the expansionist wishes of the education ministry and the cost-conscious attitude of the finance ministry, which is responsible for developing the entire state budget. During the last three years, with a high turnover of finance ministers and a steady deterioration of the economy, the discussions have continued through the autumn and winter sessions of the Council of Ministers, which is supposed to produce a budget for Parliament before the end of the year.

FIGURE 5.1

Organization for Higher Education and Sources of Funding in Spain

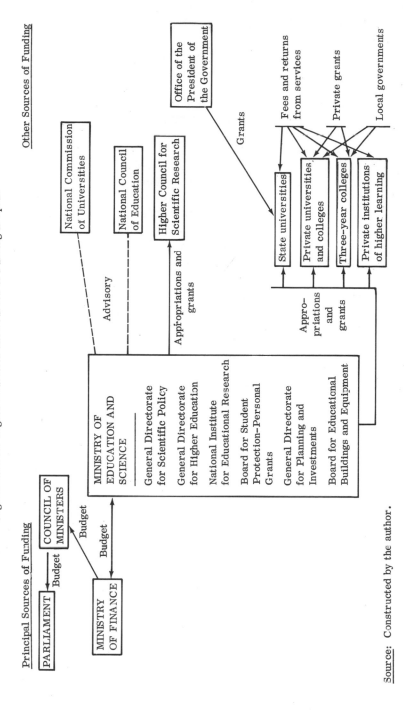

Source: Constructed by the author.

103

The educational budget, like those of the other public services, consists of a fully earmarked amount of money. Capital investments and operational expenditures are described in detail, and allocations to universities are no exception. Whereas in the past parliamentary discussion merely led to rubber-stamp approval of the decisions of the Council of Ministers, in recent years politicians have seen it as an opportunity to protect particular interests. Success in this area depends upon the politician's position on the political ladder and on his persuasive powers, but since higher education has not been of particularly high political salience, not many political records have been built on it. Now, however, with the growing demand for regional university colleges, a legislator may work hard to please his constituents by securing governmental approval for one of these institutions.

Spanish society uses the universities for various purposes besides the selection and certification of personnel in learned professions. Despite the inefficiencies, universities and university teachers and researchers are still the best resources available for strengthening the Spanish commitment to science, technology, and expansion or control of the cultural environment. Academics are used in their personal capacity to man scientific departments of the government, to advise public and private agencies, and to preside over or control most of the educational and research activities of the country. All these extra burdens, which very often clash with normal university duties, have not been matched by an increase in the number of faculty. University heads are often at a loss when trying to conduct their business without the full-time cooperation of their most qualified personnel; rectors and deans can only watch while less able and less experienced teachers perform the everyday routine of teaching and research. The government fosters or permits these extracurricular pursuits, for in many areas it is the chief employer of these moonlighting academics. It profits directly from this arrangement, as it is much cheaper than seeking broader but more indirect benefits from financing a more creative and responsible environment in institutions of higher education. Private firms are also happy with the situation for the same reason.

BUDGET CONTROLS AND DATA SYSTEMS

Because universities receive various kinds of allocations, university administrators must report on them and send specified data to the appropriate directorates of the MEC. The finance official located in each university to control the legalities of the flow of money also informs and sends operational data to the Finance Department. The Labor Department collects data about the staff and students for social security purposes.

Expenditure Control

Most of the legally prescribed information and data are used by MEC officials to implement their two main activities: the approval of every financial transaction in university affairs and the control of implementing decisions. University officials see themselves as delegates-at-large of the MEC, and they work on the assumption that every decision with economic implications must be implemented according to MEC regulations and finally approved by MEC officials. The approvals occur in two ways: when the required signature of an MEC official is obtained and when the MEC officials review and approve the procedures of university officials. University procedures can be revised only when memos, carbons, and directives are sent to the MEC, or when an actual inspection of MEC officials is carried out to control in situ the legality of some measure. The signature of the Finance Department delegate in each university is also needed on all documents related to expenditure decisions. These arrangements are prescribed in order to collect from the Treasury of Spain the monies involved in each economic operation. The treasury does not allocate funds without receiving detailed documents from the concerned departmental officials.

In 1971, the Spanish government gave a certain amount of autonomy to state universities, allowing them to make economic commitments of up to Pts 10 million without prior approval by MEC officials, to transfer monies originally allocated for other purposes, and to hire temporary nontenured teachers without MEC control, provided that a balanced budget was reached each year. Two years later, that autonomy was largely withdrawn, and academic and financial decision-making powers were again placed under the control of the MEC. That change was not prompted by economic mismanagement on the part of university officials, but mainly by the government's decision that such liberty was undesirable in view of increasing political protests by students and intellectuals.

Another move toward university autonomy was also killed in the early 1970s. Individual charters and statutes were drawn up by each state university for final approval according to the 1970 General Law of Education. The government, however, apparently felt threatened by growing campus demands for wider participation in the drafting of this university legislation and by the appeals for more autonomy than granted by most provisions of the statutes. Some of the new charters were approved after being amended to permit the maintenance of MEC control, but their actual implementation was thwarted by the government through academic and economic decisions.

In 1971 some officials of the MEC proposed more systematic information gathering and analyses for higher education allocations and won the cooperation of the minister of Education, who issued implementing recommendations to state universities. The recommendations asked for a flow of information about the cost effectiveness of higher education that, coming from universities and discussed in the MEC, would serve as guidelines for increasing university fees and adopting targets of academic excellence and administrative effectiveness. This trend produced several studies by individual universities, based mainly on Anglo-Saxon models of administration. However, when these studies reached political levels, politicians and senior academics saw in them a threat to their hold on university power, and their protests prevented the implementation of most of the measures proposed—including the consolidation of a central office of university administration intended to coordinate the new system. As a result of this political backlash, information and data from the universities, instead of becoming a tool for reform, continued to be a mere certification of how university officials observed the existing regulations on the uses of money.

Functional and Program Budgeting

When the first government of the Spanish king began to set up a rationale for the fiscal budget of 1977, in the context of the existing economic recession, both financial and educational authorities seized the occasion to begin changing from a structural to a functional accounting and budgeting system, in other words, to move toward some kind of program budgeting. Most of the experts in Spain are aware of the shortcomings and liabilities of the program approach, but apparently they prefer some kind of functional program to the old political rule-of-thumb method of allocating public money. The fiscal budget for 1977 was approved by an inattentive lame-duck Parliament, destined to be out of office in May 1977, after the general elections. The director of the budget included in the budget some blueprints for future programming without actually making any substantial change in the 1977 budget.

As for higher education, a set of rules for the economic behavior of individual universities was circulated among concerned officials, along with a formula for the devolution of responsibilities to each one. The rules included two options for discussion. The first would allow more freedom to individual universities to sell their services, with the government providing no more than half of the funds needed and student fees covering the other half. The second and more conservative one asked for greater flexibility in the allocation of public money, including a yearly revision of fees and an unspecified period of approximately five years for changing from the present centralization to the autonomy envisaged in the first option. In January 1977 these proposed rule changes had not received government sanction, but officials insisted that the program approach and the set of rules on financial autonomy were first steps for rational planning from 1978 onward. Important administrators in the ministries of education and finance and in the major universities all favor such changes, but conservative politicians and the faculty professors holding chairs appear to cling to the old forms.

As of this writing, each and every allocation is the result of a historical process: each new budget repeats the former one with some change, mostly in the form of increases. Once the allocation is established, the universities have few legal ways to transfer funds from one line to another, a practice that is supposed to change under the new approach. Negotiation at the cabinet and parliamentary levels is almost nonexistent, because of the previous staff work and negotiations among the ministries. In 1977, the only major change made by the cabinet (before parliamentary approval) was a political decision to increase the appropriation levels for higher education while holding all allocations to other levels of education at the same level. The result was an across-the-board increase, without any particular program or strategy in mind.

FORMULAS AND GUIDELINES

As noted previously, the government aids in the financing of both public and private institutions of higher education.

Operational Expenditures for Public Institutions

Recurrent incomes of the universities do not have a unified rationale. Most of the public monies that enter the university budget every year are fully earmarked, but the reason for identifying each and every allocation is, more than anything else, an outcome of ad hoc agreements between concerned parties based on the current state of the treasury.

Tenured university teachers, who form one of the most conservative forces in Spain, are privileged public servants, are part of the state bureaucracy, and are paid directly by the Spanish Treasury. Their salaries do not appear in the university budget, and their status and working conditions are based on general regulations, which allow them, among other things, to move from one state university to another without permission or control from university administrators. The total state allocation for tenured teachers is based on MEC guidelines according to which a tenured job is created when there is academic agreement regarding the need to endow a new chair because of scientific interest, or when the number of student advisees establishes the need for additional chairs in the same discipline. The senior academics form coalitions and secure the cooperation of university heads to advance such proposals to the MEC, where two committees decide whether or not to proceed with them. A decision has to be approved by the National Council of Education and the National Commission of Universities, the former being a broad platform of educational and political interests and the latter a conference of university rectors. If approved by the MEC, the Finance Ministry must then agree to include the new chair in the existing bureaucracy (civil service) of tenured teachers. Qualified full professors can apply for the job, for which final selection is by a committee of their academic peers—full professors. Once appointed, tenured teachers hold a chair in a particular university and become a part of the state bureaucracy, with all its implications.

From 1974 to 1977, mainly because of economic constraints, allocations for tenured teachers in Spain were not increased, with the result that most teaching in universities was conducted by nontenured teachers. This has been a particular hardship for the newly created universities and three-year colleges, where tenured teachers are scarce either because sufficient tenured positions have not yet been approved or because the town or locale of the new institution offers too few amenities or resources of nonacademic income to attract experienced teachers.

Each state university receives a lump sum allocation every year for nontenured teachers, who are appointed by the MEC from nominees presented by the department concerned and confirmed by the governing board of the university.

The number of appointments of nontenured teachers is based on the number of students. Every tenured teacher or department head informs the governing board of the university of new needs for teaching staff based on new student enrollment in October. The university makes a single money request to the MEC, which can be approved in full, in part, or not at all.

There is a growing awareness that the increase in nontenured teachers does not in itself produce an improvement in the quality of teaching and research, mainly because of the salaries and working conditions. Qualified graduates may see the way to a tenured position as a very long and painful process and would rather try some other more promising openings in business or industry and even in other state bureaucracies.

This situation, and the hardships imposed on Spanish higher education and culture by traditional political control, produces a steady "brain drain" toward foreign institutions of higher education. Mexico, France, and the United States host Spanish professors and researchers of the highest quality.

Administrative staff in universities have the same pattern of working conditions as teachers. Some of them have tenured positions and belong to the state bureaucracy. The remaining are hired on a year-by-year basis. Neither the nontenured teachers nor the nontenured administrators have a normal labor contract, as does the average worker in Spain. The lack of collective bargaining and other features of civil labor relations is responsible for much of the existing malaise among university personnel.

Universities receive an annual allocation for their operating costs, which include maintenance of buildings and equipment, general overhead, and teaching materials. This allocation is less specifically earmarked than other incomes and can be used by university officials with some flexibility. Since 1973, officials have complained about the small amount of this appropriation, which has not matched the increases in students, buildings, and equipment during the same period.

The universities derive research income from three main sources: from two programs administered by the Directorate of Higher Education in the MEC and from a program administered by the Office of the President of the Government.

The two MEC programs differ in goals and procedure. The first, a general program for research run by the Directorate, is in fact an extra unearmarked allowance to the teaching staff, which allows them to receive some cash and pay for some books and small equipment. The amount is small and does not foster actual research and is distributed evenly among chairs and departments. The real MEC research program is the second one, under which teachers and researchers advance research proposals every year to the MEC. The MEC's yearly allocation is distributed among the proposals, after some have been rejected and others modified. An ad hoc commission of scientists serves as the MEC umpire in these decisions.

As with all elements in the higher education economy, academics have complained about the lack of research monies available since 1973. Some conflicts arise regarding research done in universities as opposed to the Higher Council of Scientific Research, which is also funded by the state. Coordination is almost nil, and there is an increasing demand for consolidating public research funds into a single agency, at least to guarantee better use of the limited resources.

To avoid yearly limitations and to link public research with political programs, the Office of the President of the Government can also fund research projects. The procedure is almost the same as in the MEC programs: researchers, most of them university teachers, advance proposals to an Advisory Committee in the Office of the President, which decides which ones to support.

The advisory committee claims that research projects are eligible when oriented toward the national development targets of the government, but there is no available evidence to prove this. In fact, there is no publicly available evidence for the existence of any set of national priorities that could be advanced through research, because Spain is heavily dependent on Western technology and the government has not fostered workable alternatives. When research monies come to their faculty members, universities receive parallel grants for capital investment in equipment and may keep the equipment once the research is completed.

Universities are the recipients and administrators of some other governmental programs. Among these are a yearly MEC allocation to train, either in Spain or abroad, young teachers and researchers (who need the backing of university professors to be eligible for such grants) and a fund for educational research distributed to the Institutes of Education in the universities by the National Institute for Educational Sciences. These Institutes of Education also receive funds for the improvement and retention of teachers throughout the whole educational system. Most of these funds from the several sources are incorporated into the university operational budget, and others come as earmarked grants and must be used accordingly.

Operational Expenditures for Private Institutions

Private universities and private organizations of higher learning are eligible for capital grants and receive some income from the state, as previously mentioned. When they succeed in getting public funds they are accountable to the granting ministry—the MEC or some other—and are subject to the same procedures as state universities.

STATE EXPENDITURE AUDITS

Every five years, according to Spanish fiscal law, officials of a special board examine public expenditures for the legality of the flow of public monies. If, in higher education, such scrutiny reveals some mismanagement or improper use of funds, the Board of Accounts can ask personal restitution from the persons concerned. In the tradition of Spanish administration, much more emphasis is placed on formal procedures and competence in dealing with public funds than on the social usefulness of the allocations.

No provisions exist for formal complaint about the quality of teaching or of research in state universities. Nor can one protest a system in which most decisions are made by an oligarchy of academics and politicians accountable to still more like-minded academics and politicians. Only now, with the passage of more permissive laws concerning the mass media, is the public becoming aware of the problems in higher education. The process of allocating public funds to higher education may now be opened up to new standards of accountability; it may become possible to ask publicly why certain funds are allocated and what purposes they will serve.

6

THE BUDGETARY PROCESS OF SWEDISH HIGHER EDUCATION

Jan-Erik Lane

In 1975 the Swedish Parliament passed a bill outlining a reform of the entire field of higher education. As the bill began to be implemented in 1977, two new governing structures appeared: a new system for the division of units and a new system for allocating funds. This chapter deals with the changes in the budgetary process and their implications for the academic institutions.

THE ORGANIZATION OF HIGHER EDUCATION

The development of Swedish higher education since World War II is a variation on the general theme of transition from elitism to mass

---

I wish to thank Dan Brandstrom, head of the regional bureau of Norrland, and Bert Fredriksson, head of the education bureau at Umeå University, who read a draft of this manuscript and provided me with criticism and suggestions. I am grateful to Rune Premfors, research assistant in the Department of Political Science at Stockholm University and to Eskil Bjorklund of the Bureau for Education and Research at the National Swedish Board of Universities and Colleges for help in various ways. Erland Ringborg, head of the budget bureau at the National Swedish Board of Universities and Colleges provided me with a reading of a draft that has been most valuable. I am indebted to research assistant Agneta Lane and secretaries Britt-Marie Johansson and Maise Nordstrom. Other people have discussed the complexities of the budgetary process with me. Without access to their knowledge I could not have written this chapter.

TABLE 6.1

Students Enrolled in Swedish Higher Education Institutions, 1945–75

(in thousands)

| Year | Academic Units | | Nonacademic Units | Total |
	Universities and Colleges	Higher Professional Schools[b]	Lower Professional Schools[c]	
1945	9.308	4.673	4.662	18.643
1950	11.142	5.686	13.694	30.522
1955	15.928	6.648	13.827	36.403
1960	26.752	8.991	13.746	49.489
1965	49.202	14.185	18.979	82.366
1970	102.407	20.330	29.694	152.431
1975	81.107	19.762	30.465	131.334

[a]Faculties of humanities, law, mathematics and science, medicine, social science, theology.
[b]Faculties of odontology, pharmacology, technology; schools of commerce, agriculture, forestry, veterinary medicine, gymnastics, and sports.
[c]Schools of fine arts, journalism, music, nursing, social work, and teacher training.

Source: B. Fredriksson and J. -E. Lane, The Swedish System of Higher Education 1945–1977: An Organizational Approach (Sweden: Liber, 1978).

participation.* In 1945 there were about 19,000 students in all institutions of higher education; in 1975 about 130,000 students were enrolled (see Table 6.1). Traditionally, the system of higher education consisted of various types of units. Up to 1977 it was organized on principles separating academic from nonacademic units, universities and colleges from higher professional schools, and various lower professional schools from each other. At the end of the 1950s' the academic units enrolled slightly less than two-thirds of the students.

The rapid increase in enrollments during the 1960s was handled in different ways. The old elitist institutions took the main part of the expansion, and the remainder was channeled to other types of units modeled on them—new colleges and additional lower professional schools. By the end of the growth period, the academic units had increased their share of the total number of students enrolled in higher education to about three-quarters. By this time the system had become highly heterogeneous, including universities, colleges, and various types of both higher and lower professional schools.

The Reform of 1977

The reform of 1977 reduced heterogeneity to a considerable extent, although the concept of higher education was expanded to include some educational lines and courses that belonged to the secondary school system and simultaneously provided universal access to all institutions. The new system divides state higher education and communal higher education, the latter comprising one-third of the places for new students in 1977/78. Several units belonging to the state part are amalgamated and run according to the same rules.

Historically, the academic institutions had a governing structure resembling the German type. It was based on the full professor, who was responsible for a discipline. The professors were governed by the tenured faculty headed by the dean, who was usually also a professor. Along with the rector, who was a professor and elected by the tenured faculty, the deans constituted the board of the institution, the konsistorium—a professional oligarchy that elected its own leaders.

The reform of 1977 substitutes democratic representation for professional representation as the principle for governance. In the

---

*For an analysis of this transition in the Swedish system of higher education, see B. Fredriksson and J.-E. Lane, The Swedish University System of Higher Education 1945-1977: An Organizational Approach (Sweden: Liber, 1978).

reformed units, the board is composed of representatives from various groups inside and outside the institution. Some board members are appointed by units outside of the institution, and the government now appoints the rector. The governance structure of the new institutions of higher education is thus democratic and only partly self-chosen. *

Financing and Control

Public funds support most of the Swedish system of higher education. In 1975/76 the total costs amounted to roughly Kr 2,890 million. Around 75 percent, or Kr 2,200 million, were allocated to higher education and research, excluding the institutes of agriculture, forestry, and veterinary medicine (Table 6.2). Of the 75 percent of total funds allotted to academic units, 90 percent comes from the government and 10 percent from the research councils. The private sector provides less than 10 percent of the money. As this financial situation suggests, the institutions are mainly public, the development of mass education having been accomplished through the nationalization of private institutions.

TABLE 6.2

Funding of Swedish Higher Education, 1975/76
(in millions of kronor)

Academic units	2,200
Institutes of agriculture, forestry, and veterinary medicine	210
Nonacademic units	480
Total	2,890

Source: National Swedish Board of Universities and Colleges.

---

*Before 1964 there was a governance system comprised of two konsistorier, one small and one large, and an academic senate. All three bodies were composed of or elected from the full professors. See B. Fredriksson and J. -E. Lane, The Swedish System of Higher Education 1945-1977: An Organizational Approach (Sweden: Liber, 1978).

FIGURE 6.1

Outline of the Decision-Making Process in Sweden

From 1964 to 1977, Academic Units Only

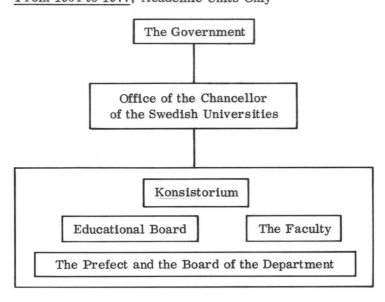

After 1977, All State Higher Education Units

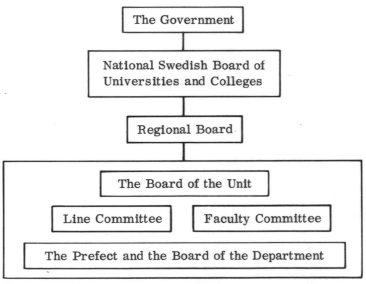

Source: Constructed by the author.

Up to 1977, Swedish academic institutions were autonomous in choosing their own governing boards, but their operations were controlled by detailed government regulations. These regulations, however, were by no means always unfavorable to educational interests; by a refined system of participation and representation, educational institutions had considerable influence on governmental policies and decisions. The system implemented in 1977 increased the amount of operational control held by the institutions, but it decreased their influence because the government now pays more attention than before to the views of the groups in society outside the institutions.

Public financing and public control imply bureaucracy, and bureaucracy means hierarchy. The organization of higher education in Sweden has been and remains hierarchical. Between 1964 and 1977, the hierarchy had separate structures for academic units and for non-academic units, with only the academic units run according to uniform rules. The reform of 1977 brings all state higher education units under one hierarchical system, in which each level is run uniformly. *
The levels in the decision-making process are shown in Figure 6.1.

THE HIGHER EDUCATION GRANT

The state budget is presented by the government to Parliament, whose acceptance—after additions and minor alterations—makes it law. Technically, the financing of higher education and research is accomplished through a grant called "higher education and research," a functional category in the budget of the Ministry of Education. Until 1977 the grant covered only academic units (with minor exceptions), but as of the reform it covers most of the research and service activities of the institutions. The institutes of agriculture, forestry, and veterinary medicine, and the research councils, which are not under the authority of the Ministry of Education, are still funded from appropriations awarded to other ministries.

The Outcome

The grant for higher education and research has increased seven times since 1945 in current prices and five times in fixed prices. In the 1945/46 budget, Kr 15 million went to higher education,

---

*For details, see B. Fredricksson and J. -E. Lane, The Swedish System of Higher Education 1945-1977: An Organizational Approach (Sweden: Liber, 1978).

TABLE 6.3

Percentage of Sources' Budget Allotments of the Grant for Higher
Education and Research, 1945/46-1975/76

| Years | Sources | | |
	Ministry Budget	State Budget	GNP
1945/46	4.39	0.43	0.07
1950/51	8.55	0.90	0.16
1955/56	8.33	0.95	0.19
1960/61	10.41	1.35	0.29
1965/66	12.40	1.77	0.44
1970/71	15.78	2.76	0.68
1975/76	17.40	2.20	0.70

Source: B. Fredricksson and J. -E. Lane, The Swedish System of Higher Education 1945-1977: An Organizational Approach
(Sweden: Liber, 1978).

whereas in the 1975/76 budget Kr 1.995 million were allocated. The
relative expansion of the grant is obvious when its share of the budget
of the Ministry of Education, the government budget, and the GNP
are considered. Table 6.3 reveals that by 1961 the grant's share of
the budget tripled and more than tripled its share of the GNP. In
these years the rate of growth (10-20 percent) was far greater than
that of GNP (5-10 percent). Also, while the grant for higher education and research grew 19 percent on the average, the budget for the
ministry for all types of education grew 14 percent on the average.

The lion's share of the grant goes directly into the universities
and the higher professional schools. A considerable though smaller
amount goes to the research councils for reallocation to the universities and schools.

Table 6.4 shows the fundamental position of the research councils and institutes since the mid-1940s. The bureaus, councils, and
institutes have two independent funding sources: the state through
the Ministry of Education and the state through other ministries on
contracts for research with the university.

TABLE 6.4

Percentage Distribution of the Grant for Higher Education and
Research, 1945/46-1975/76

Years	Central Bureaus	Universities and Professional People	Research Councils and Institutes
1945/46	0.3	94.9	4.8
1950/51	0.4	85.2	14.4
1955/56	0.3	87.7	12.0
1960/61	0.4	86.7	12.9
1965/66	0.7	83.5	15.7
1970/71	0.9	85.7	13.4
1975/76	1.0	85.1	13.9

Source: B. Fredricksson and J.-E. Lane, The Swedish System of Higher Education 1945-1977: An Organizational Approach (Sweden: Liber, 1978).

TABLE 6.5

Distribution of Appropriations for Universities and Higher
Professional Schools, 1970/71 and 1975/76
(in millions of kronor)

	1970/71	Percent	1975/76	Percent
Undergraduate education	310.0	33.9	446.8	28.3
Graduate education and research	157.7	17.2	296.5	18.8
Operating expenses of faculties	180.6	19.7	307.0	19.4
Common functions (costs for libraries, university administration, et cetera)	265.8	29.0	528.2	33.5
Total	915.0	100.0	1,578.5	100.0

Source: IKÄ:s förslag till anslagsäskanden för budgetåret 1970-71 och 1975-76 [Proposal for those requesting appropriations for budget years 1970-71 and 1975-76] (Stockholm: University Chancellor's Publication Series).

Universities and Higher Professional Schools

These institutions use their appropriations to pay for salaries and operating expenses (Table 6.5); over 28 percent is spent on salaries in undergraduate education, and slightly less than 20 percent is spent on salaries for graduate education and research. The operating expenses of the faculties—the costs of paper, copying, travel, and equipment—account for almost 20 percent

The Research Councils

The various research councils established during and immediately after World War II are vital to the institutions of higher education. Some are under the authority of the Ministry of Education, and some are under other ministries. The councils that are subordinate to the Ministry of Education get appropriations through the grant as shown in Table 6.4. Some other ministry councils allocate money to institutions as part of their grants. This is true of the largest council, the Board for Technical Development, as well as for the Council for Research into Forestry and Agriculture.

A dramatic expansion occurred in the funding from the several research councils in 1950/51, when they were allocated Kr 6.7 million, to 1975/76, when they had Kr 465 million at their disposal. In the 1960s appropriations grew at an average annual rate of 32 percent; in the 1970s the rate dropped to an average of 15 percent.

The three big councils are those dealing with technology—the Medical Council, the Natural Science Council, and the Board for Technical Development. The Medical and Natural Science councils receive about the same allocation—an amount more than four times what is given to councils for social sciences and the humanities. The Board for Technical Development allocates most of the government funds it receives to institutions outside the field of higher education; the funds received by the Council for Research into Forestry and Agriculture go to the schools of agriculture, forestry, and veterinary medicine.

In 1975/76, a total of Kr 1.6 million were allocated by other ministries to applied research. However, most money that goes for specific research areas does not go to the institutions of higher education.

THE BUDGETARY PROCESS

Since any budgetary process takes place within an organizational frame, if the framework changes the process will be affected. To oversimplify somewhat, there was one basic organizational frame in Sweden until 1977, an elitist one; since 1977 a fundamentally new organizational frame has been under construction. In the following discussion, the elitist structure is referred to as the old system.

The Preparation Time

To create a grant for higher education and research in Sweden takes roughly 19 months. Under the old and new systems, the process starts in December of Year 0, and ends a year and a half later, in June of Year 2.

At the beginning of December of Year 0, the institutions receive budget guidelines from three sources: the Ministry of Education, the state agency (National Swedish Board for Universities and Colleges or UHA), and the advisory boards within the board agency. The guidelines from the ministry, based on general guidelines for budget work proposed by the Ministry of Finance, contain the technical regulations for making requests for appropriations. The state agency also sends practical recommendations on how to build the budget, but its proposals also contain references to what it believes should guide the establishment of priorities—which are, first, the agency program, followed by declarations of the government in its budget for Year 0, and finally statements by the parliamentary committee for education. The guidelines from the advisory boards are concerned with the priorities followed in the budget proposals from the local units; their advice is usually based on the agency's long-term programs, and they seek to force the local units to pay attention to certain areas or issues, or to provide arguments defending their proposals.

Toward the end of January of Year 1, the basic units in the local institutions decide upon their requests for increased resources for undergraduate and graduate education and research. These demands are sent to coordinating boards within the local institutions. These boards set their priorities in February. In March UHA receives these proposals, together with a statement from the institutional governing boards containing their priorities from among the proposals of the internal coordinating boards.

Under the new system, one more level is added. A regional board sends the UHA a comment on the proposals of the governing boards at the beginning of May. Then the whole process moves to the central level. While the local institutions are setting priorities, the UHA (having given guidelines to the institutions), continues its work, and in March it evaluates the proposals coming in. After a series of meetings, the UHA comes up with a budget proposal for its area in June. In August the documents go to the Ministry of Education. From

then on the budget process is part of the political process in the ministries and Parliament.

Up to the top of the hierarchy—the Ministry of Education—a great number of people have been involved in making decisions, putting forward demands, and building arguments for their cases. Now, all the issues are resolved by a few persons from the Ministry of Education, the Ministry of Finance, and Parliament's committee for education.

At the beginning of September of Year 1 the Ministry of Education lists and reviews the proposals from its various subordinate boards and agencies. The unit for higher education and research goes through the requests within its area and provides a preliminary estimate of the grant. Then the Ministry of Education sends its estimate to the Ministry of Finance, which has been working on the total budget since the beginning of September; it reviews the proposal and returns it with comment. In mid-October the Ministry of Education returns the proposal to the Ministry of Finance with a statement of what it is prepared to accept. Meanwhile, there have been meetings within the government and among higher officials. After the bid from the Ministry of Education there is a period of negotiation between the staff in the budget bureau of the Ministry of Finance and the staff in the Ministry of Education. Negotiations end in a preliminary proposal on the part of the Ministry of Finance, which is sent to the Ministry of Education around mid-November. The final bid from the Ministry of Education usually comes at the end of November. The remaining discrepancies are then resolved through negotiations between the ministries or within the government. On December 13 the budget proposal goes to the printers, and it reaches Parliament about January 10 of Year 2. During the spring Parliament deals with the budget through various hearings, and by the end of May the whole procedure ends after discussion of minor additional budgetary proposals from the government and members of Parliament. In June of Year 2, the Ministry of Education sends letters of appropriations to its subordinate units.

The Ministry of Education

The Ministry of Education controls almost all types of institutions for higher education, and is responsible for most of the allocation of funds to the institutions. The ministry is made up of six units, one of which is the unit for higher education and research. The bureaucracy at the ministry has expanded substantially during the postwar period, with the number of bureaucrats growing from 14 in 1946 to 85 in 1976. Each unit is built up hierarchically with different layers of nonpolitical staff. Above the heads of the units there are three officials—one of whom is a political appointee—responsible for the coordination of the work of the whole ministry and subordinate to the minister.

The government is very much involved in the operation of the institutions of higher education. It allocates most of the funds; it sets the objectives of institutions and regulates their implementation (by prescribing the organization of studies, the number and types of teachers, and decision-making procedures); and it appoints full professors, associate professors, tenured undergraduate lecturers, and higher administrative staff.

The State Agency

Since October 1976, most of the institutions of higher education have been coordinated by one state agency, the National Swedish Board of Universities and Colleges (UHA). This agency is an amalgamation of the Office of the Chancellor for the Swedish Universities, set up in 1964, and other boards. The institutes of agriculture, forestry, and veterinary medicine remain outside the authority of this agency. With the expansion of its operations and the development of a philosophy that stresses uniformity and equality in higher education, the central administration of institutions increasingly stresses homogeneity.

The UHA now has a board of 11 members: the chancellor, who is chairman; a planning director; the chairmen of new planning commissions (replacing the old advisory boards); and 4 other members. The 5 planning commissions, which still maintain advisory positions, have a maximum of 17 members each. Their areas of concern are:

education for technical professions, natural science, and technical science,
education for administrative and social professions, social science and faculties of law,
education for medical and nursing professions, medical science, ontological and pharmaceutical sciences,
education for teaching professions, and
education for cultural and informative professions and faculties of liberal arts and theology.

Within the UHA, three administrative bureaus serve as secretariat to the advisory boards; the Bureau for Planning carries out their administrative functions. The UHA administers government regulations, conducts long-term planning of education and research, coordinates the budget proposals from local institutions, and is involved in the appeals system concerning issues in higher education.

The Regional Boards

The reform of 1977 introduced a system of six regions for post-secondary education. Each regional board consists of a maximum of 21 members appointed by various bodies representing public interest groups, local institutions, organizations of employees within the local institutions, and students. Each board serves its region through a permanent administrative staff and a system of educational advisory committees. The main work of the boards is to coordinate the activities of state higher education with those of communal higher education. They promote cooperation between institutions that have research capacity and those that do not. In the budget process, they comment on proposals from institutions and faculties, and they allocate funds to certain courses in the institutions.

The Local Institutions

Under the new system, most institutions of postsecondary education continue to be universities and higher professional schools. Under the old system, each was run by the konsistorium of tenured professors and by two types of coordinating bodies subordinate to it —the faculty and the educational committee. The konsistorium was responsible for the activities of local institutions. In the budget process it added a statement of its own priorities to proposals from faculties, and it allocated funds to operating expenses and to certain areas of undergraduate and graduate education. The educational committees were oriented toward undergraduate education. The faculty had a broader range of responsibilities, some important in the budgetary process: it made the first coordination of the institutions' budget requests and delivered them to the state agency, along with its own comments.

The new system is a radical break from the full-professor power system. The prefect-dean-konsistorium structure is replaced by:

a governing board of 15 to 18 persons comprising representatives for public interests (one-third), the rector (now appointed by the government), the administrative director, and for the teachers, employee organizations, and students,

line committees (replacing educational committees) consisting of one-third representatives for teachers, one-third for the students, and one-third for occupational groups,

the faculty, which is made up of all types and levels of teachers and will be governed by a committee elected by the faculty (the faculty committee includes one representative of the graduate students), and

the prefect, who can be selected from nontenured people.

The functional changes tend to be in the same direction; that is, the faculty committee has less power than the old faculty. Its budgetary responsibilities are narrowed to graduate education and research. The line committee draws up proposals for budget requests for undergraduate education. The governing board takes over the responsibility for budgeting undergraduate education and delivers the line committee's budget requests to the state agency, adding its comments to the faculty committee's requests for graduate education and research.

State Agency Personnel

There are three kinds of people involved in the budget process at the state agency—bureaucrats, professionals, and laymen. They represent the interests of the bureaucracy, the professions, and the public. The bureaucracy of the agency is firmly hierarchical. Members of the regional board of the agency—representing organizations of employees and employers, the national student organization, the UHA, and the Ministry of Education—have academic experience, but only a minority (about one-quarter) hold higher academic degrees. Professional representation is on the advisory committees. Under the old system, the faculties at local institutions nominated their own people to four of the nine seats. Under the new system, the government appoints the members of the advisory committees, who are first nominated by the UHA staff. A maximum of 16 members plus the chair represent the various interests on each advisory committee.

In the old system, most of the people on research councils were professors recruited by a combination of two techniques: election by professional groups and appointment by the government. Under the new system there are only three councils instead of five: one each for the humanities and social sciences, medicine, and the natural sciences. A new body, the Council Committee, coordinates the activities of the research councils and the various other bodies oriented toward applied research. It has special responsibilities for initiating and supporting interdisciplinary research. A majority of the Council Committee consists of nonacademic people.

Although the Ministry of Education is run by people with academic experience, not many have high academic degrees: of the 41 top officials who have served since World War II, only 9 have had doctoral degrees.

BUDGET TECHNIQUES

How people behave in the budget process is a function of how appropriations are determined and how funds are allocated. Appropriations can be based on items of expenditure or on functions. What is included in the grants can be the result of different decision mechanisms: automatic procedures (the application of regulations and formulas), negotiations, or submission-control (one party makes requests and another makes the final decision, thus controlling the outcome). Appropriations may be dependent on a parameter that pushes the amounts up or down, or they may be independent of any such parameter.

The old budgetary system produced itemized budgets with specific rules governing the use of the funds listed for each function (line). The lines resulted in part from automatic procedures and in part from the submission-control mechanism. Some funds were dependent on the number of students who entered each year, while other funds were not. The new budget system produces functional budgets, a result of the submission-control mechanism.

The Appropriations System

Under the old system, the grant for higher education and research was basically a system of line-item appropriations. Before 1967 it was split up into 140 appropriations; after 1967 there were 68 appropriations, and there are 30 in the new system. With each reform, rules governing the use of funds have moved steadily toward less regulation. Before 1967 the system provided detailed rules; for example, salary appropriations were broken down into five main parts and operating expenses were equally detailed. Under the new system, appropriations are not oriented toward items of expenditure but toward functions. There are two basic types of appropriation: one for graduate education and research and one for undergraduate education. Within these two categories are special appropriations for the various types of education and research. Funds are allocated directly to local institutional governing boards or to regional boards, which make the final allocations.

The reorientation of funds allotment away from items of expenditure and toward functional categories, intended to provide better information and to promote more decentralization, is part of the general movement toward program budgeting within the Swedish government. Two institutions have practiced program budgeting for some years. However, few consider the new budget system more than a first step in program budgeting, primarily because the people behind the reform seem aware of the difficulties of adopting program budgeting for higher education. There seems to be no reliable indicators of the achievement of educational goals and research programs, and no satisfactory means for clearly separating different programs or comparing them in terms of a general program structure.

The relation between the new functional system and the achievement of better information and decentralization is not clear. Politicians may perhaps get a better overview of the activities of institutions if they allocate money to programs rather than to items of expenditure; and they will be able to compare allocations that go to undergraduate education programs and to graduate education and research. But difficulties in obtaining reliable information persist: for example, how can one measure the amount of time a faculty and staff spends on undergraduate education as opposed to graduate education and research?

Reform of the budget system has been accompanied by reform of the undergraduate curriculum. The old curriculum was controlled to a large extent by the government and the state agency. The reform of 1977 considerably decentralized decisions on curriculum organization. Substituting functional for line-item budgeting also removes certain rules from the old system. Local institutions may decide what departments they want and will be able to allocate resources into new courses, new lines, and new institutional arrangements.

These changes are conducive to innovation and variety. However, the government retains control over the number and types of positions at the local units. The forces working for inflexibility have been strengthened by the labor laws of 1974 and 1976, which make it almost impossible to fire academic personnel and involve employee organizations in decision making at each institution.

The Allocation System

Automatic Procedures

An allocation system based on automatic procedures requires the fixing of unit costs for the achievement of specific educational purposes, such as a schedule of costs per full-time student. The procedure in Sweden prior to 1977 was based on "organizational plans." These originated in the late 1950s and outlined the number of students in a class, the type of teacher, and the course hours for undergraduate instruction. The mechanism was based on a simple equation: number of students times the number and types of hours times the salaries per hour.

However, the realities of higher education created two problems related to the number of students and the number and types of hours, which brought an end to the use of this device. First, the government did not limit the number of entering students for faculties of arts and sciences; this meant that the Ministry of Finance had no control over the amounts to be allocated to higher education, because it could not safely predict how many students would enroll and in what programs. When enrollments declined, departmental faculty started talking about job security and the need for basic independent resources. What finally made the mechanism obsolete was the passing of a law in 1974 that in effect prohibited laying off faculty and staff. Such a law is not congruent with a fund-allocation system oriented toward maximum flexibility.

The second problem relating to the formula mechanism is how common functions are to be counted. To get the equation going, it must be possible to pinpoint the number and types of hours necessary for the achievement of specific educational goals. In effect, the Swedish enrollment schedule was based on an elitist assumption that students come from secondary schools and stay until they get a degree by taking full-time courses in a department. By the early 1970s this assumption was no longer adequate. The 1977 reform removes the use of automatic procedures as an allocation mechanism.

Submission-Control

Under the old budgetary system, the submission-control mechanism was used to arrive at decisions concerning yearly incremental increases in resources. Under the new system, the whole grant is determined by the use of this mechanism.

Planning Frames

In the 1977 system, open access for education was replaced by a government-imposed system of "planning frames," which determine the number of students for each institution and outline the types of instruction to be given. This procedure solves the problem of meeting the demand for higher education. But the other problem remains: What are the operations going to cost? As long as a workable procedure relates the number of students to an educational plan, no problem occurs. But if such plans are not available or not used, how are amounts to be generated?

The answer to these questions is that the automatic procedure is replaced by a system of indicators. Instead of the state agency allocating funds to institutions in accordance with government regulations for courses and number of students, local institutions submit requests to the state authorities in accordance with their educational programs. The local institutions offer comprehensive plans for all educational activities and a cost analysis for them. These plans and the calculation of costs enter into the budget process. The new system allows using resources for functions other than instruction, such as the introduction of new courses. An entire new area for educational planning at the local institutions has opened up.

The question remains whether the planning frames are instruments of prognosis or mere qualified conjectures as to what the de-

mand will be. If they are conjectures, the government has no more
control than it had before, under the old system. If they are really
instruments of control, it means the elimination of unlimited admission, which has been a pillar of the system, at least in the faculties
of arts and sciences. The solution adopted after the fall of the Social
Democratic government in 1976 was a compromise: the planning
frames are to be mainly plans, but also conjectures to some extent.
Some lines and courses will have free entrance, but if the frames for
these lines and courses turn out to be inefficient, the local institutions
will have the right to apply for additional resources from the government. The government deals with such applications at its discretion.
If the government turns down the application, the frames will be plans;
if the government accepts the application, they will be conjectures.
The government has promised to follow the second alternative, but it
should be stressed that the route to any additional money is not a simple one.

By means of the planning frames, the government has an instrument to control the volume of activities at institutions, which it lacked
under the old system. No longer is there any need for strict supervision over the use of funds. Furthermore, the government still has
an effective instrument of control: it determines the number and
types of tenured and nontenured positions as well as the main outlines
of the organization of studies.

THE BUDGET PROCESS

The budget process for Swedish higher education is based on the
submission-control mechanism for allocating funds. Some people put
forward demands, others coordinate the demands, still others make
final decisions, and various groups implement them. These various
people have different roles, expectations, and tactics.

Local Institutions

The making of requests by local institutions is influenced by
guidelines and priorities from the higher levels of the hierarchy and
by the previous year's practices. Within the institutions, budget work
goes on at all levels—in departments, faculties, education (line) committees, and the governing board. Institution personnel have ideas of
what the unit should be like and what new resources it needs; but the
government, through plans and priorities, controls what claims for
new resources will be granted and provides a definite time perspective for expansions. Both long-term plans for an institution and re-

quests for the current year are heavily influenced by the higher levels. The institutions search for clues about supportable items in the government's proposals to Parliament, in Parliament's debates in the budgetary proposal for the preceding year, and in the programs of the state agency. Also, since employee organizations are a strong influence in Swedish politics, the institutions pay close attention to their desires.

Under the new system, requests are expanded to include all resources going to the institutions. That is, the institutions do not merely make demands for additional research resources or increased appropriations for operating expenses; they also request funds for the education lines and courses already being given.*

The National Swedish Board
of Universities and Colleges

The budget work of the National Swedish Board of Universities and Colleges (UHA) consists of planning and setting priorities, using a combination of bureaucratic and professional expertise.

Planning and Priorities

The UHA uses certain formal procedures to build the higher education budget according to incremental norms. It starts from a base, shows what it will cost to keep the base intact, and calculates the costs of decisions already made. Finally, it adds new demands.

The size of the UHA's budget proposals are a function of calculation, planning, and tactics. The agency calculates the effects of inflation on the base and asks for an increase that will protect the base (Alternative 1 in Table 6.6). Some demands ensue from decisions already made (Priority 1)—for example, if the government has decided to build a new institute of technology, that decision will have budgetary consequences for many years. The final part of the yearly

------

*The undergraduate curriculum implemented in 1977 is based on lines and courses. It comprises: (1) general lines, introduced by the government, which decides the outline for each line—oriented toward occupational preparation; (2) local lines, introduced by the local units; (3) individual lines, introduced by the local units; and (4) single courses, introduced by the local units. The government allocates the funds to five occupational sectors, which comprise the roughly 90 general lines. The regional boards allocate funds for local lines, individual lines, and single courses.

TABLE 6.6

Yearly Percentage Changes in Requests by the UHA,
1970/71-1977/78

Years	Unchanged Level of Ambition	Alter- native 1	Priority 1	Priority 2	Total
1970/71	8.0	3.0	5.0	5.7	13.7
1971/72	9.0	2.2	6.8	7.6	16.6
1972/73	5.4	0.8	4.6	6.4	11.8
1973/74	7.7	3.8	3.9	3.4	11.1
1974/75	7.9	2.4	5.5	1.4	9.3
1975/76	11.5	7.9	3.6	2.9	14.4
1976/77	17.5	14.9	2.6	3.0	20.5
1977/78	8.2	4.9	3.2	3.9	12.7

Source: UKÄ:sförslag till anslagsäskanden för budgetåret 1970-
71 och 1977-78 [Proposal for those requesting appropriations for
budget years 1970-71 and 1977-78] (Stockholm: University Chancellor's Publication Series).

request is for new funds, beyond those for inflation or for programs
already decided upon (Priority 2). The placement of an item in Priority 1 or 2 is significant. Backers of a request might press for having an item placed in Priority 1 to be sure it will be funded or because
it might enable them to put forward new requests in Priority 2.

In recent years Swedish higher education has been able to do
more than cover the costs of inflation. Agency personnel speak of
good and bad years for increased appropriations, depending on the
economic situation, but they have consistently made demands for new
resources of no less than 5 percent, and usually at least 3 percent of
the demand is an increment unrelated to earlier decisions.

Agency budget proposals are based on five-year plans, which
were introduced around 1970 to create continuous and comprehensive
budgeting. These prescribe the planned development for most fields
of higher education. There are, for example, long-term plans for
internationalizing Swedish higher education, for teacher training, for
the development of positions at the faculties, and so on. Budget work
at the agency is oriented toward rationality, comprehensiveness, and
continuity.

TABLE 6.7

Long-term Budget of the UHA, 1975/76-1980/81
(in thousands of kronor)

Years	Unchanged Level of Ambition	Reforms	Total
1975/76			1,578,515
1976/77	+276,353	+47,934	+324,287
1977/78	+40,050	+65,200	+105,250
1978/79	+35,950	+57,900	+93,850
1979/80	+32,150	+55,000	+87,150
1980/81	+31,900	+51,000	+82,900

Source: IKÅ:s förslag till anslagsäskanden för budgetåret 1976-
1977 [Proposal for those requesting appropriations for budget year
1976-1977] (Stockholm: University Chancellor's Publication Series).

Both the long-term and the annual budgets are preferential:
everything that goes into them has been ranked on the basis of specific priorities (see Table 6.7). When the agency requests additional
tenured or nontenured positions, it states clearly the types of positions
it wants and in which unit they should be placed. When the agency demands funds for new programs or courses, it states their priority
and gives detailed instructions for implementing them. Agency work
is oriented toward explicit preferences and incremental innovation,
that is, toward putting the amount of new resources into specific new
areas and structures.

Decision Making: Bureaucratic
versus Professional Authority

The UHA's decision-making process reflects its internal structure, which blends bureaucratic and professional authority. Formally,
the agency is run by a lay board, but in practice it is dominated by the
higher bureaucrats—the chancellor, the planning chief (in the new system), the bureau chiefs, and other high-ranking bureaucrats who become involved in particular issues. The bureaucracy formulates its
position on the issues at regular Monday meetings, and agreements
reached at these meetings are often passed on as proposals by the
lay board, which generally accepts them.

The UHA uses an advisory system to formulate recommendations from experts with professional authority. The advisory boards produce long-term programs for their particular areas and communicate with institutions through reports on studies that have been made by the government or the agency. Each board has a secretary who reports the board's professional opinions to the bureaucracy at the Monday meetings. The boards also participate in the budget process.

In the old "faculty advisory boards," the professors dominated, although they were in a minority of four to five. For the boards in the new system, clear patterns of influence have not yet emerged, but one could expect the professors to lose some of their influence to other groups.

The bureaucrats control the budget process from beginning to end. They set the frame, which contains a ceiling for funds within which the advisory boards must remain when making proposals to the UHA. Budget guidelines are influenced by the government's budget proposal for Year 1 and by how the government judges the economic situation in its long-term budget. These documents are read closely by the bureaucrats to determine the tactics to use in the next year.

After the bureaucrats decide on the budget proposal, requests from faculties and governing boards of the institutions as well as comments from regional boards are considered. These requests and comments are sent to the advisory boards, where the secretaries make preliminary proposals for the budgets—proposals guided by the long-term plans of the advisory boards and the programs of the agency. While the advisory boards come together to make decisions, the various bureaus in the UHA decide on requests for their internal work and on appropriations for which the advisory boards are not responsible. All proposals are then sent to the UHA.

The staff cuts the requests to fit the financial frame. Various staff members responsible for appropriations present the proposals to the chancellor, who in turn passes on the documented proposal with changes or additions to the lay board, which generally approves it after limited discussion.

Since there are many domains and many bureaucrats, all with special interests to serve, there must be some mechanism of coordination. One method is to urge staff members to state their views if they disagree with what the professionals, other bureaucrats, or the lay board members want and to oblige them to carry out all decisions arrived at by correct procedures. Another mechanism is to have someone to coordinate the work. In the old agency organization, the chief of the planning bureau took main responsibility for the budget work. The secretaries of advisory boards were under his authority, and he could keep a firm grip on the entire process; if he had trouble, it was more likely to come from other bureau chiefs who had not accepted him as an equal. Who will coordinate the work under the new system? No one knows. Perhaps the bureau for budget affairs will be able to recapture the functions of the old planning bureau, or perhaps some other coordinating mechanism will develop. In any case, what was once held together firmly will now be more fragmented.

Government Budget Policy

The government's unanimous budget proposal to Parliament is the outcome of negotiations between the various ministries and the Ministry of Finance. With regard to the grant for higher education and research, negotiations are conducted between the Ministry of Education—particularly its unit for higher education—and the budget bureau in the Ministry of Finance over demands from the various units subordinate to the Ministry of Education. The distribution of roles is clear. Throughout the negotiations, the Ministry of Education acts as the representative of special interests, whereas the role of the Ministry of Finance is to guard the people's money and to consider the general interests of the country, particularly the national economy. When the final decisions are made, all participants back the outcome unanimously.

Negotiations follow a demand-and-cut dialectic. Units subordinate to the Ministry of Education first present their demands, which are usually cut by the Ministry of Finance. In recent years, for example, when the state agency presented demands for reforms (Priority 2) that would cost Kr 62 million, Kr 17 million, and Kr 41 million, they received about Kr 7 million, Kr 8 million, and Kr 9 million. The fact that staff members at the Ministry of Finance regard themselves as guardians of the general interest does not imply that they restrict themselves to purely economic or theoretical statements about the proposals of the unit for higher education. Negotiations between the two groups are very specific. The unit presents detailed requests, and the Ministry of Finance staff returns these requests with specific cuts. The staff of the budget bureau continues and completes the work that was begun by the coordinating boards within the local institutions; they make the final coordination. In the words of one staff member: "It may be the case that in our capacity as a Ministry of Finance we are more concerned about the level of innovation and the level of investment in economic life. So we might see more reason for building an institute of technology in Norrland than for increasing an appropriation for law instruction."

The first cut in the requests from agencies and boards is made by the unit for higher education within the Ministry of Education. The expectations of people at the unit govern their negotiations with the budget bureau staff: "We know we cannot accept everything that the various units demand; we must make a preliminary cut. We will go along in one area but be restrictive in others because we know that we can never get all the demands through. Even at this stage much is cut away because we know that many requests are unrealistic. We have to pick a few requests and really stand up for them." In negotiating, the unit's staff uses the programs of the agency to back their requests. Negotiations between the two ministries begin between lower civil service bureaucrats and are successively transferred upward to bureaucrats selected politically and finally to the Minister of Finance and the government. Bureaucrats at the Ministry of Finance are usually one level above the corresponding bureaucrats at other ministries. When there is no agreement on an issue, it is passed on to higher agency levels for new negotiations. This pattern is followed up to the government level.

Budget work within Parliament and its education committee reflects the dominant position of the government. Although the committee deals with each appropriation separately, it does not make detailed investigations into how the appropriation was constructed. It may change certain proposals from the government, but its work is not oriented toward overall coordination. When the education committee makes alterations it usually adds instead of cuts. It conducts hearings but does not provide in-depth analyses. Such hearings are often used as occasions for a last attempt by various interest groups to increase appropriations. Groups outside of Parliament often initiate such hearings. The committee lacks resources to deal more comprehensively with the budget. In 1977 it had a staff of only three persons. Although the government's budget negotiations for the grant to higher education and research is guided by party affiliation, the committee sometimes operates as a nonpartisan unit.

CONCLUSION

Budgeting for the field of higher education presents a number of crucial political problems. The government and the institutions have to agree about what activities should be supported by the public purse and what these activities may cost. To reach such an understanding there must be some recognition of the amount of autonomy the local units may command.

The reform of the Swedish system of higher education in 1977 makes basic changes in most aspects of the system. It introduces new budget techniques that shift the balances of autonomy and control. Under the old system the government kept a firm grip on the local units by means of detailed itemized budgets. There was only one parameter the government could not control: the total cost of educational operations. Part of the funds were allocated by automatic procedures based on full-time enrollment schemes, which, within the faculties allowing unlimited admission, implied that the government had to supply resources to meet an undetermined demand. The government tried to gain some control of this parameter by means of conjectures into future demand, but its attempts were not successful. This system for allocating funds dissolved gradually from within, as the assumptions on which it was based became obsolete because of changes in student demand and in the employment conditions of teachers.

The new budget system is aimed at controlling total costs. By means of the system of planning frames, the government will gain almost total control over the cost parameter. At the same time the government will allow more autonomy in the use of the appropriations.

Budgeting is introduced and cost analyses are based on various indicators. The government retains some general control of the activities of local institutions. The grant to higher education is decided through the use of submission-control mechanisms, and the government makes decisions on the recruitment of tenured positions in the academic disciplines.

The introduction of more autonomy into Swedish higher education has been achieved but at the cost of a decline in professorial influence. Various groups from outside academia are now represented on the governing bodies of the institutions. Local boards are no longer run by academic deans but by people representing various legitimate social interests. The Swedish universities will henceforth be run according to the principles of democratic representation rather than those of academic professionalism.

7

WHO GETS WHAT
AND HOW:
TRENDS AND ISSUES

Lyman A. Glenny

The previous chapters presented the case studies of five European nations, each focusing on the organizations and practices through which the budgets for higher educational institutions are formulated and implemented. These systematic descriptions allow comparisons to be made with states in the United States. Each case also raises questions about certain substantive or procedural issues that have a direct impact on the allocation of resources. Moreover, personal interviews with officials in each of these nations and states brought to light many political and institutional issues. These included budget allocation processes, usually considered more as a technical means for resolving larger policy issues than as major issues in themselves. Some problems, of course, do arise from the budget process itself, such as problems with the formulas used and the data bases required. But more general problems arise from the use of the budget as a device for resolving issues that impinge on various areas, such as student enrollments, manpower requirements for the society, faculty tenure and salaries, and faculty commitments to students and institutions, and from the broad issue of how and by whom higher education should be controlled, both inside and outside the institutions.

Some issues have high visibility in one nation but remain almost unnoticed in others. Few of them seem to be universal among the five European countries and the United States or even among the European ones. Some recent issues reflect the trends toward mass and universal higher education, while others, which have smoldered for a long period (such as manpower oversupplies and rising unit costs), flare up as major policy confrontations because of new aggravating conditions. Moreover, issues unknown in one nation may be very much alive in others; or some issues that are unperceived or unresolved in the states of the United States may be "old hat" to the industrially advanced European nations. Examples are the arguments over the usefulness of the ancient but faltering chair system in Europe and, on the other hand, the uses and abuses of the coordinating agency in the United States, positioned between institutional governing boards and the government but supposedly objective toward both.

The issues selected for discussion are important either because of their implications for current budgets or because certain budget-related decisions will have long-range effects that are potentially beneficial or inimical to the society and to higher education. In each instance, the direction or practice could be changed by policy actions, possibly reversing or ameliorating unfortunate consequences.

The issues and problems that have an impact on funding allocations are divided into two groups: (1) those bearing on the organization and procedures used for formulating budgets and making allocations and (2) those relating to students and faculties, such as access, manpower needs, enrollment ceilings, salaries, faculty ranking systems, and the chair system and tenure. The first group is dealt with in this chapter and the second in Chapter 8.

POLITICAL AND SOCIAL SETTING FOR BUDGET FORMULATION

Several factors affect the way governments look upon higher education, either supporting it with increased financial resources, being indifferent to its needs, or reducing funds in order to conform with changes in enrollment or to force reform by institutions and faculty members. Certainly general economic conditions and the confidence with which the public ministries hold higher education have serious consequences for colleges and universities. The degree to which individual politicians freely intervene by proposing statutes to control institutions, or to create new ones in their districts, certainly has an effect, as does the pressure exerted on the politicians by students, professors, rectors, high administrative officials, and private economic interests, all seeking their particular goals. Perhaps the most important factor in this relationship between government and higher education is the degree of stability of the government itself, for high stability may provide the confidence to change major policies and instability may lead to vacillation, uncertainty, and status quo politics. A preliminary discussion of these factors will place our later comments on budgeting and the financing of higher institutions in a context that may explain current practice better than anything to be found in the budget process itself.

Economic Conditions

Each of the six countries discussed suffered economic depression of some severity during the early and mid-1970s. While the level of unemployment was considered high, it varied only a few percentage points from country to country. The inflation rate and the growth (or drop) in the GNP varied greatly, with Italy suffering the most severely on both counts. Greece also had a slight drop in national income in 1974 but has kept a low unemployment rate. Balances of payments in 1976 were also on the negative side in each country except the United States. Hence, the climate for increasing the funds for higher education seems rather unpromising.

In France, Italy, and some of the U.S. states, these negative signs led to appropriations for higher education that failed to keep up with enrollment numbers and inflation. France allowed only a 5 percent increase in maintenance and continuing operational expenses. It came closer to matching the inflation rate with the salaries of its civil service, to which all permanent university and institute faculty and staff members belong. But neither salaries nor operations funds increased enough to meet inflation fully. As it was projected for the 1977/78 fiscal year, funding is maintained at the level of the previous year, with no adjustments for inflation.

Italy finds itself in a financial crisis, unable to provide funds for the massive increases in enrollment or for the inflation rate of about 20 percent per year. Student-faculty ratios, as reported by Gandiglio in Chapter 4, have increased steadily over the past few years. In the United States, of the 17 states studied, 14 received funding sufficient to cover new enrollment and inflation (Colorado increased its funding by 47 percent in constant dollars), but three did not (New York lost 6 percent in constant dollars), indicating once again the striking variations between states (Ruyle and Glenny 1978).

Both Sweden and Greece provided funds to cover inflation. With the rapid increase in students in the late 1960s and early 1970s, Greece has not increased its funding sufficiently to maintain its former student-faculty ratio; but Sweden provided an increase above inflation for changes in program and salaries in 1976/77 when its enrollments remained virtually static. On the other hand, Spain increased its total allocation for higher education substantially, but gave no augmentation increases above inflation for any other governmentally supported service. Yet Spain also had a high unemployment rate and high inflation. McGurn (in Burn 1971) analyzed this investment phenomenon as follows: "The fear that under-investment in education would hinder economic growth in a period of increased labor market complexity led to the worldwide increases in national education expenditures" (p. 27).

Hence, the economic condition of the different countries does not explain the range in appropriations for higher education. In countries and states with about equal financial difficulties, some provided increases and others fell behind. The factor that may explain more fully this difference is the attitude of the public and politicians toward higher education and their idea of its place in the society.

Confidence in Higher Education

This factor, more than any other (including enrollments), appears to determine the level at which states finance their higher education systems. The same finding resulted from the 17-state U.S. study and a previous 4-state study (Glenny and Dalglish 1973). Spain obviously saw the need to provide more variety, better training, and education closer to the homes of rural youth, and it provided the funds needed to make such improvements. Greece, too, remains supportive of higher education, but the development of new secondary professional schools (junior colleges) and buildings depends on loans from international banks, which commit future state income to loan payments. It assumes that university graduates will diversify its economy, increase productivity, and decentralize its population—or at least prevent further population concentrations in its two major metropolitan centers. France and Sweden and most of the states in the United States have societies and political leaders partially disillusioned with the universities and postsecondary education, except for professional and vocational-technical training, which is where new funds are tending to go. Oversupplies of college graduates in many different fields, their subsequent underemployment or unemployment, and the high costs of maintaining students in school seemed to have been used as sufficient justification for holding higher education to minimal increases in funding. These conditions also appear to apply to certain countries not covered in this study (Germany, Belgium, the Netherlands, and Britain) that are highly industrialized and have advanced higher educational systems.

Confidence in colleges and universities, while waning or at least leveling off, may result in stagnant financing for some years to come, perhaps as many as 10 or 15 years in the United States. On the other hand, countries not as technologically advanced may arrive at the same point much more quickly, because their rapid increases in enrollment will not be matched by a corresponding growth in the number of work places available to its graduates. Spain, for example, claims to require only 10 percent of its labor force to have college degrees, but over 20 percent of the college-age group now attends higher institutions. In the United States, the U.S. Department of Labor projections for the next 10 years show only 20 percent of the labor force as needing a college education, whereas over one third of all persons between 18 and 24—along with millions of adults over the normal college age—are now in college.

More positive public attitudes can develop only if the higher institutions can convince the public of the worth of liberal, non-job-oriented education and can cease to encourage student aspirations not suited to the realities of the job market. In most countries this will take some time, especially since new social priorities will assert themselves and be funded with state monies formerly allocated to higher education. As Barbara Burn (1971) has said of Italy: "For some 25 years Italy has shown itself capable of defusing crises without undertaking radical solutions. Incremental change fits the Italian style" (p. 44).

Political Influence and Higher Education Budgets

Higher education, though seldom a subject on which a politician stakes his legislative future, nevertheless has advocates and adversaries who will attempt to influence his actions. In the United States, the presidents of large universities, associations of institutions, and student groups each attempt to influence both policy and budgets by lobbying and testifying before legislative committees. In the European countries, very similar pressures are exerted, more indirectly in most cases but much more directly in a few others.

The indirectness is a result of the parliamentary systems of government enjoyed by the five nations surveyed in this study. Individual politicians there have much less influence on any issue, because party loyalty in voting is expected and is indeed essential for the maintenance of the parliamentary system. Certainly, higher institutional leaders must support the government's budget position (or keep quiet) once that position is formally presented to Parliament. Few changes are made in budgets once they have left the ministries of Education (Higher Education in France) and of the Treasury, and fewer still remain after the cabinet and prime minister have stated the government position. Any pressure must be exerted early in the budget process and focus on the ministries, either directly or through cries of alarm in the news media. The goals of rectors, directors, and principals of higher institutions can also be officially adopted by one of the political parties, either within the government coalition or in opposition. In the end, however, after all the cries and publicity subside with the appearance of the appropriations, it is the position of the ministries of Education and Finance that most often prevail. That situation is not different in the various states of the United States.

Exceptions to ministry dominance do occur, however, and usually on major issues. In Sweden, for example, the U-68 reform came up in 1975 legislation for establishing six regional planning and administrative centers in order to decentralize higher education. It came as a result of the powerful Center party's demands and was accepted by the Social Democratic government. In the United States, several new medical and veterinary schools have been added to planning and capital budgets against the recommendations of state coordinating agencies and sometimes against the wishes of the state governors. Local gains for the politicians who help obtain a new campus or a new building lead to these aberrations of politicians following staff recommendations. Spain, in creating its new college system in order to relieve university enrollment pressures and to diversify its educational opportunities, allows local geographical areas or cities to start a college by local donation of the land, capital facilities, and a portion of the operating costs. Politicians gain by supporting such activity in their districts. One result of such a policy, already experienced in several U.S. states with the construction of community colleges and making two-year colleges into four-year ones, is an oversupply of small colleges that are weak in curricula breadth and faculty quality. Some ministry officials already worry about that outcome in Spain.

The most direct form of political involvement occurs in the three Mediterranean nations covered here—Greece, Spain, and Italy. In those countries, where professors have extraordinary influence and prestige, a great many of them hold parliamentary positions and thus dominate the education committees and the government policies on higher education. Collectively, their numbers provide formidable power that may be thrown for or against a policy. There are several concrete results of this professorial power. First, the professors can usually prevent the passage of bills introduced to limit or to change the power of the endowed chairs in the universities. Reforms in faculty ranking, salaries, internal governance, and curriculum tend to fail against the professors' political power. Second, the professors favor themselves by encouraging passage of laws that, as in Spain, give the professors up to ten times the amount of salary provided the major core of the university teachers, although they may constitute only 5 to 10 percent of the total faculty at one institution. Third, they may gain other privileges, such as holding two chairs simultaneously or, as in Greece, being required to write textbooks for each of their courses, which they profitably sell to the Ministry of Education for free distribution to students. Fourth, they maintain control of government research funds through membership on the ministry councils that allocate funds to institutes and to individual professors, with the usual result being that administrative processes are completely controlled by these same influential professors or close colleagues, as will be discussed subsequently.

No other political force in these countries has as much power in relation to higher education as the professors who sit in Parliament. Even if the government introduced important, well-planned reform measures, its bills could fail, either because of the large number of votes held by these persons in Parliament, or because they could threaten to withdraw their support from one party, which might very well topple the sort of shaky coalition governments so characteristic of post-World War II Europe. In neither France nor Sweden are there as many professors who are members of Parliament as there are in Spain, Italy, and Greece. In France, a political pressure for or against higher education measures often takes the form of public demonstrations and pressures against the government by teaching unions of faculty members and by the local communities. Students in France joined the very strong and eventually successful protests made by the teaching unions against the government proposal to reform the university curriculum by making it somewhat more occupationally oriented. In Italy, students publicly demonstrated in early 1977 to show their dissatisfaction with overcrowded conditions in the universities and the lack of jobs available to graduates.

In the United States, faculty members seldom become elected members of state legislatures, although a few may be found in most states. Faculty members exercise their meager power primarily through state professional organizations; in a few states, however (especially New York, Michigan, and New Jersey), faculty labor unions affiliated with national unions wield considerable influence. State politicians, who often look upon faculties as arrogant, overpaid, and underworked, find it hard to sympathize with faculty pleas. Students, where they are organized for state lobbying purposes (as in California and Wisconsin), have more political clout by far than professors on matters relating to higher education. In California, for example, the university student lobby is ranked by one polling organization as the twelfth most influential group in the state.

Stability of Governments

In Spain and Greece, where democratic governing processes are beginning to be reasserted after periods of dictatorship, professors play key roles in stabilizing the governments. In Italy, the government coalition is so weak that reform measures are rarely suggested for fear that one or more of the coalition parties will pull out. Pignatelli (in Burn 1973) concludes, "The most serious obstacle impeding reform in Italian higher education is not so much the absence of clearly defined strategy to bring about reform as the traditional adaptability or even acceptance of crisis in our country as an inherent and inalienable evil. To catalyze change there is no alternative but to increase existing tensions" (p. 59).

Sweden faces a somewhat similar problem, with the new Center party forming a coalition government with the conservative and liberal parties. As noted above, the Center party, which forced in the regional decentralization plan, now finds itself having to implement it. Originally and primarily a political act for showing the progressiveness of the party, the staffs of the Finance and Education ministries were a big uneasy about regionalism in 1976. By 1977, however, the government put its complete support behind the regions with full funding.

France shares with the other nations a continued instability of government, a tradition throughout the postwar era except for the Gaullist period of 1958-69. Even when the minister of the Secretariat of State for the Universities speaks out for reform of the curriculum or for changes in the financing of the provincial and urban universities, the premier takes little cognizance—ignoring a possible threat to continuance of his government.

Thus, the instability of the governments in some of these European nations may account for the lack of enthusiasm for passing reform measures or forcing their implementation. Certainly, the combination of unstable government, inflation, poor economic conditions, and the power of the professoriate in and out of parliaments all provide something less than an optimistic outlook for major change or reform in postsecondary education, however much reforms of this nature may be discussed by politicians and in the media.

Sweden's good fortune in reform lies in its U-68 report having been adopted, before these "crisis" conditions, by a socialist government in power for about 30 years. Perhaps the most that can be said is that in each of these nations small incremental changes will occur to produce more funding of vocational technical programs, a weakening of faculty power, and the provision of more aid and jobs for students. In the past year, only Spain has really increased higher education funding for new programs, new colleges, and maintenance at better levels than those already extant. The assertion of Pignatelli (in Burn 1973) on Italian change for higher education sums up the attitude in several other European nations: "However, the postuniversity schools through which industries meet their internal training needs are today in crisis. Hence it is possible that the enlarging roles of labor and industry will intensify the demand for university reform" (p. 58).

Sweden and France have already reorganized their postschool system to include labor and industrial representation in university governing and advisory bodies.

ORGANIZATION FOR BUDGETING

The greatest contrast between the budgeting process in the five European countries and the U.S. states is in the number of budget reviews that take place after the budget has been cleared through the internal machinery of an institution. Except for Sweden, where three reviews were possible because of its cabinet-level National Board for Universities and Colleges, the other nations provided only two reviews, one of which could be called detailed and the other general. In the U.S. states, a minimum of three reviews occurs in each state, and in one of the seventeen that we studied there were five reviews, some of which were detailed and others that were selective or superficial. This difference in the review process provides in the United States both an opportunity for the institution to argue its case to different audiences, each of which has influence on final budget outcomes, and also an opportunity for the staff reviewers to ask for further data and information and to make reductions in all items, some perhaps left untouched by previous reviewers. A university governing board may recommend a budget that is reviewed seriatim or concurrently by the coordinating board for higher education, by the governor's executive budget office, by the joint legislative analyst (working for the staff of both houses of the legislature), and by the appropriations committees of the senate and of the house. The appropriations committees may also divide the staff reviews, allowing each of the two major political parties to focus on items of special interest. The plethora of reviews makes heavy demands on many top administrative officials of the institutions, who must answer questions, defend requests, provide new data, and otherwise lobby for their interests. A president of a major Midwestern university stated that in one year he had spent 64 hours in actual testimony before these several agencies in his state. The average experience is not quite that taxing, but in any state at least one or two reviews will be quite thorough and detailed (probably those by the coordinating board and either the executive budget office or the legislative analyst). The other legislative committees and their staffs tend to pick out issues considered to be politically salient and press very hard on them to the exclusion of all other budget items. Of course, it makes a difference in what form the budget is presented— as will be noted in the section on Budget Forms—whether it is line-item, functional, or program. The end of a budget review cycle will find that practically every item proposed has been questioned one or more times and repetitiously defended. The end product appears no better for having experienced the several reviews, and the various costs in time spent by all the staffs, especially those of the universities and colleges, become very expensive. Moreover, the attention of presidents, vice-presidents, and provosts is drawn away from their main academic purpose into defending the budget, further subjecting the institution to political criticism for neglect of internal management, academic change, and increased productivity, and for being overstaffed at the administrative level.

In Europe, the institutional budget goes directly to the Ministry of Education (or Higher Education), where a thorough review is made, mostly to see that the preparation accurately corresponds to the instructions of the Treasury and the Education ministries. Salaries of staff and faculties, with the exception of certain part-time or adjunct persons, are not even included in the budget. (Teachers' salaries are usually negotiated by unions with the government, as are those of other civil service employees.) Research is normally not carried as an item, being administered downward from a lump-sum appropriation to the ministry or research council. Hence, what the institutional budget consists of amounts to about 20 percent of the U.S. college or university budget, what in the United States is called supplies and equipment, buildings, grounds, and maintenance. Occasionally libraries are treated as budget items, but at other times they are funded from another lump sum received by the ministry. But once they are reviewed by the education staffs, the budgets go to the Treasury minister, where under normal circumstances only the total amounts of money by institution or for all institutions in relation to other state services will receive attention. The two ministers or their chief deputies may make the final negotiations before the higher education request becomes part of the government's budget package to Parliament. (In Sweden, the National Swedish Board for Universities and Colleges may play a rather decisive role in suggesting to both ministries specific allocations within available state funding for higher education.) And in Parliament, only rarely are particular items discussed in any detail, and then not by standing committees on education or higher education. Few budgetary changes, if any, are made by Parliament.

The relatively small sums controlled through university budgets in European countries strongly encourage negotiation rather than objective criteria to determine the sums appropriated. That money contains all the flexibility that an institution may have in a time of fluctuating utility prices, rising student-faculty ratios, and the need to employ more and more part-time personnel. In several countries a preaudit of expenditures further limits alternative use of the funds. U.S. administrators would feel straightjacketed with so little authority over staff and faculty and so little money to move around within their budgets. European rectors and presidents would feel heavily belabored if subjected to the several reviews of state budgets required in the United States. The following section discusses certain issues relating to the technologies used in the several systems studied.

Budget reviews may seem onerous to Americans, but the Europeans seem destined to receive somewhat similar treatment if various plans for decentralizing authority should proceed apace.

TRENDS IN BUDGETING PRACTICE

The case study chapters (Chapters 2 through 6) discuss the processes and technologies used in formulating the government budget for higher education. Additional information on these subjects became available from personal interveiws with ministry officials. Also detected from both sources are trends in relation to budget forms and formats, basic units funded, technologies used, data bases employed, and the underlying planning practices. These elements will be discussed in this section.

Budget Forms

The case studies mention the trend away from line-item budgets toward functional and program formats, a phenomenon seemingly as universal in Europe as in the United States. Most of the states in our U.S. study continued some of the line-item approach to budgeting while also providing the newer functional or programmatic forms. While the functional format had been laid down as "good practice" in the postwar years, virtually all of the states show signs of transforming that form into the newer concept of program budgeting. Progress toward program budgets, which commenced in the early 1960s in state government, now proceeds slowly but steadily, following earlier failures in several states (such as Wisconsin) to put Planning-Program-Budgeting-Systems (PPBS) into effect full-blown during one or two budget cycles. Current practice falls far short of the theory and models developed for PPBS; and indeed, as critics of the form, such as Aaron Wildavsky (1974), have asserted with vigor, its models never can be fully operative because of the lack of definite outcomes attributable directly to higher education and the overwhelming amount of data and paper work (with concomitant costs) required of PPBS. Currently, the states proceed cautiously during each budget cycle to develop more program emphases.

This program focus appears to take the same form in Europe as in the United States. The disciplinary department or line becomes a "program" along with the functional items of libraries, student services, auxiliary enterprises (dormitories, eating halls, farms, or hospitals that produce revenue for services), administration, and physical plant (buildings and grounds) maintenance. Occasionally, specializations within broad disciplines may be identified as programs. However, in the United States the tendency is to collapse the number of programs for budgetary purposes to something between 20 and 30, although major research universities may offer degrees in several hundred different programs. This collapsing results from normative similarities in costs across programs rather than their necessarily being a closely related curricular group. The condensed program format was developed for internal management purposes during the 1950s and 1960s by the "Big Ten" (Midwest) universities and the University of California. By the mid-1960s, states such as Illinois and New York, using modifications of these developed costing procedures, moved toward the condensed program format for use in program control and for budget review of the public system of higher education. The statewide higher education agencies took the early initiatives toward these goals, usually without knowing much of the theory supporting PPBS. Since 1968, the National Center for Higher Education Management Systems has developed a series of technical products, including data element dictionaries and program costing procedure manuals, and through much fieldwork has accelerated their use in various states and institutions. These efforts, plus declining funding levels, have encouraged institutions to review operations using the program as the reviewed unit. Moreover, state governments, through their executive budget office (the governor's staff) have followed the coordinating boards in adopting program approaches. The executive budget office, which has a great deal of power behind it, often actively promotes program budgeting. The newly created legislative appropriations committee staffs also lean toward program analysis. Politicians know little, if anything, about PPBS, and for the most part believe it strengthens the hand of the executive more than it should, an observation made by many critics of PPBS.

Colleges and universities in the United States, France, Sweden, and Spain have independently begun the development of modified program systems for internal management purposes. But the national ministries, as case studies of France and Sweden indicate, have also moved or are planning to move toward programs as the budget base. The governments, as much as the institutions, see the program form as allowing closer control of inputs and outputs by the central authority, while giving a great deal of local discretion in the actual expenditure of allocated appropriations. Programs may be reviewed for effectiveness and efficiency during the construction of the budget or between budget cycles, often in the United States by a staff not directly involved in budget formulation.

Formulas and Formula Bases

While the form of the budgets is shifting toward the program, the formulas are shifting from the simple student-faculty ratio still used in rather gross form (taking the institution as a whole) in Spain, Italy, and Greece toward rough unit-cost estimates, which may also be closely tied to a more sophisticated use of the student-faculty ratio, as in France. The student-faculty ratio, as previously mentioned, has been the technical device by which most institutions of higher learning in the Western world have measured the need for additional faculty (as student numbers increased) and also supposedly measured the quality of institutions. The closer the ratio the higher the quality, so goes the assumption, although with little supporting evidence. The ratios, as the French experience reveals, may be much more sophisticated than before, providing separate ratios for each discipline, line, or department, and then the number of needed faculty aggregated for salary purposes, and the number of students aggregated for financial aid and student services. In Sweden, these ratios by discipline have been negotiated within universities and then with the Office of the Chancellor of the Universities and the Ministry of the Treasury. Negotiation and current class-hour costs prevailed, with some results that would appear surprising in the United States. For example, in Sweden the sciences were able to show a need for relatively low ratios, as might be expected, and the humanities and social sciences had high ones. However, when mathematics was considered, after many other ratios had been determined, the professors made a case from their historical cost base for getting roughly the same ratio as for teaching physics or chemistry. (In the United States, mathematics is considered one of the less costly programs with relatively high student-faculty ratios.)

When data bases for unit costs or criteria for establishing ratios have not been developed, the role of negotiation soars as the means for arriving at final decisions. Those with power within the university and those from universities who exercise power in the larger political society seek and get a lion's share of state funds rather than a just or equitable share. The National Swedish Board for Universities and Colleges (UHA) began in 1977 a thorough study of the costs of all academic programs in order to reduce the amount of negotiation on annual budget increases. France plans to use unit costs as a budget base. It begins with the student-faculty ratio by program and then determines the direct costs of instruction for each ratio. In 1976, the Ministry of Higher Education was already attempting to obtain costs by class hour of instruction in order to analyze more fully the costs for each discipline in each institution. The ministry goal is a norm or standard (perhaps to be flexibly applied) applicable to the system as a whole in developing the budget and allocating funds to each institution and program. Moreover, the ministry began the attempt to derive and apply similar principles to the technical institutes in early 1977, also with the aim of establishing a formula for budget and allocation purposes.

However, in Spain, Italy, and Greece, the prevailing pattern for seeking state money is neither through unit costs nor a strict student-faculty ratio. The number of students has some influence, but officials in Spain and Italy were unanimous in their opinion that negotiation by the chairs with the rector (president) and the rector with the ministries and the government really determined who got what and how much. Greece, too, performed similarly but relied more on the ratios and less on negotiation than did the other two countries. Nevertheless, Spanish and Greek officials expressed interest in achieving a much more equitable system of allocation by use of unit costs and program budgeting. The fact that in Spain both the universities at Madrid and Barcelona are experimenting with costing (and other management) devices gives encouragement to the ministry officials of Education and Treasury that necessary data banks can gradually be established and formulas created using costs as the critical base.

Unit costs may be derived from institutionwide data or by school, program, or student-hour (student-credit-hour). The smaller the unit to be used, the more data and technology are required. The level of instruction can also be added, compounding the complexity and cost. In the United States, unit-cost studies based on the credit hour usually encompass at least three to five levels of instruction. For small institutions elaborate processes such as these are a luxury, whereas for complex universities they are a necessity. Computers, excellent programmers, and experienced analysts are essential to the effective costing of large institutions and to state systems of institutions. The costs of compiling data, from the initial stages of defining operational terms on through to routine data collection, after three or four years of experimentation, may be staggering. Effort and cost can be reduced, however, if an institution or system adopts an existing "package" of definitions of data and program elements and methodologies for deriving costs. Also available are simulation models. Such packages may require modification, but that is much cheaper than starting from scratch. While the U.S. technologies are validated for state-college types of institutions, they have not yet reached the same stage of perfection for community colleges, private liberal arts colleges, or for the large, complex research university, public or private. In Europe, according to Goldberg (in letter to author, 1977), the French secretary of state for the universities never thoroughly studied nor understood the U.S. models; and the decision reached by

Sweden and Spain is that U.S. models and technologies are too elaborate and expensive, or do not comprehend appropriately their own typologies of courses and programs. However, the ministry officials stated that many, if not most, of the conceptual ideas being promoted for management systems had come from U.S. or Canadian (Toronto) sources, but they were revising the technologies in fundamental ways to suit their particular purposes, which are bound to be diverse and to create more differences like those that exist among the states in the United States.

In Europe, as in the U.S. states, the gains from program budgets and unit costs first appear as new means for formulating budgets, or for allocating appropriations, or both. However, as soon as these goals are achieved the more fundamental goal of accountability appears and henceforth dominates the process. The direction taken in Sweden and France toward costing and programmatic budgets has the ulterior goal of taking authority away from the chair professors and delegating ministry powers to the administrators of the university, college, or institute. The ministries wish to make the institution the accountable agency, instead of the ministry, as in traditional practice. Hence, the governments in Sweden, France, and Spain each take definite measures (unit-costing, program budgeting, university hiring) that, collectively, are expected to achieve both a higher degree of decentralization and more accountability.

A rather neat set of managerial ploys enables ministry staffs to initiate and carry through this transfer of power. Through the budget and the technologies used in its formulation and allocation, and given the conditions or ties that may be attached to the monies, the staffs of the ministries of Education and Treasury can often bring about desired changes without new statutes. New laws, as we have observed, often face formidable opposition in the Parliaments of some nations because of the number and power of the professors seated there. For the most part, these people can be bypassed sufficiently to achieve in part the goals of the central professional staffs. The influence of central staffs grows rapidly as they develop complicated technologies for resource allocation. The former "automatic" procedures used in Sweden and France have given way to greater and greater complexity, which is easily understood by the technician but much more difficult for the ordinary academic to grasp. Even so, as Goldberg states, the actual changes in past practice brought about by the new, more complicated formulas progress toward the goal of equity and yet fall short of making allocations entirely according to real need.

Professional staffs, however, remain entranced with the theoretical goals of the new technology and encourage its application. As in the United States, the European central staffs appear to take the specialists' perspective, somehow overlooking or choosing to ignore how some practices aggravate rather than smooth out issues on allocation fairness, due process, equity, and other desirable goals. They seem to believe that technology can bring about these ends without applying the evil or uneven hand of human beings, except their own.

Data Bases

While the case-study chapters discuss the use of data in applying the new budget methodologies, they fall somewhat short in indicating the depth, scope, and quality of the data used in formula calculations. The omissions no doubt reflect the authors' inability to examine data bases, either because they are kept secret or because they are nonexistent. The authors are also skeptical of the extent to which the known data bases reveal more than a passing acquaintance with the reality they aim to describe.

Within the United States, as indicated previously, some states have extensive validated data banks on higher education, whereas others closely resemble European nations in the study. In the U.S. study, Illinois, Tennessee, Florida, New York, Wisconsin, and Washington stood out as having many routinely collected data available, a fact that directly affected their use in resource application and policy analysis.

Only in France, among the European nations, did the central ministry attempt to collect a similar kind of data and apply it. Goldberg describes some of the deficiencies of the data themselves and further points to the failure of this technological approach to achieve certain policy goals of the government. Until recently, data in France, however copious, however valid, and however applied, were for the most part closely sequestered in the Ministry of Higher Education. Even the presidents of the institutions had little or no access to it. Such secrecy called into question the validity of the data base as well as the fairness of the processes used in allocation. Finally, a special committee drawn from the Conference of University Presidents was formed to oversee the formula calculations and participate in the hearings. The results of some calculations were communicated to presidents on a systematic basis, and other data analyses were obtainable by special request. The Secretariat of State for the Universities feared, and still does to some extent, that the revelation of the data and formula calculations encourages institutions to use fund-generating bases for internal distribution of funds, especially in the new institutions that were formed by federating groups of existing autonomous faculties. These centripetal tendencies were thus avoided by the practice of secrecy. It was also feared that public disclosure of all data and calculations would diminish the already contested authority of the relatively new ministry and lessen the limited power of the university presidents represented by the conference and its special advisory committee. By 1976, the Secretariat chose to reveal more detailed information to all institutions while attempting to maintain financial order in the more financially fragile institutions.

Goldberg verifies that current outcomes in France are not much different than formerly, although ostensibly the government seeks to aid the innovative institutions, the new ones, and especially the ones in the provinces as opposed to those in Paris. The more open presentation of data and methodologies may provide the healthy criticism necessary to make these institutions serve the objectives assigned to them. It is the people in the institutions and universities who have the self-interest and competitive capacity to review the details, seek the loopholes, and invent methods for data validation and use that would more nearly achieve the state goals. Goldberg verifies that the state does obtain a great deal of its data from the responses of the institutions in justifying their claims for funds. The accumulation of all these data along with those regularly collected could provide, if the will to do so were present, the base for setting policy objectives or standards to achieve not only equity but also appropriate funding for the demonstrated "real" needs of the individual institutions. As Goldberg states in a letter, "Only a policy developed at the level of the central authority could be properly imbued with the procedures and criteria for a 'fair' allotment—that is, in conformity with legal standards" (letter to author, August 18, 1977).

France furnishes the best example in the study of a nation in which much more data are available than are made public. Other nations fall short in collecting pertinent data for operational decisions. Sweden seeks quick means to improve its data bases for accountability purposes, but one is surprised—given the Swedish reputation for quality higher education and the national penchant for innovation and change —that it does not have better data bases to evaluate its operations. The UHA recognizes these data needs and plans to study better and more valid means of collection.

Italy appears to have very little data, even on enrollments, and no state official interviewed had much faith in the validity of the available data. The base was narrow, suspect as to accuracy, and not used except in the loosest way for resource allocation. Data bases will no doubt remain in poor condition as long as favoritism and friendly negotiations continue to dominate allocation processes. An abundance of valid data would be an anathema to those cherished practices.

Spain presents a picture somewhat similar to that of Italy. The difference lies in the government's intent and in the excellent training of some top administrators in the ministries of Education and Treasury, as well as in the universities. A fair-sized core of higher education administrators has received common training in the national institute for career governmental officers. They know the language and uses of modern technologies applicable to higher education. They want to implement some of the managerial techniques and to bring about a much more rational process for resource allocation, getting away from the friendships and favoritism that have traditionally settled questions of who gets what and how much. If the Spanish government moves ahead as some of these administrators plan, the data systems and the technologies used would match any in the five countries under study in Europe, and would approach advanced practices in the United States.

Greece publishes more data on its higher institutions than any of the other five European nations. In this respect, its practice parallels that in the United States, where large amounts of data may be published and where every institution not only knows the technical bases for budget formulas but probably has a representative on the committee that establishes them. The Greeks, however, have not yet chosen to adopt the more advanced costing and allocation techniques available in the United States, and so their published data base is quite narrow in comparison. Negotiation, favoritism, and friendships still play the leading role in Greek allocations, as in Italy and Spain.

One must keep in mind that in discussing institutional budget allocations in these nations, the funds dealt with comprise only a small proportion of the total operating budget. All salaries of permanent faculty and staff come from the ministry or government civil service budget, and research funds (as opposed to instruction) come down to faculty members and research institutes through different channels. As a result of these practices, which in themselves are being subjected to reevaluation in Sweden and France, the European nations have far fewer of the kinds of data bases required in the United States for allocating all state funds. The United States Higher Education General Information Survey (HEGIS) alone would seem to produce more data about higher education by institution, by type of institution, and by state than is available in any of the five European nations. Yet the U.S. Survey, according to most state coordinators and executives, falls so far short of state needs that with few exceptions state data systems must be made entirely different and more elaborate in order to meet perceived requirements.

Positive forces working toward better data systems are the international conferences and working committees, sponsored by the Organization for Economic and Cultural Development (OECD) and UNESCO, that focus on management practices. They will have an important and continued impact on what the European nations finally use. Both Canada and the United States, as well as some German states, also seem destined to influence the new practices adopted.

Allocations of Research Funds

The issue of how research funds should be allocated grows out of the pleas of younger, inexperienced faculty members for a much greater share of state funds made available to the professors. As it stands in each country in Europe, research funds are distributed by a different route than operating funds or salary funds. Research money in each country comes primarily from the government. The sums available generally are those of the previous year with some amount of add-on. No budgets are submitted, nor are projects reviewed before the funds are appropriated. Once they are appropriated, a national research council may allocate them among the several ministries; or, more likely, that decision has been made before the appropriation, and the share for each function goes to the appropriate ministry. The ministry in turn has connected with it, not in a hierarchical sense but as a semi-independent body, a council for the distribution of these funds. This council then allocates lump sums to a number of other research councils, each of which represents a discipline (perceived nationally rather than according to an institution's own definition). These councils in turn review the project proposals of professors and institutes and make priority decisions among them.

The issue boils down to a conflict between the chair professors and the young, lower-ranking faculty members. Each research council, from the national one down through the disciplinary ones, is dominated by the most powerful and well-known chairs in the universities of the nation. Government officials admit that the money is substantially divided among the better-known chair colleagues, and that little of it is made available to those without established reputations as good researchers. Without a chair mentor, formidable obstacles confront the neophyte researcher; once successful research has been conducted, however, funds from the higher education ministry are likely to continue to support further research efforts. The French national research office plans to withhold a small percentage of the total research grant to made "seed" grants to young but promising faculty members, thus encouraging a new group of researchers not under the direct control of the full professors.

While the above description applies primarily to the European nations, the methods and results of distributing research funds in the United States appear similar. Most of the large state research universities permit faculty members to carry lower teaching loads, so as to free some time for research. This amount of time for research, converted to dollars, accounts for the vast majority of state research funds. However, it is not all, since the state often funds projects that relate to agriculture and to the main industries within its boundaries.

The greatest amount of research money used in conducting projects (paying assistants, purchasing equipment, using computers, and so on) comes from various federal agencies rather than from the states. Dozens of agencies distribute such funds and most of the larger ones, such as the National Science Foundation, the National Institute of Mental Health, and the National Institute of Education, receive lump sums, which are occasionally broken down into broad program categories. They award these funds to university researchers and to those in private and nonprofit research institutes, such as the Brookings Institution, Battelle Institute, and the Rand Corporation, on the basis of competitions and fairly specific guidelines for research goals (which sometimes even specify particular methodologies). In virtually all cases, the funds are legally awarded to the institution, not to the principal investigator for the project; this gives the institution some control (if desired) over the types of personnel employed with project money, and some control over accounting, and assures the granting authority that the funds are being expended according to the regular rules and regulations of the receiving institution.

The next largest source of research funds for U.S. higher education faculties comes from the private philanthropic, nonprofit foundations, such as the Ford Foundation, the Carnegie Corporation, the Lilly Endowment, the Russell Sage Foundation, and the Sloan Foundation. Usually foundations have their own special priority interests, but in contrast to government agencies, after the grant is made they impose few, if any, guidelines and rules on the researcher. These grants, normally awarded at specified intervals each year from field-initiated proposals, receive review by three or more experts in the field to be researched—another form of peer review.

Against both the governments and foundations, the community college, state college, and younger university faculty members complain, as in Europe, that only the well-known and successful researchers at the most prestigious institutions get the funds. The denial of this conclusion by the granting authorities is generally discounted by the affronted groups.

An issue apparently not present in Europe but omnipresent in the United States is the controversy over faculty members spending too much time on research and not enough on teaching, particularly of undergraduate students. This issue will not be further dealt with in this book because it appears often in the literature on higher education in the United States.

Planning as a Basis for Budgeting

Plans and planning have become bywords in the heavily industrialized nations, where the complexity of the economy and the society
appear to require planning; for the developing nations, planning appears as the high road to industrial status and increased GNP with the
least amount of waste. Nations provide plans for their total future
economic development, for correcting major societal ills, and for
speedily achieving specific intermediate and long-range goals. The
development and funding of higher education has not always escaped
this planning euphoria.

During the 1950s and especially in the 1960s, almost every state
in the United States produced one or more documents called a "master plan," which was supposed to guide state policy in creating new
institutions and programs, providing increased access, meeting the
needs of minorities and women, and otherwise producing guidelines
for "the orderly development of higher education in the state." In the
period of rapid enrollment expansion, these plans served many of
their stated purposes, especially in building new campuses, developing community college systems, and transforming former teachers'
colleges into comprehensive state colleges or "emerging" universities.
The plans that were made often had an impact on larger public policy;
and in a few cases they also set the broad parameters within which
budget decisions for operations were made. But such bases were exceptional. Most plans did not guide the annual or biennial operational
budgets, not even for the agency (usually the state coordinating board
or statewide governing board for higher education) that had developed
the plan (or had it formulated by outside consultants). After 1968, as
enrollments began to fluctuate among institutions and funding began to
decrease, plans of earlier vintage quickly became obsolete and were
shelved in favor of ad hoc decision making based on current exigen-
cies. Planning for higher education by the states has not regained its
former status or form. Most plans in use today concern specific
problems and their solutions, such as whether a need exists for a new
medical or veterinary school, or whether some doctoral programs
ought to be cut back or eliminated. Comprehensive plans have fallen
into disuse in favor of pragmatic courses of action that reflect the
immediate concerns of politicians. But even politicians who once seldom thought about plans now want to know about consequences of decisions going beyond the next budget cycle (Bartley 1975).

European countries, especially those in the north, have a much
longer history of national and state planning than exists in the United
States. The socialist parties have always insisted on planning, and
Sweden, Greece, and France in this study have long attempted national
planning on a grand scale. However, planning in Spain and Italy has

been very limited, in much the same way it is in some Mountain and Western states of the United States; it is undertaken only if it seems necessary to solve a particular problem. The national plans have worked only indifferently (or not at all, according to some U.S. scholars, notably (Aaron Wildavsky); manpower forecasts for higher education, especially, have fallen short of anticipated goals. Nevertheless, all the nations in the study except Italy intend to plan for higher education or are in the midst of it.

For the socialist nations, the planning process used by the Soviet Union tends to provide the model. The Economic Research Institute of the State Planning Committee of the USSR Council of Ministers (1972) describes the mode of planning in the Soviet Union as follows:

> Local economic bodies and local planning commissions engage in territorial planning. Regional, territorial, city and district planning commissions draw up draft plans of economic and cultural development and submit them for approval to the corresponding executive committees of local Soviets. After approval, these plans are sent to the higher planning agencies.
>
> They then go to the planning agency of each Soviet for revision and then on up to the State Planning Committee of the USSR (Gosplan) which has three divisions: all Union, Republican, and Local.
>
> State national economic plans are designated for long periods (long-term plans) and also for short periods (current annual plans) and are primary instruments for guiding all the sectors and spheres of the national economy.
>
> At present, the five-year plan with a breakdown of major assignments by years is the basic form of planning. Annual plans specify the assignments contained in the long-term plan, new requirements of society and the achievements of science and technology.
>
> But naturally, even given very high precision in formulating the long-term plan all changes in economic life cannot be foreseen. Therefore the adjustment of annual assignments is inevitable. [Pp. 183, 182, 10, 188, and 189]

The Swedish Ministry of Finance provides state planning through a continuous planning process. It is no longer enamored of periodic plans and now prefers to make adjustments in plans as new societal factors dictate. Gunnar Petri (1976) states:

There is no special independent apparatus in Sweden for
long-term planning, which is instead undertaken as part
of the regular activities of the Government. . . . The
aim is to maintain a "rolling plan."
The central planning body is the Government, and
below this primarily the Ministry of Finance. The
Ministry of Finance is responsible for the general coordination of economic policy and planning. The central
document for economic planning is the Budget Statement
[(worked out twice a year by the Finance Ministry)] . . .
a cyclical policy but also with long-term policy. [(Long-
term budget is five years, short-term is one year.)]
[P. 8]

The results of such state planning influenced the very substantial planning process and end product called the U-68 (1968) plan for
postsecondary education, which began to be implemented in 1977.
The U-68 plan provides for decentralization to regions and to institutions and limits the power and control of full professors over curricula, personnel, and research. It also seeks to provide greater diversity in educational opportunity by creating different types of institutions, offering more adult programs, and placing more emphasis
on vocational and technical education. The UHA will provide continuous evaluation of U-68 outcomes and practices and will make necessary modifications to achieve long-range planning goals.
France, too, conducted educational planning and as a result
built new types of institutions and tried establishing "innovative" universities, as well as opening up places for adult or continuing education. However, no current plan governs general public policy in
France, as Goldberg reports in Chapter 2, and previous goals established through planning are far from being achieved through the current budget process. Goldberg observes that both the bases and the
processes for fund allocation seem to thwart rather than to help
achieve publicly stated goals for higher education.
Of the remaining countries, Spain, as Moncada reports, hopes
to engage in more planning and to improve management techniques,
but political realities there have blocked actions that could thwart the
people currently holding power, including the full professors, especially those in Parliament. Greece, on the other hand, considers itself more as a developing nation in attempting to lay the base for a
more diversified economy and a decentralization of population. The
government contracted with one of its major research organizations
to formulate its fourth five-year national economic development
plan; in this plan higher education will play a critical role, both in
supplying appropriate manpower and in providing training in various
geographic locations in the country.

Despite the planning mentioned above, we find that, just as in the United States, the annual budget cycle, the priorities inherent in the budgets, and the amounts of money appropriated for various functions appear to have little relationship to plans. Specific planning goals and means suggested for achieving them are rarely made explicit in the budget. Consideration may nevertheless have been given to a plan, particularly by the agency that developed it, if the agency also reviews and influences recommendations on budgets. Even without specific reference to a plan, the attitudes and values of officials already embedded in a plan may come through in recommendations on budget allocations. This simply means that people tend to follow their values and attitudes rather consistently in plans and action.

Despite this caveat to the belief that planning actually does help control budget formulation, this study has produced little evidence that planning or plans have much impact on current operating budgets, including the hiring of faculty and the funding of research.

In both France and Spain, the governments through central ministries established a set of national priorities for research. Funds were even earmarked for research in specific areas. However, the officials interviewed indicated that once funds were allocated to professors for research, there was no checking to see if fund expenditures matched the national rather than the professorial preferences. Funds awarded to institutes with specific missions of research in the priority areas (atomic energy in France, for example) could be expected to spend funds according to plan because the interests of the researchers, the institute, and the government all coincided. But in all five European nations, research funds are largely controlled, in initial as well as in subsequent allocation, by the best-known researchers, and national priorities may or may not remain the focus of the research.

The situation in the United States is again similar to the one in Europe, except that the sources of funds are far more diverse. Most researchers are employees of a private or public university or a research institute. Administrators for federal research programs and foundations are drawn from the talent pool located in the active research organizations. However, in the United States the researchers in the agencies allocating funds are not concurrently working as professors in the universities, but instead are full-time administrators of the research programs, though some are only on leave from a university for two or three years or more. Also in the United States, governmental research is much more closely monitored than in the European nations. On the other hand, the "peer review" process makes possible the direct intervention of professors and researchers who have a self-interest in the outcomes of fund allocations. Favoritism, reputation, and the school represented all are said to have in-

fluence on who gets research money, how much, and for what purposes. Yet the monitoring and the receipt of a grant under the auspices of an agency with specific program priorities limits the researcher in pursuing personal rather than public or foundation purposes in the research.

8
STUDENTS AND FACULTY: ISSUES AND TRENDS
Lyman A. Glenny

The previous chapter dealt with the political and organizational setting for making budgets, the means for producing budgets, and the impact of the budget process on the power structures of institutions and on state goals. This chapter focuses on certain issues and trends relating to students and faculty that have vital importance to public policy on the funding of postsecondary institutions.

STUDENTS

Students are the very reason for higher education and the issues relating to them seem endless, especially as one reflects on the student activism of the late 1960s and early 1970s, which continues in a few nations today. Three major issues will be discussed here, although many others in one way or another affect the lives of students or potential students. The three issues are: student aspirations and civic intelligence versus state-planned manpower needs; social policy affecting higher education enrollments; and government policy concerning continuing education for adults. Each issue focuses on the central element in formulating university budgets, that is, the number of students to be enrolled. In each of the nations studied, higher education relies far more on student numbers to generate funds than it does on research or public service work.

Student Aspirations versus
Projected Manpower Requirements

This topic, representing two of three methods for planning higher education, might well be labeled manpower planning versus the free market system. Under either label, only a few major ramifications for budgeting will be considered. The third method, the cost-benefit approach, was mentioned only once by officials in Europe (Spain) and only a few times during the study in the 17 states in the United States. The possibility of using such an approach arose in discussions, but no state was trying it, for while identifiable benefits were plentiful, the means of measuring them were either completely lacking or available only for benefits of marginal impact. At best, process variables such as degrees granted (some people consider degrees as outcomes) or student-credit-hours produced could be compared with resource input. Even politicians in the United States have cooled to the cost-benefit approach as a means of gaining effective control of the universities; they have turned instead to controlling student input by limiting budgets for specific schools or programs or by setting ceilings on the numbers of enrolled students.

Manpower planning, as opposed to the free market approach, appears to be a real issue in most countries. It derives principally from an oversupply of trained specialists in a variety of fields at a time when student aspirations for professional and graduate training continue at an extraordinarily high level and is further aggravated by student frustration with employment problems. Oversupplies first hit the United States in some fields in 1968 and have accelerated to the present time, when few major traditional fields of study foresee a shortage in the immediate future. Medicine and certain other specializations in the health care field appear to remain short of practitioners, and whatever the number of graduates, that number may continue to be short until a more efficient health care delivery system brings nonurbanized people the level of care enjoyed in the large cities, where the money income is and the doctors go. Yet, medicine remains the principal specialization to which most industrialized countries apply enrollment limits, for such reasons as high training costs and the influence of practicing professionals in trying to limit competition.

The oversupply condition now has spread to Sweden, Belgium, and France among the countries studied. European newspapers, as well as Far Eastern ones, take notice of the warning on oversupply and "over-education" explicated by leading education and budget ministries. The Chronicle of Higher Education (United States), in the last year alone, has carried headlines such as "Denmark to Call a Halt to College Growth," "Teacher Unemployment Rises in Some European Countries," "The Ruinous Plight of Italy's Universities," and "Peril of 'Over-Education.'" Accompanying these cries of alarm· are reports of the further leveling of enrollments in industrialized Europe and impending reductions in Sweden and in several sectors of U.S. higher education.

The alternative to forbidding students to enroll in oversubscribed programs reduces their opportunities to enter universities and opens new options in the vocational-technical fields, part-time enrollment, work-study programs, and short intensive courses. Pressures to shift financial support in this direction arise from the generally recognizable shortage of middle-level technicians, service, and repair people. The special needs of industry receive attention, and in the United States especially, the industries themselves train thousands of their own employees for better jobs within the industry or for new jobs as the old ones become obsolete. George McGurn (1974) speculates about the recent tendency to bring persons from industry into the universities:

> Is there some relationship to the planning failure (manpower planning) and the movement to recruit students from working situations rather than secondary school systems? Swedish, French, and German approaches to recurrent education suggest that they are, in part, an attempt to import specific job characteristics into the educational system through students rather than through providing skills implied by manpower projections that are dependent on a job market more flexible than educational programs. [P. 36]

Considering the longer term, planners cannot accept recent headlines as evidence of future societal needs. Yet in no industrialized Western country has manpower planning achieved much success in giving direction to universities for producing particular specialists. Although politicians and central government officials limit resources and enrollments in certain fields, they do so knowing that even the most expertly made projections of manpower requirements have widely missed the mark. Hence, one problem is projection. What techniques can be employed in societies where so many independent, uncontrolled variables exist? Most socialist governments, such as those in Sweden and France, have tried to act on manpower forecasts along with national economic planning goals, but with little success. Assumptions about the future vary as much as past experiences do and can be taken seriously by policy makers only as a matter of personal preference rather than of scientific accuracy or validity. McGurn (1974) observes: "Industrial countries which have traditionally had a much tighter link between academic training and job-oriented knowledge than in the United States . . . are tending to explore ways of loosening this linkage and find the U.S. model of great interest" (p. 33-34). The looseness of the U.S. model was well illustrated in a conference on manpower forecasts as they relate to university program planning conducted in Washington, D. C. by the American Council on Education in 1973. The manpower specialists from federal and private research agencies agreed that universities should use available projections, but cautiously and without gearing programs directly to projected needs.

While public controversy over manpower needs continues to be debated in newspapers, legislatures, and other public places, the students remain relatively unaffected in their aspirations. In the United States in the fall of 1976, more than twice as many first-year college students aspired to become members of the leading professions as were estimated to be needed by the U. S. Department of Labor. Research evidence indicates that some students of course change their career aspirations (Cross 1971); but since the United States has well over 30 percent of the 18- to 21-year-old age group in college at a time when the U. S. Department of Labor states that no more than 20 percent of future positions in the work force will require a college education, surpluses seem bound to occur.

Given the discrepancy between student aspirations and the planners' estimates of need for future specialists, what should the public policy be, and who should decide? These questions are particularly hard to answer in a democratic society, where the politician often must face irate parents whose sons or daughters are refused admission into a program because of oversupply, current or projected. Regardless of forecasts, parents want their children to be enrolled. The market–demand model of planning thus comes directly into conflict with the planned manpower model. Which serves society better and why? Do we have good evidence with which to answer these questions?

Probably the free market system for education has its best working example in the United States. The advantages of that model are often stated somewhat as follows. The student in a democratic society should be able to choose the occupation he wishes. If the competition for jobs in the occupation is severe, that becomes his problem to solve, particularly if he is informed about job opportunities as he continues his training. The government is supported by his family's taxes as much as by the next family's. If two students are equally capable, why should only one be admitted, if justice is to prevail? The young person turned down might turn out to be a better practitioner than the one allowed entrance, but no one will ever know unless he is given the opportunity.

Ond distinct disadvantage for the student competing in the market system is that social phenomena create fads for entering certain fields of study as against others (biology and psychology in the United States being good recent examples). The student enters partly because his friends do, or because of a current shortage in the particular specialty. But the shortage may well have disappeared by the time a student completes his studies, leaving him and his comrades competing in an oversupplied area. Engineering in the United States has experienced this out-of-phase productivity, at least since the 1930s. The market-model response to these issues argues that although the market will absorb the graduates at a somewhat lower level than they expected when entering college, they will not remain unemployed for long, but will obtain other lower-status and lower-paying positions. This process, while traumatic for the individuals concerned, upgrades the general educational level of the society and its work force, which in the Jeffersonian view of a democratic society should be a goal to be sought rather than a dragon to be slaughtered.

The planning model also has its advantages and shortcomings. By planning the number of specialists needed in a given area of work, the state assures itself of sufficient people to operate its economy and services without unexpected shortages. Resources, maximized by not being oversupplied, can be put to more productive uses. This prevents the creation of a class of frustrated surplus specialists, compelled to seek work at a level below that for which they were trained. Selecting the most promising students through examination and past performance is a reasonable way of choosing between those allowed and those denied entry. Waste and inefficiency in the entire economy are minimized; productivity and efficiency maximized. Errors in forecasting manpower needs may be corrected on an ongoing basis and appropriate adjustments made in educational inputs.

These arguments, much oversimplified (and not necessarily supported by evidence), provide the fundamental differences between the two systems. What then have the nations in the study done about the issues?

Sweden has experienced oversupplies of specialists despite the fact that it has probably done more manpower and economic planning than any other country in the study. The Swedish safeguard, to provide flexibility in supply, may be partially accomplished by the 25-4 system, whereby any person 25 years or older, with 4 years of work experience, may enter a university without having completed secondary school. This option could bring in a fresh group of students whenever shortages appear, perhaps people with considerable practical experience in the field of shortage. Also, the Swedish government has imposed or allowed numerous clausus (enrollment ceilings) in the field of medicine and is currently studying other fields to which enrollment ceilings may be applied. Even more than in the past, this society apparently intends to use manpower planning and to implement the planning through the educational systems. One result is the definite shift in attention and resources away from universities toward the technical offerings of other institutions.

The French, too, engage in manpower planning and recently saw a need for more persons with technical competencies rather than those trained in theory or traditional fields at universities. The government wants the university curricula to shift toward more practical objectives and also intends to support with additional funds those universities that would meet regional manpower requirements. However, the students appear to agree with the professors—with resulting demonstrations against changing the university curricula—regardless of the fact that many currently enrolled students seem destined to graduate in fields of oversupply for the French economy. Students refuse to give up their aspirations because planners think they should; Gallic independence once again asserts itself. At the same time, the French provide more opportunity for adults and for part-time students to attend school—an attempt to fill shortages that may also create additional surpluses.

Some Spanish officials speak of a cost-benefit type of education rather than manpower needs, although the two are not unrelated. Having just left a dictatorship and being in a state of uneasy transition toward a more democratic form of government, the education and finance ministries appear reluctant, despite their strong beliefs in program budgeting (and thus manpower planning), to take strong immediate action. Nevertheless, the nonpolitical administrators in the ministries and universities see the need for substantive changes in curricula and in student enrollment in particular university programs. The Spaniards have become as enamored with costing and with measuring benefits of education as any of the other countries, some of which have already tried these devices at least on an experimental scale (see Chapter 7).

Italy not only has no manpower planning for its university inputs, it also has little accurate data on the number of persons actively enrolled in the various specializations currently offered and only a remote idea of current enrollment for the whole system of higher education.

Greece is now in the final stages of its fourth national economic development plan since the end of the military dictatorship. Just what effects it will have on the old university practices can only be conjectured. The planners are, however, relying on the higher education system to supply specialists for economic development. Also, the selectivity process for university entry to roughly one in five or six applicants sets limits on overall enrollment as well as for some disciplines. No oversupply problems presently concern the officials.

In the United States, some state coordinating agencies for higher education have conducted manpower studies; a few have covered many specializations, but most have dealt only with medicine, other major professions, and with doctoral-level specialists. The doctoral-level studies have probably had priority over all others, and have caused much public debate (and in New York, court cases) when certain doctoral programs have been forced to close. The state of Washington has considered the closing of as many as 50 graduate programs on the recommendation of its Council on Postsecondary Education. Indiana recently completed a full-scale manpower study, and more specialized studies of single professions or occupational clusters go on almost continuously in many of the large industrial states. However, the trend in student enrollment toward technical and vocational courses in the community colleges (two years) seems to coincide closely with the wishes of the political leaders, who, disillusioned with the universities for turning out too many doctorates, would rather produce more service-repair people and those who can fit directly into industrial jobs. State-imposed campus enrollment ceilings have become rather commonplace, though ceilings on disciplines or departments have been few. Local, state, and national economies all play important roles in holding down enrollments in some institutions and encouraging increases in others, often in different locations. Politicians talk a good deal about better manpower planning, but seem aware that no one has accurate forecasts of need in a society as dynamic in unanticipated variables as the United States.

In October 1976 the author visited the Soviet Union on a scholar exchange sponsored by the U.S. State Department on the subject of manpower planning and continuing education ("correspondence education" in the Soviet Union). The Soviet ministry officials insisted that their planning worked, and that there were no oversupply problems, and in fact an undersupply in some fields because of new needs or great technological changes. Nevertheless, from private conversations with officials, it seems that after graduation from some Moscow universities and institutes, only about half the young people know what jobs they want or can get, primarily because their training allows them specific job offers in Siberia or other outer republics, but few in Moscow, which they did not wish to leave. A major change in policy in the Soviet Union, effected in 1976, placed limits on the number of active agricultural and industrial workers who could return to school under industry or government sponsorship. The state plans not to allow further increases in the numbers of adults in higher education. Officials stated that adult returnees were insufficiently theory-oriented, and they said they preferred limited expansion of regular daytime enrollments for youth. This restrictive policy on adult or continuing education, however, was in contrast to that of all other countries visited or studied. The last USSR five-year plan allows graduates of universities and other people to have more freedom in the selection of their jobs than previously. Indeed, the bulletin boards at the entrances to offices where many degree-holders and technical specialists work are posted with notices of job opportunities, indicating that such flexibility in placement (characteristic of a free market) must add to uncertainties in planned manpower requirements. Setting planned quotas for the number of students who may enter institutions of higher education markedly reduces the cost of education in comparison with costs in nations where open access and mass entry prevail. The wealth of the United States continues to provide constant dollar equivalents for the number of students entering (Ruyle and Glenny 1978). No measure of the share that higher education contributes to the GNP of a nation has been agreed upon by international or even national economists (although several have tried). However, almost all persons who think about the future assert that education must encourage the ability to be flexible, adaptable, and ready to make major changes in occupational skills rather than obtaining a narrow specialization that epitomizes most of modern higher education, especially in the Soviet system. No one knows if the costs in productivity and GNP are higher in the United States, with its wide-open universal system, than in the planned quota systems of the Soviet Union. By Soviet estimates, however 27 to 30 percent of the country's productivity can be attributed to higher education (Zhamin 1973).

If these results are valid, one may wonder why adult education enrollments have been frozen and why the new openings in higher education remain so limited. Zhamin also states:

> Among tool makers with a five-year service record, those
> with an eight-year education have 35 percent higher labor
> productivity than those with a lower education. The out-
> put of workers who have completed secondary education is
> 25 percent greater than that of those with no more than an
> eight-year education. . . . Each extra class in the work-
> er's general education resulted in an increase in labor
> productivity averaging 1.5 to 2 percent in the engineering
> industry, 0.4 to 0.7 percent in the ferrous metal in-
> dustry, and 1.5 to 2.2 percent in light industry. [P. 111]

One should not leave this topic without saying that the entire discussion above relates to manpower and to economic considerations. Education for its own sake and for the development of the individual in self-confidence, self-esteem, and ability to adjust to changing societal features may prove more important to the individual and society than the number of properly trained people for the work force. But with few exceptions, the pressures appear to be on economics. The French students in 1975/76 (among more important issues such as the large tuition increase) rebelled against making their curricula more professionally work-oriented; and, because they see few new employment opportunities, they continue their opposition to this day. The Italians have done no planning; they continue to let the traditional curricula and chair systems determine university offerings, and no major changes have occurred to meet what might be called "national manpower needs." The Spanish, too, have been slow to make changes in a similar "baronial" system, although the opinions of professional administrators in the ministries and universities indicate that there may be substantive changes as new governments achieve more stability. The instability of government certainly accounts in part for Italy's conservatism, and to some degree for the conservatism in France and Sweden. Major reforms are watered down during implementation, or shelved entirely by party leaders determined to stay afloat on fragile coalitions that break up over minor social issues.

Social Policy and Student Enrollments

In most if not all industrialized countries, postsecondary and higher education enrollments are already affected, or will be affected in the near future, by three factors: the drop in number of births; the tendency toward income equalization except for the very unskilled; and changes in life styles and requirements for lifelong learning.

Live Births

The baby boom of the postwar years appears most pronounced in the countries that now have the greatest drops in number of live births, that is, Northern Europe, Britain, the United States, and Canada. Plans made in the late 1960s and early 1970s for expansion of higher education enrollments into the indefinite future now seem so grossly outmoded that newcomers to the planning field are astounded at the misjudgments in forecasting and the size of the error in estimating enrollments. While the economic depression of the first half of the 1970s has affected higher education enrollments adversely, it merely presages a further leveling off or even a major downturn in the 1980s, which will last for at least another 15 years, to 1995. This is an incontrovertible fact, since the babies are already born who will be attending colleges and universities during those years, and only a mass immigration of low-age groups into a country, or an increase in the college attendance rate can change the situation. The data given in Chapter 1 on live births and their changing rates show, for the six countries studied, what the college-age group will look like until 1995. However, the data also show that the change in number of live births that occurred 18 years ago should still be feeding an increased rather than a decreased number of young people into the higher institutions;

but only in Spain is the rate of attendance still increasing. The year
of enrollment turnaround will vary from nation to nation, but for
most it will be between about 1980 and 1985 when the number of college-age young people actually drops from the preceding year. But
what factors account for the drop or leveling of current college enrollments while the number of young people increases? The depression and lack of sufficient funds for students to attend seem to be factors. The trend might be reversed with a world economic recovery
(which at the moment of writing is not fully realized) that may increase
the need for highly skilled and trained specialists at all levels in the
work force.

Convergence of Wage Levels

Another factor causing dropping enrollments, however, has
been very powerful in the United States and in certain of the industrialized Western nations, where labor unions force the wages of skilled
workers to converge with those of university-trained specialists. Potential students for universities are discouraged from entering or are
drawn off into the skilled labor class. When street sweepers and
garbage collectors in San Francisco are paid an annual wage equal to
that of an assistant professor at the University of California in Berkeley, a young person may indeed rethink his plans for a future vocation. This picture in the United States is not the extreme; the tendency
to equalize wages is even more pronounced in nations having long his-
tories of postwar socialist governments. With the changing life styles
of the young infiltrating the older generations, status (especially status epitomized by the accumulation of wealth) comes to mean less,
because many amenities, such as a house, one or two automobiles, a
vacation home, a trailer or camper, a boat, or a nearby tennis court,
are now owned by both white-collar and blue-collar workers alike.
An emphasis on material possessions seems to be returning, but the
families of organized labor as well as the families of professionals
can acquire these assets almost equally, although they may differ in
quality or chic.

Adult and Continuing Education

The recent projections of enrollments made by planners in Europe and the United States took into consideration the adults who
wanted further education. In some cases, plans for more new adult
enrollments compensated entirely, or almost entirely, for the drop
in the numbers of young people available for entry. The Swedish 25-4
plan, the French continuing education plan, and the upward spurt in
the average age of community college students in the United States
give support to this assumption. However, if resources to higher

education remain tight for the indeterminate future, the adult level of education may be hard hit, as evidenced in the United States. While adult education in the United States has come about almost fortuitously (primarily as the result of planning at the local institutional level), the national plans of Sweden and France promote continuing education as an official alternative to forcing the young to remain in school from 11 to 13 years and then, without a break, to go immediately into higher education for another 2 to 8 years. However, this planning in Sweden and France has not succeeded in keeping up enrollments in higher education, especially in the universities. Only time will tell whether such plans that tinker and adjust will bring about the desired results. Evidence from the United States indicates that there is a high correlation between the most educated and the wealthiest people, those being the ones who most often return for adult and continuing education. The number of persons who have not completed high school who take continuing education turns out to be a relatively small, 6 to 7 percent (National Center for Educational Statistics 1977), of the total.

Therefore, more than other factors, keeping the young in school for longer periods of time seems to encourage the rate of recurring education. How, then, can adults with little previous education be brought into recurring or continuing education? Retention rates can and should be improved for both secondary and higher education. In some nations the two-track secondary mode is being changed to allow vocational-technical and academic groups into higher education at a later time, instead of restricting entry to those with academic preparation. This kind of change depends on the commitment of higher education faculties to alternative education models appropriate to the adult level. Change would also depend on the commitment of a nation to education as such, and not exclusively to manpower planning.

The Proportion of Age Groups in Higher Education

The outcome of efforts to make continuing education a reality will also depend upon the percent of the college-age group who attend college. The changes mentioned above would improve that proportion, but even in the United States, where the percentage of age cohort in college reached a peak of about 41 percent in 1968, it has dropped steadily to about 38 percent of the age group in 1977—a percentage just above that of several European nations that built up their proportions as the United States percentage skidded downward. Can it be that only one-third of the population can be attracted to higher education, or are intellectually capable of handling the work? Or would new and different programs of study, no less rigorous than the traditional ones, attract further enrollments of both the young and adults?

As mentioned in Chapter 1, the data about the proportion of secondary school graduates, of an age group who go on to higher education, must be considered suspect until higher, tertiary, and postsecondary education have been more clearly defined and data reported on them by the various nations of the world. (The Organization for Economic Cooperation and Development has made significant studies and suggestions in this direction.) Similar problems of definition must be solved at the secondary school level in order to lay the base for appropriate definitions at the higher levels. Hence, little reliability can now be attributed to the reported data.

Other Budget Considerations on Student Issues

Financial costs to the public and to students participating in the market model tend to be heavy compared to those costs in the planned model, which allows money only for the manpower and exact specializations needed in the society. Waste from oversupply or from education for its own sake becomes greatly reduced in the planned model. And of course the number of students, or proportion of the age group in higher education, is also reduced.

Planners insist that costs to the student, both hidden and direct, are very high in the market model: the expenses of attending in terms of tuition and books, the cost of income that is lost unless the state provides exceptionally high subsidies, which would then increase the costs to the state, and always the psychic costs for those graduates who are surplus and are forced to take jobs of lesser status and income than their degrees prepared them for. Moreover, the argument could now be put forth that shifts in students from one discipline to another—such as the 58 percent increase in biological sciences and the 30 percent drop in physical sciences in a five-year period in the United States—do not accurately reflect market needs, create unnecessary costs to the state, and simultaneously lay the base for surplus manpower.

In addition to these quite practical arguments, the states with planned manpower production indicate that their economies could not stand the financial drain the market model imposes. This assumption was partially validated by the phenomenon of the states in the United States cutting adult education budgets and imposing ceilings on programs and institutions during the recent economic depression.

Also, in the United States, against all tradition, politicians increasingly insist on planning to aid them in making decisions. At the moment, the market model is far from doomed, but recent modifications are bringing it closer to the practice of European countries that exert manpower control by limiting access to training. When students have gone to court claiming discrimination because they were excluded by enrollment ceilings, the courts have so far supported government planning and controls.

When enrollments level off or decrease, the budgets do not go down in proportion to the number of students; they often increase to provide new programs to attract students or to provide new types of specialists needed in the economy. Maintenance of buildings, libraries, and other service facilities continue to be costly whether or not student numbers decline. The resulting high unit cost per student in such institutions precludes the growing, more popular institutions from receiving the traditional "fair share" per student characteristic of the 1960s (Ruyle and Glenny 1978). Italy is an outstanding example of student numbers outstripping funding because of open admissions policies. Growing institutions, in these situations, may have more difficulty launching new programs than the waning ones. In Italy, the increasing gap in student-faculty ratios indicates that in at least one market model, the costs do not rise to anything like the level necessary to maintain former standards of quality. The resulting increase in student-faculty ratios, together with an absolute shortage of facilities and a high rate of unemployed graduates, also seems to bring about student riots, as occurred in early 1977.

This discussion of student issues in relation to the amount of funds needed for higher education has shown that public policy alone may have very significant consequences in terms of the numbers of students in college. The support for continuing education, the imposition of enrollment ceilings on programs and institutions, and the tracking system in secondary schools all result from asserting a public policy that may be changed—again by man's will. The birthrates and the willingness of students to attend college when they see oversupplies of skilled persons seem less subject to policy intervention; but even here, tax incentives, student financial support, and employment opportunities can be sufficiently manipulated by government so as to improve or discourage the numbers of students in higher education.

FACULTY

Students are the reason for having institutions of higher education, but each institution in reality consists of its faculties. Certain faculty issues, too, have a direct bearing on the allocations made to higher education, and current practices result in large part from policy of governments. Salary levels, the faculty ranks, the proportion of part-time faculty, and tenure policies all result from policy decisions that can be changed, albeit in some nations with extreme political difficulty. Nevertheless, change can occur, as Goldberg asserted in Chapter 2, if the government has the will to act. Some of these faculty issues are discussed in the following pages.

Salaries of Faculty

Salaries of teaching faculty and support personnel constitute the major portion of all funds appropriated to the operation of higher education institutions. In the United States, these funds are found invariably in the budget of an institution or individual campus. In Europe, on the other hand, funds for faculty salaries are found in the general salary budget of the national government (civil service) or of a ministry, and are not mentioned or cited in the budgets of the individual colleges or universities. This situation, so puzzling to U.S. citizens, comes about because professors and most other permanent members of a university staff are employees of the government, fall within its civil service and retirement systems and are subject to state rules and regulations rather than those of the universities. Thus, when one examines the budgets of a university in France or Spain the salary item will be small (although it is growing larger), for it represents only those few positions (usually of a part-time or short-term contractual nature) that are appointed by the university itself. This feature of so many European countries makes it very difficult to calculate "the budget" of a university, or even of the whole national system of higher education, for comparative purposes. One must comb the government budget for items pertinent to higher education and add them to those in the university budgets in order to get rough comparability with the United States.

It is true that in many of the United States the retirement funds and health-care benefits are represented as they are in Europe, where the monies for these purposes are neither listed nor footnoted in institutional budgets. But not so with salaries. Salary levels for college and university professors are high, usually in the upper 10 percent of all income levels. In the United States, their relative position has been dropping for the past few years. The salary levels in the industrialized countries of Europe, particularly northern Europe and the British Isles, are roughly comparable to those in the United States; but the salaries of teaching staffs in Spain, Italy, and Greece are much lower, so low that one can assume that each faculty person must have one or more "moonlighting" jobs in order to make a comfortable living. It should be noted that full chair professors are paid up to ten times as much as the average teacher in the universities. Ironically, the social image and prestige of a faculty member in low-paying countries is at least as high or higher than in the well-paying nations.

With this image, the professor finds little difficulty in being on one or more boards of directors of banks or industrial corporations, holding legal counseling positions, engaging in consulting, or holding a second teaching position in another university.

The tendency for the lower-paid faculty to hold more than one job diverts their attention away from students and instruction in search of alternate means of income. Students get short shrift everywhere, according to reports of student opinion in the news; and in these nations the facts seem well validated by the activities of the professors.

A second tendency resulting from this practice is that it makes the professor even more independent from the university than the common practice of making him an employee of the government rather than of a university. Both practices lead to the dissembling of the university as a "community" of scholars and students and makes it a place to run a quick class and then get out to other jobs to make a living. This division of faculty attention limits feelings of commitment to the students' welfare as well as to the university itself. Low pay for teaching has its costs even if substantial sums are "saved" by the state. The negative effects on the social organization of the university subject it to the pressures of students and outside organizations, and, as we will discuss further, the chair or professorship itself comes under fire from these same groups.

Still another problem occurs when university personnel are civil service employees of the government. Civil service normally results in a structured salary system so that persons would get the same pay in whichever university they worked, whether faculty members or staff. Graham Richards (1977) recently commented on this practice:

> In countries with state-regulated uniform salary scales it is impossible for a newly-created institution to attract the talent from older established centres to rise to the first division of quality. In the American capitalist system it is open to any institution to try to attract talent and to develop good research by means of simple financial inducement. In this way centres of excellence are created by a natural process rather than by government decree.
>
> A particularly important aspect of this process is the speed with which American science can become involved and pre-eminent in new fields. [P. 648]

In summary, while faculty reputations and image throughout the nations in the study were high, they appeared to be highest in nations that paid the lowest salaries; and there, the image itself was capitalized upon, being the chief selling feature in obtaining one or more other positions for additional compensation.

Faculty Ranking Systems

Budget officers in the ministries of Education and Finance in the European nations increasingly look upon the structure of the faculty as unfair, wasteful of resources, and inefficient in its operation, regardless of the size of the total budget for salaries. In the United States, the budget officers in many states believe that the faculties are paid too much (often more than the budget staffs), but they have seldom attacked the structure of faculty rank or faculty privileges, except for sabbatical leaves. In the United States, and to a somewhat lesser extent in other English-speaking nations, the ranking of teachers in colleges and universities falls into a regular hierarchy: from instructors at the bottom level, moving upward through assistant professors, associate professors, and full professors. Except in prestige universities, young instructors (who, because of surpluses, now have Ph.D.'s) expect to move to assistant professorships after three or fewer years of service with automatic regularity, merely because of acceptable performance and longevity. Promotion to associate professor, in most universities and many colleges, also provides tenure, so that review can be very stiff indeed in the more prestigious universities whereas approval is almost automatic in some of the lesser universities and colleges. In some institutions tenure is based almost entirely on longevity (usually seven or fewer years), and in some cases may be achieved in the rank of assistant professor. Nevertheless, each rank has status as part of the faculty; and only in the most elite of public and private institutions do the tenured faculty (usually from 40 to 70 percent) consider themselves a group separate from the other ranks for governing, elective offices, committee work, graduate instruction, or dissertation supervision. All members are employed by the institution in which they teach or conduct research, and the sense of being a single faculty is at least moderate to high not only for their own department and school or college, but the university itself. In other words, faculty members in the United States tend to be more informal with each other, and generally a communal spirit bridges the gap between their salary ranks. Administrators of U.S. universities might not share this charitable view of faculty colleagueship and commitment to an institution, but in comparison with their counterparts in the European universities, they are better off in this respect than they realize.

All five European nations in the study use the chair system as the basis for the appointment of full professors and the means for directing a department, discipline, or program. With a few reservations about Sweden and France, this person normally holds the only professorship in the unit, heads it, gives direction to its curriculum, and conducts himself as an oligarch slightly superior to his equals or

outright dictatorial and authoritarian. He is the chair and he is also
the department or discipline. He personally selects the other members of his teaching and research staff, assigns their work loads, determines which courses they teach, and otherwise runs the unit. His
subordinate teaching staff hold titles that give little hint that a career
ladder exists up which each might be expected to climb, given reasonable competence and time. Some positions are not considered
"faculty," even though the many persons holding faculty titles may
teach the majority of all classes and meet more students than the
people holding superior titles. Some teachers are not considered to
be part of the faculty even though they may have tenure under the labor
laws or laws of the Ministry of Education. The rank-consciousness
of teaching staff members and the pecking order of privilege prohib-
its the much freer comradeship found in the United States.

Regardless of a faculty member's experience or qualifications
for research and teaching, assessment of competence falls to the
chair or to a chair-dominated group decision process. Each subordinate teacher must rely on the chair for advancement, and when such
a subordinate applies for a better position at another university the
chair can effectively veto the move by fiat or by indicating his wishes
to the hiring chair. Especially during long periods of leveling or declining enrollment and restricted growth, the next lower-ranking faculty members wait for the chair to retire or to die; but as they say of
the justices of the United States Supreme Court (whose judges are appointed for life): "They never retire and are a long time a-dying."
Younger faculty members in European universities are at least as discouraged and demoralized about becoming full professors as those in
the worst circumstances in the United States.

Officials at high government levels recognize that many young
teachers may be more up-to-date in their fields and as professionally
competent as the chair. They also see the chair as the person who
receives the financial resources, faculty, and support staff for the
unit and maintains them in a fiefdom from which they may not be ex-
tracted for changes in program, new programs, or other services the
university might better provide to serve the students and the community. Collectively, the chairs control the internal governing and bud-
get-making pattern of institutions and spend the resources after appropriation. The university administration is delegated very little separate power by the state, except for maintenance of buildings, and
hence cannot control the allocation or reallocation of funds without
the consent of the chairs. (In the future, this situation may not apply
to Sweden, as noted by Lane in Chapter 6.

Moreover, the chairs have the same tenure under civil service
as the teaching "faculty" of almost all the universities. This makes
them employees of the government rather than of the university, and

as little subject to university control as the professors. Ministry officers believe this independence to be inimical to curricula change and to student relationships with the department, as well as to the university as a whole. They want more flexibility, adaptability, and accountability from the universities.

While university budgets as such include funds for some support services (often referred to as "stuff") and for maintaining grounds and buildings, these funds constitute such a small part of any departmental budget or chair domain that real control can seldom be exercised by manipulating those funds, even if a university rector were to be so headstrong or nonacademic as to try.

The results of this study show strong disillusionment with the chair system, and a widespread desire to modify or do away with the system altogether. Some authors give most of the credit for this waning influence to student activism since the late 1960s. The case studies, and my own interviews with high government officials, indicate that the student cause has been taken over by government officials, but for quite different reasons. Staff members and high semipolitical officers seem fairly unanimous in their desire to further weaken the chairs while strengthening the university administrations. These officials have undoubtedly influenced Parliament members, and Britain and the United States appear to them to have models that could be modified for local use. They see the academic disciplines in these countries as being less autonomous from the universities and more an integral part of an overall set of interconnected curricula and research programs that encompass a number of departments and schools.

The desired goal of continental reformers is to make the universities responsible and accountable for the activities of the chairs and their staffs, even to the point of having the university appoint or nominate the professors and other faculty rather than having them appointed, as they are now, by the Ministry of Education (sometimes with concurrence by the Ministry of Finance) or by parliamentary action (as formerly done in Sweden).

The chairs are being weakened, for the evidence in this study is clear enough for several countries. However, the process is very slow. Sweden is in transition toward the goal of transferring (or delegating) to the universities and other institutions of higher education the power to nominate members for teaching appointments approved by the government. Lane provides details for just how the reorganization is to take place. The French partially broke the power of the chair by arbitrary government action in appointing more than one, and sometimes several, professors to a single department or discipline formerly controlled exclusively by a single professor. This change is a result of student activism, according to officials. Naturally, one must assume that the ministry staffs were already sympathetic to the reform for reasons of their own.

Now that enrollments have leveled off or are dropping in some of the European countries, they too will be reconsidering the organization of their systems. Also the subprofessorial types (under a mélange of titles) have organized and joined the students in protesting the existing system. Government officials, with outside pressure from the public and from the universities, have found it opportune, under the reality of fiscal constraints, to encourage organizational and curricular changes. In periods of uncertainty, of course, higher authorities tend to shift the uncertainty down to lower levels. With the chair system in operation, they cannot do so. But through reorganization that makes the university administration the accountable unit, they succeed in both endeavors, that is, creating responsible decentralization and reforming the chair system.

However, the chair system has yet to be fully broken in any of the countries under study, although various attempts and plans have been effected to greatly limit the power of the chair in all countries but Italy. Their degree of success cannot be assessed for several more years at the earliest.

Faculty Tenure

In all of the European countries, faculty tenure is automatically provided under the same laws that apply to other government civil servants. Faculty members receive the same retirement, job security, cost-of-living increases, and pay adjustments as the classified employees of the government; indeed, they are classified employees of the government. This practice still prevails in isolated cases in the United States in state college systems and for nonacademic staffs in state colleges and universities, although some states such as Illinois have set up a separate "civil service" system for nonacademic employees of higher institutions. Even in the past, when many more faculties were under civil service regulations in the United States, they were seldom treated the same as other state employees; they were usually regarded as special and given different status than other government personnel.

In addition to the civil service laws that apply to European faculties, certain general labor or social security laws may also apply. Statutes of this sort do not allow a faculty member (or any other public employee) to be fired or dismissed for lack of work or because of the abolition of a program. These "rights" have often been gained at the insistence of labor unions who have succeeded in getting them included in the legislative programs of socialist parties.

In the short run, this kind of labor-law tenure (which applies to almost all employees working in the university, including faculties), provides for an indefinite regular salary level in lieu of unemployment compensation, as in the United States. In the United States the faculty member is laid off and then given only a portion of his salary as unemployment compensation. The practice in the United States is surely inimical to the welfare of the individual, but the university may look upon it with favor since the unemployment compensation paid to the person laid off does not come directly out of the university budget.

In the long run, these devices for providing indefinite employment regardless of work load have several consequences that could hurt the interests of higher education and have special ill effects on the size of the budgets for higher education and the inability to shift existing funds to new or expanding programs.

One example will suffice to illustrate these possible consequences. At one new European university, the department had 8 faculty members (a chair and 7 others) and 40 students at its peak enrollment. State planning had anticipated a much higher enrollment but as in other countries, enrollments declined. Even worse, enrollments dropped to a point at which this department had only four students and the same eight faculty members. A faculty member, however, could not be laid off or transferred by the university to other work unless he himself requested it, and even then the reallocation of manpower could be vetoed by the chair. These faculty members remained on regular salaries, received cost-of-living increases, and the regular increases for longevity under the civil service. Some taught no classes and indeed most had been underemployed even at the time when the department had 40 students. Hence the unit costs of maintaining this department (and other departments in similar straits) continued to rise spectacularly as enrollments declined. The faculty wanted the government to solve the problem by putting them to work on research, but with sums of money over and above the regularly appropriated funds for current research.

If such conditions continue over a long period of time, the normal operating costs that could be attributed to the university budget (including the faculty salaries in the government or ministry budget) would greatly increase, to make the unit costs exceedingly high. Worse, they would force higher education to consume a larger and larger proportion of the state funds available for public services. It is higher education rather than health or welfare or other services that in the public eye is leveling off in importance and in enrollment. Yet, as new money is added for new educational programs (and must be added since it cannot be reallocated from departments that are declining in enrollment and relevance), the old programs continue to increase in cost, thus compounding the cost problem. Over a long period of time the institutions become parking lots for the faculty and staff who remain to teach the diminishing number of students.

The other more serious consequence (since governments may raise sufficient funds to allow the extraordinary expenditures just mentioned) is the negative impact on the quality of the programs offered. The lack of constructive work with a rotating and challenging group of students soon leaves the average faculty member with little incentive to keep up in his field or to contribute to its development. Students generally enroll in popular or successful programs and will drop out of programs that are failing if they can do so without sacrificing years of previous education toward a degree. Faculty stagnation thus inevitably lowers the quality of a program.

A third important consequence of tenuring all faculty and staff, rather than allowing the surplus personnel to be thrown on the open market, is the loss of a well-trained pool of faculty manpower from which new and growing institutions could draw. Under current conditions, such persons may be found in one of these dying departments, but the longer they stay the less qualified and the less visible or desirable they become for being hired into a more productive situation. If forced into the open market, individual faculty members would make greater efforts to improve their skills and knowledge in order to compete for the good positions that become available.

Common Problems, Converging Outcomes

In 1977 David Babcock suggested, at a seminar at the Australian National University at Canberra, that educational trends in Europe and the United States were converging in goals and in practice. He argued that as the U.S. faculties become more and more tenured, as younger faculty members find it more and more difficult, if not impossible, to advance in rank, and as more part-time faculty members are employed (to save money and to prevent their possible tenure), U.S. practice more and more resembles the European chair system with its traditional and well-known deficiencies—an aging professoriate that controls the development of the curricula, the promotion of young faculty, and the decision process within the university.

The argument seems to have a great deal of validity. The facts support it. So does the reaction of younger faculty, of students who seek curricula changes, and of the permanent faculty who protest the increased hiring of part-time instructors. In both the United States and Europe, higher ministry officials and even politicians express grave concern about these conditions and appear willing to make substantive changes to correct them. The principal difference between the United States and Europe, however, is that U.S. faculties have

virtually no power to influence public policy. But during the coming
period of falling enrollments and oversupplies of doctorates, the politicians alone may take action to limit the percentage of faculty on
tenure, to limit the rate of promotion to tenure, to provide funds only
for part-time instructional help, and otherwise to take control of a
situation that in the European countries has often been largely thwarted
by the professors acting in consort. Only faculty unionism on a large
scale in the United States could produce anything resembling the power
of the European professors. In the more distinguished research universities, collective bargaining has not yet occurred and does not appear to be on the horizon. Hence in the United States, direct governmental action may solve problems that are indeed very similar to
those of the European nations. In Europe, with its plethora of coalition governments conditioned to the status quo, quick action to solve
common problems appears highly unlikely, even in Sweden, which has
already made the most progress toward constructing a more "rational"
model for control of the universities and the professoriate.

CONCLUDING COMMENT

In Chapters 7 and 8 we have attempted to analyze some of the principal issues that government officials in the five European nations and in the United States discussed during the course of our interviews with them. These issues arose also in part from the funding allocation problems dealt with in the individual chapters on the European nations.

We find that some problems are fairly common to all the states and nations. Each state and each nation approaches the solution of its problems from a historical context unlike that of any other state or nation. The solutions used in one of these nations may have great relevance for the solutions to similar problems in another nation or state. Certainly the trends seem to indicate that none of the problems discussed here have easy solutions and that the normal negotiating, bargaining, and procedural due processes of democratic societies tend to produce slow rather than sweeping change on any given issue. On both student and faculty issues, as well as on the technologies used for funding allocations, a tendency for opinion and practice to converge seems in the making between the states of the United States and these nations of Europe.

One should not conclude that the objective of this book has been to provide ready-made solutions to problems. Our objective has been to provide, through the case studies and the analyses of allocation procedures and issues relating to the funding of students and faculties, some insight into how the same problems or issues can be dealt with in different ways and yet achieve somewhat similar results. Some solutions can be borrowed from another state or nation and applied with little change in another political entity, but the evidence would indicate that more benefits derive from an understanding of how and why other nations deal with the same problem in diverse ways. Those insights may help any political entity in better comprehending its own problem and arriving at a solution entirely appropriate to its own traditions and practices. Inept borrowing of practice only complicates a problem and does not lead to the "right" solution. An understanding of the many dimensions of a problem seen from a variety of state or national perspectives may put a nation on its own internally constructed path to glory.

APPENDIX A

HISTORICAL BASES FOR
THE STUDY

During 1976/77, the Center for Research and Development in Higher Education at the University of California, Berkeley, completed a three-year study of budgeting practices and decision making in relation to higher education in 17 states of the United States.

This state budget study, resulting in six volumes, culminated 20 years of Center work on studies of state governmental coordination, planning, and financing of higher education institutions. The initial study, published in 1959, comparatively examined the operations, the strengths, and the weaknesses of 11 state-level coordinating agencies and statewide governing boards for public baccalaureate and graduate institutions, including in some states public community colleges. Following in 1966 and 1968 were case studies of Wisconsin and California by Gilbert Paltridge, who also evaluated the effectiveness of their two coordinating mechanisms. In 1962, T. R. McConnell published his Patterns of State Higher Education, generalizing on his own and the Center's previously published work, and on British higher education and coordination, which he had researched over the previous ten years. Ernest Palola directed a five-state study in 1968-70 comparing state planning practices, evaluating their effectiveness, and suggesting guidelines for the improvement of postsecondary education planning. In Public Universities, State Agencies, and the Law (1973), Dalglish and Glenny conducted a study of the four major state universities with constitutional autonomy and compared them with four similarly prestigious universities in other states that had only statutory powers. Finally, all of these Center authors, during intervening years, published journal articles and chapters for other books and gave addresses that further analyzed their research and ideas on relationships between higher education and the state.

SELECTION OF EUROPEAN NATIONS

In negotiation with the Ford Foundation, we agreed that one person in one year could make a fairly thorough examination and analysis of no more than five countries. The countries chosen were something of a compromise between those most like and least like the United States. The European ones assumed to have sophisticated, modern budgeting techniques most like those in the United States were Britain, some states in West Germany, Sweden, and France. At the same

187

time, we agreed that other nations not so advanced in budgeting technology, such as Spain, Italy, and Greece, should be included.

We agreed without much difficulty on five countries: Sweden, France, Spain, Italy, and Greece. Sweden, after seven years of discussion and political game playing, was finally decentralizing its universities and forming regional agencies for some planning and financing of universities and institutes. France was in the midst of attempts to decentralize to universities certain personnel and curricular matters formerly highly centralized at the state level. The Spanish tradition of centralism also seemed on the verge of being abandoned. Italy was assumed not to have changed a great deal in 20 years or more (Burton Clark 1976 and Barbara Burn 1971, 1973), and Greece was an unknown quantity in regard to governmental relationships with its universities.

PROCEDURES

The study of budgeting practices in the United States, which preceded the European component, consisted of investigation and analyses of 17 states. A moderately elaborate questionnaire was first sent to the heads of each of the state agencies that had some major responsibility for the operating budgets of public colleges and universities. In most states these agencies consisted of the governor's executive budget office, the legislative analyst, and the statewide coordinating or governing board for higher education. In addition, some legislators had staffed their appropriations committees to carry on very much the same kinds of budget analyses and reviews as the other agencies; these, too, were sent questionnaires. The questionnaire asked for basic information about the agency, the number of people working there (especially on higher education budgets), their education and experience, the legal documents delineating the authority of the agency to review budgets, and documentation of the exact role played by the agency in arriving at recommendations on higher education budgets.

The six-member team reviewed these materials at the Berkeley Center and later visited each of the 17 states for periods of one to two weeks, during which time every person from the lowest state analyst to the highest staff member was interviewed for an hour or more. For this purpose we prepared interview schedules appropriate to the level of decision making of the persons to be interviewed. Each interview was conducted by two or three members of the team, with two teams operating simultaneously in the state. During the interview, one or both members took notes (we did not tape record the interviews, hoping to obtain freer responses), and later dictated or wrote out the responses to the interview schedule and our evaluation of the persons interviewed. My own dictated notes on the interviews, which were primarily with the chiefs and deputies of each of the agencies, ran to about 500 typewritten pages. Each interviewer filled out an elaborate debriefing form consisting of some 50 pages of items from his notes for each state. These debriefing forms were used to produce a digest of some 84 tables of data and were also used by the persons writing the six-volume study that resulted.

The six-volume U.S. study investigated the complete decision-making process by staff members (not by politicians), from the time the budget left the institution until after the appropriation was signed by the governor. In preparing the present volume, comparing U.S. with European practice, we considerably changed the scope of research. Instead of examining with equal effort each element in the staff decision process, we decided first to focus somewhat more on the technical means used to construct or to review budgets and, second, to find the trends and issues that appeared likely to have a decided impact on budgets. In the United States, we found that in one state a formula was used to develop 90 percent of the operating budget; in other states a combination of formulas or guidelines and negotiation served; and in one state negotiation alone provided the means for arriving at the government figures. We also found that while the backgrounds of the staff reviewers differed according to the type of agency that employed them, an even wider disparity appeared in the training and experiences of staff members among the different states. We also determined which salient issues had heavy impact on the process and which subjects received detailed analyses. What would be found in Europe became the focus of the new investigation.

Since science and research bend toward the biases of the perceivers, we designed our research to avoid applying one person's perspective to all of these states. In each of the European nations, a contract was made with a scholar who would be familiar with the government, with its organization for budgeting, and with the problems of finance of colleges and universities. Each of these scholars wrote the case study for his own country. Two are political scientists, as I am, one is a sociologist, and two are economists.

In order that the case studies prepared by each of these professional researchers have some uniformity, an outline was provided of the major areas to be described and the data to be furnished. The outline left room for individual interpretation and for inserting factors and dealing with dimensions not included in the outline itself. Thus, the case studies take individual approaches but preserve the basic elements of the outline. As editor of the series of case studies and author of the comparative chapters, I reviewed each case report, eliminated extraneous material (such as descriptions of budgeting for building and capital purposes), and attempted to impose some uniformity in the use of the English language. The cases were then returned to the original authors, and also to one of the other officials in the nation whom I had interviewed, for final review and comment.

My role in each country was to read available documents about the system of higher education, particularly higher education issues and budget and finance practices; then to read the preliminary draft of the case study prepared by the contract author; and finally to interview the principal persons in ministries directly involved in making staff decisions on higher education budgets. Many of these persons spoke fluent English, but for others the contract scholar or a hired interpreter aided in the interviewing. The schedule of interviews was first suggested by the case study author, and then revised as I thought desirable. With the exception of a few people in the five European nations, I believe the persons interviewed were indeed those with the knowledge I sought. Notes were taken during the interviews and then elaborated on later the same day. After completing the above procedures, some additional data seemed necessary in order to deal adequately with budget issues. The authors willingly agreed to furnish it if possible. In some countries, records of higher education operations are not made public, and in others data are several years behind the current year. Even enrollments for the fall of 1976 could not be obtained for some nations when this manuscript went to press in 1978.

As a final note on procedure, one should be aware that the fieldwork in the United States was done during 1974/75, and the fieldwork for Europe during the fall of 1976 and the winter of 1977. (We have tried to make as uniform as possible all data for fiscal year 1974/75 and, where possible, 1975/76.) Data, however, do not appear to be as important to budget practice as the resolution of policy issues confronting the states. Data give only a statistical picture. For example, the cost per credit hour for a course may be determined and compared with much higher costs of similar courses in other colleges, but the policy decision as to the "reasonableness" of the different costs falls back on a judgment of quality in staff, faculty, and student output. Another example is the numbers of students attending a college. If the number falls 40 percent in a year or two, a major policy question of whether to keep certain programs or even the courses open must be decided. The data are clear—the decision on what to do may be very unclear. Analyses beyond data provide the content of the budget and hence reflect the technologies used to budget that content.

APPENDIX B

THE U.S. CASE STUDIES
AND DATA

This appendix deals with budgeting for public four-year colleges and universities. The budget process studied in each state was that which led to the development of the budget for the fiscal year 1974/75. Unless the context clearly indicates otherwise, the concern here is only with budget formulation for four-year colleges and universities and for those two-year campuses whose budgets are reviewed in a similar manner. In each state, budget practices, procedures, and structures—the state's budget process as a whole—form the unit of analysis. A major assumption, nevertheless, is that these processes operate through the interaction of three types of organizational or administrative structures present in most states: an executive budget staff, a legislative budget staff, and the budget staff of a state-level higher education agency. Specific dimensions of these three agency structures are used here to display and explain the descriptive data.

STRUCTURAL CLASSIFICATION OF AGENCY STAFFS

To simplify description of the 17 states in our study, 3 major agency structures are collapsed in the discussion that follows. In general, the data relate to 51 agency staffs in the 17 states: 16 executive budget offices, 29 legislative fiscal staffs, and 16 staffs of state higher education agencies. A brief discussion of each of these is required.

Executive Budget Staff

Every state but one, Mississippi, has an executive budget office. The staff that serves the Joint Executive-Legislative Commission on Budgeting and Accounting in Mississippi has at least one characteristic of an executive budget office: responsibility for allotment and control of funds. However, during budget development this commission is clearly responsible to the legislature rather than to the governor, who lacks a budget staff of his own.

Legislative Fiscal Staff

Staffs of the legislative committees are less easily categorized than those in executive budget offices. A state legislature may or may not employ a staff for a joint fiscal committee. Staff members may be assigned to individual committees from a central pool. Whether there is joint staff or not, the fiscal committees in either or both houses may or may not employ staffs. Committee staffs may be further divided to support the minority and majority party members. As a further complication, neither the staff of the unicameral legislature in Nebraska nor that of the executive-legislative commission in Mississippi really belongs to any of these classifications. For this descriptive report, categorization is simplified.

Joint Legislative Fiscal Committee Staff

In six states, joint legislative fiscal committees are served by a staff, and none of these staffs is divided along party lines. In addition, the commission staff in Mississippi, the legislative staff in Nebraska, and the single staff in Kansas are treated here as joint staffs.

Separate House Fiscal Committee Staff

In nine states, both houses of the legislature have staff support, and in one other, Tennessee, only the upper house is so served. In three of these states—Illinois, Pennsylvania, and Washington—each of the separate house staffs is divided along party lines. In general, however, we shall disregard this party division.

The organizational "units of analysis" for description, therefore, are:

Joint legislative staff, including staffs in Mississippi, Nebraska, and Kansas	9
Separate legislative staffs	
Upper-house staffs, disregarding majority and minority divisions	10
Lower-house staffs, disregarding majority and minority divisions	9
Total separate staffs	19
Total legislative fiscal staffs	28

Among the 17 state legislatures, 7 were supported only by a joint staff, 8 only by separate house staffs, and 2 by both a joint staff and a separate house staff.

State Higher Education Agency Staff

State higher education agency staffs are somewhat easier to describe because the agencies themselves have been subject to several
classifications in the past.[1] The possible dimensions can be reduced
to three to simplify display of data about their staffs. The voluntary
structure in Nebraska lacks a state-level staff. Whether state higher
education agencies that do have staffs also have statutory budget responsibilities is a major factor in the overall process. However, the
precise nature of such responsibility and the manner in which it is
exercised varies greatly. Categorization based only on statutory budget responsibility can thus be misleading. With this reservation in
mind, the three classifications are:

Consolidated governing board staff	5
Separate coordinating agency staff	8
State department of education staff	3
Total agency staffs in study	16

As useful as the above classification is for data presentation,
it does not do justice to the rich diversity of organizations interested
in the budget process. Florida, for example, is classified as a state
with a consolidated governing board. Yet that board is in fact an
agency of the state Department of Education, through which its budget
is submitted for perfunctory technical review. In Michigan, Kansas,
and Washington, administrative councils of institutional chief executive officers have substantial budget influence.

Summary

Although state budget <u>processes</u> are the ultimate subjects of
our analysis, our published report and this appendix generally display descriptive data according to the structural criteria of these 60
administrative staffs in the 17 states:

16 executive budget office staffs
28 legislative fiscal staffs, comprising
   9 joint legislative committee staffs
  10 upper-house committee staffs
   9 lower-house committee staffs
16 statewide higher education agency staffs, comprising
   5 consolidated governing boards
   8 separate coordinating agencies for
   3 state departments of education

STAFF ORGANIZATION

The organization of the state administrative agencies that review higher education operating budgets is inseparable from the
broader context of state government. The traditional political and
governmental roles of the governor and legislature (usually implicit)
are major factors in executive and legislative staff organization. On
the other hand, the staffs of the state higher education agencies, which
have lacked the long tradition of political roles, are far more likely
than executive or legislative staffs to have their responsibilities ex-
plicitly mandated by statute.

Executive and Legislative Staff

Organizational structures reflect the differing political roles
of the governor and the legislature in several ways. Because executive budget staff members formulate the entire governor's budget during each budget cycle, they must, if only to check their numbers, review higher education budgets on a regular and routine basis. Legislative review, on the other hand, is often less structured and more
selective. However, in states such as California, Colorado, Michigan, and Texas, the legislative fiscal staffs engage in comprehensive
reviews of budgets.

Staff Size and Effort

Organizationally, executive budget staffs are larger than the
others, both in their entirety and in the number of analysts specifically
assigned to higher education (see Table B.1). Among legislative
staffs, as would be expected, a joint staff utilizes more analysts than
a separate house staff. Even if a state higher education agency has
budget responsibilities, staff assignments for them can rarely be
fixed with certainty. The assignment of only one or two analysts for
budget review in Illinois, for example, does not reflect the redirec-
tion of program analysts or capital budget analysts to the operating
budget task at "budget time." Among the three types of staffs, the
growth in numbers and influence of legislative fiscal staffs in almost
all of the 17 states is distinctive. In Kansas and Virginia such staffs
have been recently created, and in these states and elsewhere legislative staff growth seems certain to be an important influence on state
budget procedures for higher education in the future.
Less difference is found in contrasting staff perceptions of how
time is spent in budget review (see Table B.2): although executive
budget staffs perceive a great amount of routine and technical budget

TABLE B.1

Full-time Professional Staff Assigned to Higher Education
Operating Budget Review, by Types of Staffs

	None or a Fractional Position	One Posi- tion	Two or Three Positions	Four or More Positions
Executive budget office (16 states)	n.a.	2	5	9
Legislative staff Joint staff (9 states)	1	2	3	3
Separate staff (10 states)	4	7	7	n.a.
State higher education agency (16 states)*	2	3	5	6

n.a.: data not available

*State higher education agency figures do not include Florida's
other agency, the state Department of Education.

Source: Compiled by the author.

work (such as recalculating formula factors), so do legislative and
higher education staffs. Four legislative staffs (in New York, Florida, Hawaii, and Wisconsin) and two executive budget office staffs (in
Colorado and Nebraska) perceived their time as equally divided between policy and routine review.

Organizational Distance

The state budget office may be located either in the governor's
office or in a separate department or agency.[2] Regardless of the location, however, an analyst in the executive budget office is inevitably farther removed organizationally from the governor, the elected
official to whom he is responsible, than is a legislative analyst from
the legislators.

State Higher Education Agency Staff Functions

The staffs of the state higher education agencies are very different from those of the governors and legislatures. Although it is possible to generalize from the governmental roles of the latter to the

TABLE B.2

Staff Perceptions of Budget Review Effort as Routine or Policy

Type of Staff	Number of Agencies Perceiving			
	More than 50 Percent of Time Spent in Routine Review	More than 50 Percent of Time Spent in Policy Review	Equal Time Spent on Both	No Re-sponse
Executive budget office (16 states)	9	4	2	1
Legislative staff				
Joint staff (9 states)	2	2	1	4
Separate staff (10 states)	4	3	3	8
State higher education agency (16 states)*	7	5	1	3

*State higher education agency figures do not include Florida's other agency, the state Department of Education.

Source: Compiled by the author.

budget roles of their supporting staffs, such generalization about state higher education agency staffs is precluded by the wide variations in structure and responsibilities of the agencies themselves. The budget responsibilities of a consolidated governing board may be implicit in its governing authority, but those of a separate coordinating agency or state board of education usually result from statutory mandate. Higher education master planning; determination of campus role, scope, or mission; and review of academic programs are common statutory functions of state higher education agencies (see Table B.3). Although statutory provisions are usually a reasonable guide to the budgetary role of a state higher education agency, this is not always the case. Historically, in California the coordinating agency has deliberately chosen not to exercise the advisory budget authority given it by statute. On the other hand, the coordinating agencies in Texas and Washington are seen as having a substantial budget role despite their limited statutory powers.

TABLE B.3

Statutory Responsibility for Information, Tuition, and Budget
Formulas, by Types of State Higher Education Agencies

| | Statutory Responsibility | | |
| | | Review or Approval of | |
Type of Agency	Information Collection	Tuition Levels	Budget Formulas
Consolidated governing boards (5)	4	5	3
Separate coordinating agencies (8)	8	4	5
State boards of education (3)	1	1	n.a.
Total (16 agencies)	13	10	8

n.a.: data not available

Source: Compiled by the author.

STAFF PERSONNEL MATTERS

The differing personnel policies of state executive, legislative,
and higher education agencies influence, we must assume, the differing budget processes in the states. The formal aspects of civil service and recruiting policy discussed here are fairly easily classified,
yet less easily classified factors may be of equal or greater importance. Both formal policy and conventional wisdom tend to stereotype
agency personnel: the executive budget analyst is a career professional in his particular state; the legislative analyst is an aspiring
politician; the higher education analyst is a career professional also,
but in a national arena. The grain of truth in these stereotypes should
not obscure the fact that in some states an individual may hold two,
or perhaps all three, of these positions over a relatively short period
of time. Personnel are people, and they live as well as work in Al-
bany, Sacramento, and Austin and move among the agencies as opportunity presents itself.

Civil Service

The applicability of civil service or similar statewide regulations to executive and legislative staffs is fairly consistent across

TABLE B.4

Applicability of Civil Service Regulations to State Higher Education
Agency Staffs

	Applicable	Not Applicable
Consolidated governing boards (5)	1	4
Separate coordinating agencies (8)	3	5
State departments of education (3)	3	n.a.
Total (16 agencies)	7	9

n.a.: data not available

Source: Compiled by the author.

states (see Table B.4). As might be expected, executive staffs are
generally subject to such regulations and legislative staffs are not.
Executive budget staffs in Illinois and Tennessee are the only such
staffs not covered by civil service. The joint executive-legislative
commission staff in Mississippi is considered a legislative staff in
this report, and is the only such staff covered by civil service, although the legislative fiscal bureau in Wisconsin adheres to the state
civil service regulations. Greater variation, however, exists in the
applicability of these regulations to the state higher education agencies. Robert O. Berdahl has suggested that qualified persons may be
discouraged from serving on coordinating agencies by state salary
schedules and other civil service restrictions.[3]

Academic Background and Recruiting Policy

Allen Schick has suggested that the type of budget review a
state agency performs may be revealed by the academic background
of the staff.[4] While it is possible that such a relationship will emerge,
the descriptive data alone offer little direction for further analysis.
Executive and legislative budget agencies are generally less interested
in recruiting specialists than in hiring a "good man" regardless of
academic background. Public or business administration, political
science, and economics are preferred backgrounds for both agencies.
More legislatures than executive agencies seek an accounting background for staff members, but neither shows any great interest in a
disciplinary background in educational administration. Although state

higher education agencies are, of course, more likely to look for background in educational administration for their staffs in general, they appear to be as likely as other agencies to prefer a business administration background for members of budget staffs.

General policies or tendencies with respect to other aspects of recruiting allow limited generalization: executive budget offices, followed by legislative committees, are more likely than other agencies to recruit professional staff members directly from college. With only two exceptions, state higher education agencies appear to expect their staff to have had experience before they are recruited. Similarly, although both executive and legislative agencies look to their own state as the recruiting pool, state higher education agencies in most states appear willing to go outside the state for higher education budget staff members. More than other agencies, legislative fiscal staffs look to other state agencies for staff members, but this is characteristic of only 6 of the 17 state agencies. Campuses within the state are not often considered a source of staff personnel for executive and legislative agencies, and only slightly more than half of the state higher education agencies see campuses as a source. Few executive and legislative agencies and only one state higher education agency look to business or industry as a source of staff personnel.

PROCESS AND PROCEDURE

State budget organizations are difficult to describe because of their numbers and variety. Description of the budget processes across states not only encompasses structurally based difficulties but compounds them: the activity of each agency interacts and relates to that of another. Moreover, as Robert D. Lee and Ronald W. Johnson note, and as our study confirms: "Though the same institutional units may exist over time, both procedures and substantive content vary from year to year."[5] They ascribe the protean nature of the formulation procedures to the many efforts at budget reform. Evidence of procedural instability because of such reform is found in five states: Hawaii, Michigan, New York, Pennsylvania, and Wisconsin. Curiously, higher education budgets appear to be the earliest targets of reformers. But for higher education budgeting, at least, procedural changes from year to year may be equally attributable to less formal causes: when, as in Colorado or Connecticut, for example, legislative staff analysis is largely the province of one person, the professional interests of the individual holding the position will influence the process as a whole. In addition, political and policy differences between the governor and the legislature, as in New York, or within the legislature itself, as in Illinois, may have substantial impact on the budget process even though that impact is merely a by-product of other concerns. The influence of these three compounding factors, that is, deliberate budget reforms, the interaction of the several agencies, and professional or political concerns, is best understood descriptively in the context of the individual states. Moreover, the increasing impact of revenue constraints in every state requires staff adaptation.

Subject to these important limitations, describing the major phases of budget processes is less difficult than describing the organizations that participate in them. (The processes and procedures of all 17 states can generally be classified chronologically.) Tables B.5 through B.8 are presented to show the variation among the 17 states in budget analytic and allocation procedures. Each is self-explanatory. Some states use more than one type of analysis and may use three or four different ones in order to gain various perspectives on the budgets. The flow of information and data from one agency to another is shown in Figure B.1, which follows the four tables. Again, one should observe the differences among these states, differences that typify all states in the United States.

Rather than providing a summary of procedures in all 17 states, 4 case studies to show the diversity of the agencies and the analytical and review procedures utilized are briefly described in the following pages.

CALIFORNIA (1974/75)

Formulation of higher education operating budgets in California is characterized by: (1) large staffs of those agencies actively concerned with budget review and analysis; (2) the strong budget role of the three multicampus systems vis-à-vis the coordinating agency and individual campuses; (3) ambiguity concerning the budget role of the new California Postsecondary Education Commission in relation to the roles of the Budget Division and the Office of the Legislative Analyst; (4) lengthy legislative hearings; (5) the policy of staff rotation between budget cycles in the Budget Division; and (6) the role of the Director of Finance as the representative of higher education in the governor's cabinet. California has an annual budget with a fiscal year beginning July 1 (see Figure B.2). The responsible state agencies are as follows.

Executive Branch

The Budget Division of the Department of Finance (DOF) has a professional staff of 101, with 9.5 professional positions assigned to

TABLE B.5

State Agency Review of Higher Education Operating Budgets: Computerized Data Bases

State	Executive Budget Office Tabulation	Analysis	Legislative Fiscal Staff Tabulation	Analysis	Constitutional Governing Board Tabulation	Analysis	Coordinating Agency Tabulation	Analysis	State Department of Education Tabulation	Analysis
California	x									
Colorado	x									
Connecticut	x		x				x			
Florida	x	x	x	x	x	x				
Hawaii	x				x	x				
Illinois							x	x		
Kansas										
Michigan			x	x						
Mississippi					x					
Nebraska	x	x	x	x						
New York										
Pennsylvania			x						x	
Tennessee							x	x		
Texas							x	x		
Virginia	x	x					x	x		
Washington	x	x		x			x	x		
Wisconsin					x	x				x
Total	8	4	5	4	4	3	6	5	1	1

Note: "Tabulation" is the use of a computerized running account of budgetary data to provide data arrays and totals. "Analysis" is the use of computerized data bases to evaluate budget decision alternatives.

State notes:

Illinois: Both the legislative and executive budget staffs can use Board of Higher Education data.
Nebraska: The 1202 Commission has an enrollment projection model that will be used by the Legislative Fiscal Office.
Pennsylvania: The State Department of Education uses a computer to aid in the calculation of budgets for the state colleges.
Texas: Data collected by the Coordinating Board are available to the governor's Budget Office and the Legislative Budget Board.
Virginia: The Council of Higher Education is converting its extensive data base to machine-usable form.

Source: Compiled by the author.

TABLE B.6

Factors or Formula Elements Used in Review of the Instructional Portion of Higher Education Operating Budgets: Student Credit Unit per FTE Faculty

State	Identification by Levels of Instruction of Student					Program or Discipline
	Lower Division, Upper Division, M.A., Ph.D.	Lower Division, Upper Division, Graduate	Undergraduate, M.A., Ph.D.	Undergraduate, Graduate	None	
California					x	x
Colorado	x					x
Connecticut					x	
Florida	x					x
Hawaii						
Illinois						
Kansas						
Michigan						
Mississippi						
Nebraska	x					
New York						
Pennsylvania					x	
Tennessee						
Texas						
Virginia						
Washington	x					x
Wisconsin						
Total	4	0	0	0	3	4

State notes:

California: The State University and Colleges use formulas to generate a portion of their budget, but the state agencies that review CSUC budgets do not use them as the basis for their analysis.

Connecticut: The budget indicator (SCHLDE's) equates all student contact hours to a lower division equivalent; consequently, levels are taken into account but not specifically identified. SCHLDE ratios are calculated for each constituent unit and are applied with some uniformity across institutions.

Nebraska: Although the staff of the Legislative Fiscal Office is now philosophically opposed to formulas, it appears to have made adjustments in the past on the basis of a formula that specifies lower division, upper division, and graduate level ratios.

Pennsylvania: Individual campuses are not identified in the universities' budget submissions.

Washington: The basic faculty staffing ratios apply to all programs except engineering, architecture, fisheries, and forestry, which use a lower ratio.

Source: Compiled by the author.

TABLE B.7

Factors or Formula Elements Used in Review of the Instructional Portion of Higher Education Operating Budgets: Student-Faculty Ratios

State	Identification by Levels of Instruction of Student					Program or Discipline
	Lower Division, Upper Division, M.A., Ph.D.	Lower Division, Upper Division, Graduate	Undergraduate, M.A., Ph.D.	Undergraduate, Graduate	None	
California						
Colorado						
Connecticut					x	x
Florida						
Hawaii						
Illinois	x					
Kansas					x	
Michigan						
Mississippi		x				
Nebraska						
New York	x					
Pennsylvania						
Tennessee						
Texas			x			
Virginia	x					x
Washington						
Wisconsin						
Total	3	1	1	0	2	2

State notes:

Illinois: The Board of Higher Education uses a weighted student-faculty ratio.

Kansas: The student-faculty ratio is 15:1 at universities and 20:1 at state colleges.

Mississippi: For the 1975/76 budget request, the student-faculty ratio based formula will be replaced by a unit-cost formula in which 1973/74 student credit-hour costs by lower, upper, and graduate levels and field of study for each of three clusters of institutions will be used to generate the instructional portion of the operating budget.

Source: Compiled by the author.

Factors or Formula Elements Used in Review of the Instructional Portion of Higher Education Operating Budgets: Unit Costs

State	Costs per Student Credit Unit	Costs per FTE Student	Costs by Program or Discipline
California			
Colorado		x	
Connecticut			
Florida	x		x
Hawaii	x		x
Illinois	x	x	x
Kansas			
Michigan		x	
Mississippi			
Nebraska			
New York			
Pennsylvania			x
Tennessee	x		x
Texas	x		x
Virginia			
Washington		x	x
Wisconsin	x	x	x
Total	6	5	8

State notes:

Colorado: Unit costs are used in determining the level of tuition for each campus.

Florida: Unit costs are used only for generating community college budgets.

Illinois: Unit costs are by weighted full-time equivalent student (FTES).

Michigan: The legislative fiscal staff uses unit costs to adjust base budgets for enrollment changes.

Pennsylvania: Unit cost data are collected from the state-owned institutions.

Tennessee: Program costs are identified at seven levels of instruction. Organization aggregation of data is "state" in the sense that formula rates are based on a weighted statewide average.

Texas: Unit cost data from out-of-state are used in the development of formulas.

Washington: Unit cost studies, conducted by the Council on Higher Education, have not been formally incorporated into a statewide formula or indicator but are available for state agencies to use in their budget analyses.

Wisconsin: The formula applies to the budget increment only by level of student (four levels).

Source: Compiled by the author.

FIGURE B.1

Data Information and Analytical Flow among Agencies in Four States

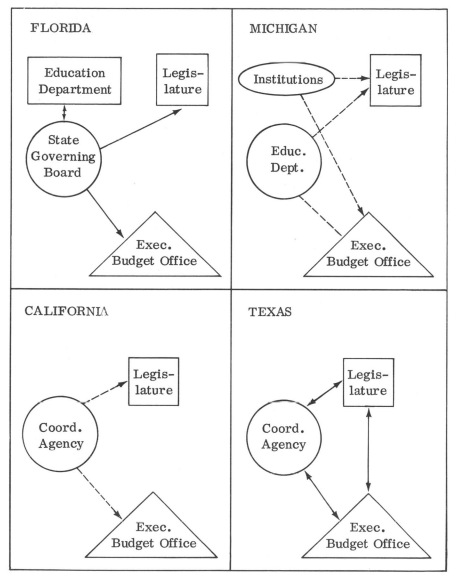

Key: Solid lines indicate greater volume of communication than the dotted lines. Arrows indicate the dominant direction of information and data flow.

Source: Compiled by the author.

FIGURE B.2

California: Higher Education Operating Budget Flow Chart, 1974/75 Budget

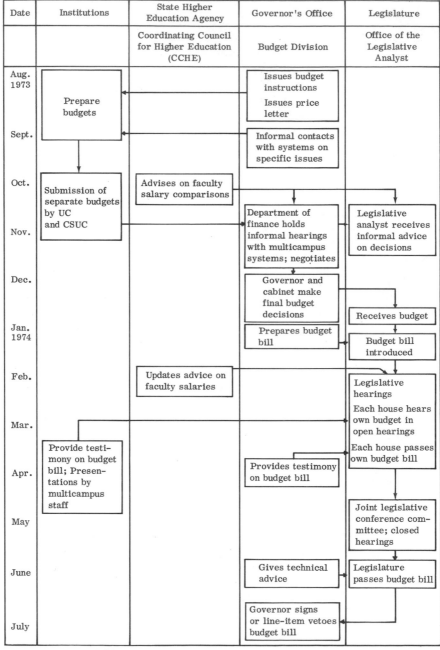

Date	Institutions	State Higher Education Agency	Governor's Office	Legislature
		Coordinating Council for Higher Education (CCHE)	Budget Division	Office of the Legislative Analyst
Aug. 1973	Prepare budgets		Issues budget instructions Issues price letter	
Sept.			Informal contacts with systems on specific issues	
Oct.	Submission of separate budgets by UC and CSUC	Advises on faculty salary comparisons		
Nov.			Department of finance holds informal hearings with multicampus systems; negotiates	Legislative analyst receives informal advice on decisions
Dec.			Governor and cabinet make final budget decisions	
Jan. 1974			Prepares budget bill	Receives budget Budget bill introduced
Feb.		Updates advice on faculty salaries		Legislative hearings Each house hears own budget in open hearings
Mar.	Provide testimony on budget bill; Presentations by multicampus staff			Each house passes own budget bill
Apr.			Provides testimony on budget bill	
May				Joint legislative conference committee; closed hearings
June			Gives technical advice	Legislature passes budget bill
July			Governor signs or line-item vetoes budget bill	

Source: Compiled by the author.

higher education operating budgets. The Audit Division in DOF has 40 professional staff members, 8 to 10 of whom engage in program audits of higher education.

Legislative Branch

The Office of the Legislative Analyst for the Joint Legislative Budget Committee (Legislative Analyst) has 42 professional staff members, of whom 3 are responsible for higher education operating budgets. In addition, the lower house fiscal committee has one full-time staff member with higher education responsibilities. Staff members of the Office of the Legislative Analyst also engage in program audits of higher education. In addition, the auditor general, with a professional staff of 50, also conducts program audits of higher education.

State Higher Education Agency

The California Postsecondary Education Commission (CPEC) replaced the Coordinating Council for Higher Education (CCHE) in 1974, retaining all CCHE staff members except the director. CPEC has 18 professional staff members. Prior to 1974, CCHE staff analyzed faculty salary data and prepared an analysis of the costs of instruction. CPEC is continuing these studies. Findings are available to budget review agencies. CPEC staff organization is still under development.

Higher Education Coordination and Governance

CPEC is a coordinating agency with limited budget responsibility for advising on institutional budget priorities, student financial aid, and tuition. Historically, CCHE did not exercise budget authority other than through its annual or other special short-term studies. It is not yet clear what budget role the new CPEC will play. CPEC coordinates 28 four-year college and university campuses governed by two multicampus boards: the University of California (UC) with constitutional status and the statutory California State University and Colleges (CSUC). It also coordinates 100 two-year campuses, which are governed by 70 local district boards and loosely supervised by a statewide board. The state provides a portion of the funds for two-year campuses through a foundation program that employs an ADA equalization formula.

Major Elements of the Budget Process

Presubmission Activity

Procedural budget instructions are issued by DOF in August, first with a general policy letter and later by a "price letter" indicating general cost increases for utilities and commodities. Overall percentage increase targets are provided for each of the three segments. Informal contacts between DOF, the Legislative Analyst's staff, and the two senior segments are frequent. Contacts are usually structured around specific policy issues that have been identified by budget staffs or other agency staffs and reviewed by political leaders.

Budget Requests

Budget requests differ among the segments of higher education. The UC request is a consolidation of the campus requests, after review, without identification of individual campus amounts. The budget is presented in seven major program categories that resemble the WICHE/NCHEMS PCS[6] elements, but those contents differ significantly. The CSUC request has adopted the seven PCS program elements. The budget for each CSUC campus is presented employing this format. The requests from both segments identify separately "base adjustments" and "program maintenance and new program proposals." Both UC and CSUC system budget requests contain considerable narrative justification. All requests are submitted simultaneously to the Department of Finance and to the Legislative Analyst.

Review and Analysis

Review by the Department of Finance entails, first, an analysis of adjustments to the previous year's "budget base," such as price changes and salary increases. Then an analysis is made of "program change proposals," such as improvements of existing programs and the initiation of new programs. Analyses are buttressed by intensive short-range policy studies initiated by staff but approved by top officials. These studies are available to institutions but not generally published. The Legislative Analyst's staff does not find the broad program categories used for review by DOF useful for their analysis; it looks at specific increases and singles out particular priority items for examination. An analysis also is made of the governor's changes in the system's requests. The Legislative Analyst provides the staff for the Senate Finance Committee and works closely with the staff of the Assembly Ways and Means Committee. Studies undertaken by the Legislative Analyst's office become public documents. No formal statewide information system exists, although CPEC is being encouraged to develop one. The budget instructions and routine and special requests made during the budget process provide the core of basic data utilized. These data are supplemented by the findings of the special studies. Although statewide analytic procedures based on student credit units per FTE faculty member have been proposed by DOF, they are yet to be fully implemented. A 1960 statutory master plan for higher education provides a general policy framework for budget review. The new CPEC has been given continuing planning responsibilities and is developing a five-year statewide plan.

DOF Hearings

In November the director of Finance holds hearings from one-half to one full day on the budget requests of the two senior segments. Hearings are based on DOF staff special studies and are preceded by extensive informal staff negotiations. Legislative staff members currently do not attend these hearings, although there is a good deal of informal communication on issues at the staff level.

Governor's Budget

The governor's budget, submitted to the legislature in January, contains both narrative and less extensive quantitative justifications. It is in program form, similar to the institutional requests. Operating budget requests are by segment with the request for the UC system shown only in total, and for the CSUC system by campus.

Legislative Hearings

In March and April the fiscal committees in each house hold hearings on the governor's budget, those in the lower house extending over several weeks. The legislature is advised by specific recommendations in a formal report of the Legislative Analyst as well as by the fiscal committee staffs. The staff of the Legislative Analyst presents its recommendations to the committees. Multicampus system administrators testify, and DOF staff members attend and defend the governor's budget. Final decisions on particular items are made as the hearings proceed.

Budget Bill

The budget bill is drafted by the DOF and appropriates funds by segment rather than by campus, with the bulk of funds in a single line for each.

Control and Veto

The budget bill contains specific control language desired by the executive and legislative branches. In addition, the conference committee issues a report to further express legislative intent, often in substantial detail. The governor has line-item veto authority and can reduce appropriations within lines.

FLORIDA (1974/75)

Formulation of higher education operating budgets in Florida is characterized by: (1) an unusual governance structure, with a single governing board and chancellor for the senior public institutions, and a separate board for the community colleges, with both boards under an elected commissioner of education; (2) use for the last five to six years of an extensive productivity-based formula that generates approximately 80 to 90 percent of the budget requests of the senior institutions; (3) a reasonably even division of influence and power between the various state-level agencies involved in budgeting; and (4) a recently inaugurated "Programs of Distinction" plan, whereby resources beyond those generated by formula are allocated to designated disciplines. Florida has an annual budget with a fiscal year beginning on July 1 (see Figure B.3). The responsible state agencies are as follows.

Executive Branch

The Division of Budget, Department of Administration (DOA) has a professional staff of 29, four of whom are responsible for higher education operating budgets.

Legislative Branch

The House Appropriations Committee has a professional staff of ten, one of whom is responsible for higher education operating budgets. The Senate Ways and Means Committee also has a professional staff of ten, one of whom is responsible for higher education operating budgets.

Major State Higher Education Agency

The Board of Regents (BOR) of the State University System of Florida (SUSOF) has a professional staff of 43, 11 of whom have responsibility for higher education operating budgets.

FIGURE B.3.

Florida: Higher Education Operating Budget Flow Chart, 1974/75 Budget

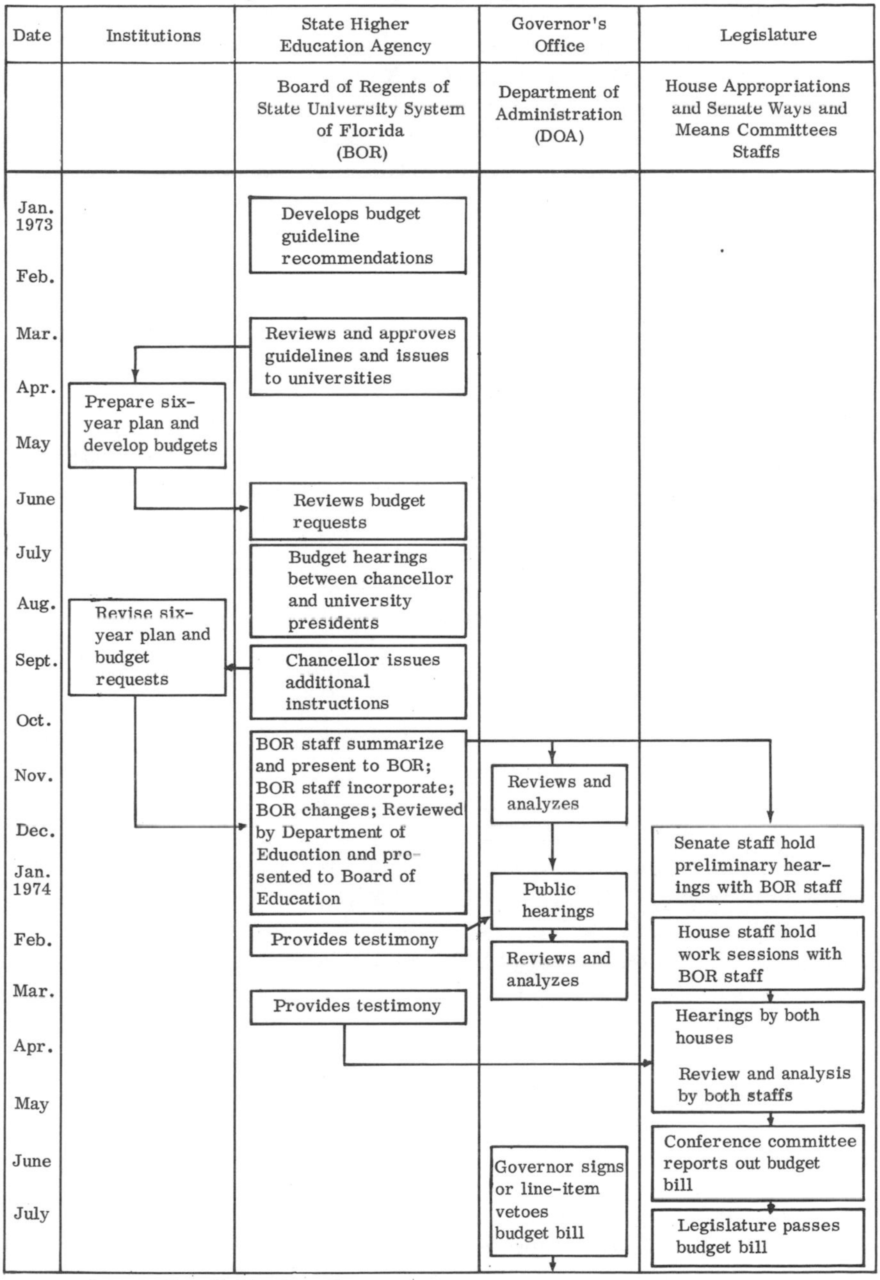

Date	Institutions	State Higher Education Agency	Governor's Office	Legislature
		Board of Regents of State University System of Florida (BOR)	Department of Administration (DOA)	House Appropriations and Senate Ways and Means Committees Staffs
Jan. 1973 Feb.		Develops budget guideline recommendations		
Mar. Apr. May	Prepare six-year plan and develop budgets	Reviews and approves guidelines and issues to universities		
June		Reviews budget requests		
July Aug. Sept. Oct.	Revise six-year plan and budget requests	Budget hearings between chancellor and university presidents / Chancellor issues additional instructions		
Nov. Dec. Jan. 1974		BOR staff summarize and present to BOR; BOR staff incorporate; BOR changes; Reviewed by Department of Education and presented to Board of Education	Reviews and analyzes / Public hearings	Senate staff hold preliminary hearings with BOR staff
Feb. Mar.		Provides testimony / Provides testimony	Reviews and analyzes	House staff hold work sessions with BOR staff
Apr. May				Hearings by both houses / Review and analysis by both staffs
June July			Governor signs or line-item vetoes budget bill	Conference committee reports out budget bill / Legislature passes budget bill

Source: Compiled by the author.

213

Higher Education Coordination and Governance

The BOR is a consolidated governing board that reviews and approves campus budget requests and prepares and submits a consolidated budget to the Department of Education (DOE), the State Board of Education, the governor, and the legislature. The BOR is responsible for the governance and coordination of five four-year universities and four senior level institutions (which offer third- and fourth-year baccalaureate programs). The BOR is one of four divisions in the DOE and reports to an elected commissioner and the Board of Education. The Board of Education is composed of the governor and six elected state officials, with the governor serving as chairman. The six officials are members of the governor's cabinet. The SUSOF is a state agency subject to all state regulations. The 28 community colleges are coordinated by a single board, which is one of the four divisions in the DOE. The community colleges have local boards, yet are fully state-funded on the basis of a cost-per-student formula. The community colleges are not subject to the same state controls as the SUSOF.

Major Elements of the Budget Process

Presubmission Activity

Budget instructions are issued to the BOR by the DOA in late July. The DOA emphasis is on format, but the instructions do include guidelines for inflation factors, replacement costs, and the like. The DOE issues instructions and guidelines that are supplemental to those issued by the DOA. In May the DOA gives the BOR staff an estimate of the state general revenues. A Program-Planning-Budget committee, with one representative from each institution, meets 15 to 20 times each year to discuss budget procedures. The committee is advisory to the chancellor. A PPB subcommittee on enrollments makes forecasts of total SUSOF enrollments. The institutions adjust their forecasts to fit the total. Another PPB subcommittee on budget preparation develops guidelines and formats for use within SUSOF.

Budget Requests

The SUSOF generates a total budget request for all institutions, using formulas and data supplied by campuses. Institutions are given budget base figures, so that their requests to the BOR staff in June or July include only requested increases over the base amount. The institutions do not submit a comprehensive budget request but, instead, submit a narrative listing of issues, special problems, proposed program changes, and priorities that are negotiated with the SUSOF. Institutions had previously been required to submit six-year plans, but this exercise was abandoned beginning with the 1975/76 fiscal year. Priorities set by the university presidents are documented between July and September using the institutional staffs as a resource. The legislature has mandated the use of the NCHEMS/PCS format for the BOR request. Individual institutions are not identified in the education and general (E&G) portion of the BOR recommendations. The E&G request represents the major portion of the budget. The DOA receives a preliminary budget in October, makes changes, and returns it to the BOR for correction. The BOR request is reviewed by the DOE and presented to the Board of Education in October, prior to final submission to the DOA by November 1. The legislature receives copies of the request at this time.

Review and Analysis

The BOR builds a budget base largely with the aid of formulas. The BOR reviews new programs, then decides upon a dollar total that would be available for new or expanded programs over and above what the formula generates. Productivity criteria are used to eliminate ongoing programs. In general, productivity factors and workload coefficients have remained reasonably constant. The DOE staff read all budgets for consistency, mathematical accuracy, and readability. The focus of DOE review is on dollar totals; it is not a substantive review, and the DOE staff usually does not make changes on issues. The DOA first conducts a preliminary analysis, checking the technical accuracy of the BOR requests. It relies on the latest fall enrollments for its work, and uses these to adjust the BOR figures if necessary. Issue papers are prepared, and a policy group within the DOA makes decisions on the issues identified and provides the DOA analysts with guidelines for further evaluation. The DOA staff does not look at data from individual institutions; for information needs, it deals primarily with the BOR staff. The House Appropriations Committee staff members start with the BOR request and, from their own data, develop their recommendations. The Senate Ways and Means Committee staff members prepare an analysis of the agency request and the governor's recommendation for each budget entity, identifying decision points, major policies and issues, and dollar implications. These analyses are presented to the subcommittee responsible for education budgets for its consideration, action, and recommendations. The staff members do not make explicit recommendations.

Hearings

The BOR staff budget hearings between the chancellor and the university presidents are usually held in late July and last at least two days. The BOR staff is present and makes presentations by budget program. Institutional staff members are also present. Priorities are set and voted upon by the presidents. The chancellor and the president develop a gross estimate of need, based upon student-drive models, inflation factors, and special needs. The institutions are not involved in any hearings after these negotiations with the BOR staff. In December or January, the DOA holds a conference with high-level officials from both the BOR and the DOA staffs; these negotiations are an opportunity for the BOR staff to plead its case for programs eliminated or reduced during budget review. The governor holds public hearings early in January.

Governor's Budget

The governor's budget is submitted to the legislature in March. The budget is in program format: education and general (E&G) is the major budget entity with 13 major components, which include instruction and research activities, administrative support, and physical plant management. The E&G entity, however, is summarized by object of expenditure, for example, in terms of salaries, other personal services, expenses, operating capital outlay, and special categories. In addition to the primary E&G entity, there are seven other entities, mostly consisting of organizations such as schools of medicine, the engineering experiment station, and the agricultural experiment stations and extension service. There is no narrative justification, but the DOA changes in the BOR request are shown.

Legislative Hearings

A subcommittee of the Senate Ways and Means Committee holds preliminary hearings with the Board of Regents' staff in December or January. These hearings are structured to determine the impact of actions taken by the prior legislature on institutional operations, to review the current legislative request, and to identify major problems, policies, and issues of special interest to the Board of Regents or the subcommittee. The hearings generally are not adversary in nature. The DOA staff is present. The BOR staff determine which institutional staff shall attend. The House Appropriations Committee subcommittees and staff hold daily meetings with the BOR staff two or three weeks before the legislative sessions open and begin to focus on key issues. (Because of the personalities involved in 1974/75, however, this did not, in fact, occur.) All sessions are open to the public. Both houses hold hearings in March or April, when testimony is presented by the BOR, DOE, and DOA staffs.

Budget Bill

Each house passes a budget bill. A conference committee negotiates the final bill. There is a single consolidated bill for all state activity. Funds are appropriated within the E&G program according to object of expenditure. The number of allowable positions is also indicated. The appropriation is made to the SUSOF. Accompanying the budget bill is a statement of legislative actions and comments.

Control and Veto

Legislative control is exercised partially through the expression of intent in statements accompanying the budget bill. The legislature appropriates positions; the DOA maintains rigid position controls. Legislative intent also sets the growth rates for enrollments at the "beginning graduate" and "advanced graduate" levels. The governor has line-item veto authority but cannot reduce items within lines. His veto powers have a marginal impact on action, because it is rarely practical to veto an entire line of the SUSOF appropriation.

MICHIGAN (1974/75)

Formulation of higher education operating budgets in Michigan is characterized by: (1) the considerable autonomy of the institutions; (2) the ambiguity of state agency functions in budget review, resulting from the constitutional status of the public higher education institutions; (3) the uncertain division of responsibilities among the state agencies that review higher education budgets; and (4) the sizable effort of the legislature to monitor campus operations through routine information submissions. Michigan has an annual budget with the fiscal year beginning July 1 (see Figure B.4). The responsible state agencies are as follows.

Executive Branch

The Bureau of the Budget (BOB) in the Department of Management and Budget has a staff of 30, four of whom have responsibility for higher education operating budgets.

FIGURE B.4

Michigan: Higher Education Operating Budget Flow Chart, 1974/75 Budget

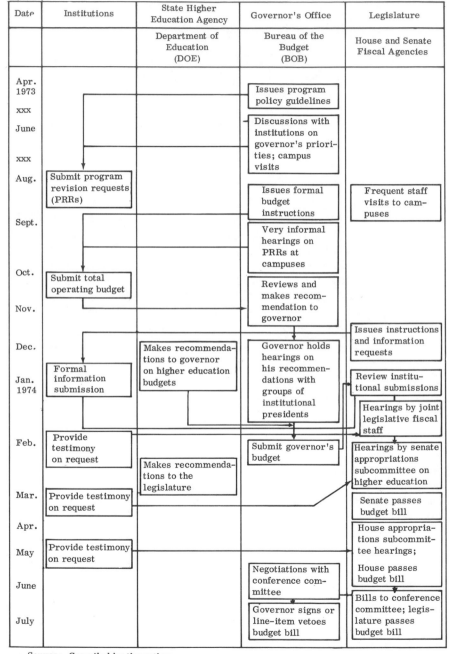

Date	Institutions	State Higher Education Agency	Governor's Office	Legislature
		Department of Education (DOE)	Bureau of the Budget (BOB)	House and Senate Fiscal Agencies
Apr. 1973			Issues program policy guidelines	
xxx				
June			Discussions with institutions on governor's priorities; campus visits	
xxx				
Aug.	Submit program revision requests (PRRs)		Issues formal budget instructions	Frequent staff visits to campuses
Sept.			Very informal hearings on PRRs at campuses	
Oct.	Submit total operating budget		Reviews and makes recommendation to governor	
Nov.				
Dec.		Makes recommendations to governor on higher education budgets	Governor holds hearings on his recommendations with groups of institutional presidents	Issues instructions and information requests
Jan. 1974	Formal information submission			Review institutional submissions
				Hearings by joint legislative fiscal staff
Feb.	Provide testimony on request	Makes recommendations to the legislature	Submit governor's budget	Hearings by senate appropriations subcommittee on higher education
Mar.	Provide testimony on request			Senate passes budget bill
Apr.				House appropriations subcommittee hearings;
May	Provide testimony on request			House passes budget bill
June			Negotiations with conference committee	Bills to conference committee; legislature passes budget bill
July			Governor signs or line-item vetoes budget bill	

Source: Compiled by the author.

Legislative Branch

Each house has a fiscal agency staff that serves its Appropriations Committee. The Senate Fiscal Agency (SFA) has a staff of 12,
two of whom have higher education budget responsibility. The House
Fiscal Agency (HFA) also has a staff of 12, one of whom has such responsibility.

State Higher Education Agency

The Higher Education and Adult Continuing Education Office of
the Department of Education (DOE) has a staff of six, one of whom
has responsibility for higher education operating budgets.

Higher Education Coordination and Governance

The DOE is a coordinating agency with statutory authority for
general planning and coordination of public higher education and for
advising on the financial requirements of higher education institutions. However, a series of court decisions on ambiguous sections
of the 1963 state constitution has resulted in the DOE's actually exer-
cising only a limited coordination role. Each of the 13 four-year colleges and universities has its own governing board, and 29 junior and
community colleges have local governing boards in addition to a single state community college board. The two-year colleges receive
local support but request state funds in essentially the same manner
as the four-year institutions.

Major Elements of the Budget Process

Presubmission Activity

In April the BOB issues to all agencies a set of Program Guidelines (PPGs) that delineate issues and priorities by state program for
the coming budget cycle. The institutions respond by submitting Program Revision Requests (PRRs). These are discussed informally
with the BOB staff prior to the submission of separate base budgets.
In September, shortly before the budget submission is due, the BOB
sends out formal instructions specifying information requirements.
Legislative fiscal staff members make frequent visits to institutions
during August and September.

Budget Requests

Each campus submits a request for state appropriations with the base budget request in WICHE/NCHEMS PCS program format and with the PRRs separately identified. All programs and PRRs are shown by objects of expenditure. The requests are supported with data on enrollments, credit hours, degrees, positions, and salaries. Requests are submitted to the BOB, but are forwarded simultaneously to the DOE and the legislative fiscal staffs. Prior to their own review, legislative fiscal committees have required additional lengthy information submissions from each institution. In fiscal 1975/76, the BOB and the legislative fiscal staffs achieved some coordination of information submissions.

Review and Analysis

The BOB budget review for fiscal 1974/75, begun in October, was incremental and structured by programs. Their review focused on the institutional PRRs, using analyses of costs by object-of-expenditure classification and by fund source. In most instances, base budget requests were approved by the BOB at the level of current year expenditures. Information submitted to the legislative fiscal agencies in January is used principally in preparation of a net state appropriations tracking summary. This summary relates state appropriations to organizational units rather than program structures. The legislative fiscal agencies use this summary as the framework for reviewing institutional base budgets and the budgets for program changes. In preparing its recommendations on financial requirements, the DOE relies on formulas to emphasize equity considerations.

Executive Hearings

The BOB recommendations for individual campuses are usually made known to the institutions in individual hearings with the director of Management and Budget in November. Later the governor meets with the presidents of all institutions in groups of three to five to discuss final recommendations.

Governor's Budget

The governor's budget, submitted in January, displays individual campus recommendations in WICHE/NCHEMS PCS format, with instruction divided into 12 subaggregates of the HEGIS taxonomy and financial aid separated from student services. Explanations of incre-

mental budget changes and of historical enrollment data are included
for each institution. Budget narrative and justification are limited.

Legislative Hearings

Hearings with the president and staff of each of the 44 institutions are held from January through April by both fiscal committees.
Traditionally, the senate originated the higher education budget bills
and held its hearings first. The house worked from bills passed by
the senate and tended to work within the framework established by
senate staff review. For the 1974/75 fiscal year budget, house hearings were moved ahead of the senate hearings, but this practice is
not expected to continue. The BOB and DOE staffs attend these hearings but rarely participate. Appropriation Committee members rely
on issue papers and analyses of alternatives prepared by the staff,
in addition to the tracking summary.

Budget Bill

There are five budget bills for the operating and capital expenditures of public higher education. All are written by the Senate Appropriations Committee. The bill for four-year colleges and universities is in a modified WICHE/NCHEMS PCS program format. Libraries are separated from general support and financial aid is separated from student services, with instruction broken down according
to the organizational structure of the individual campuses rather than
by HEGIS disciplines. The community and junior college bill shows
a lump sum for each campus.

Control and Veto

Control language in the budget bill is extensive, ranging from
information reporting and auditing requirements to authorization of
specific campus programs. Because of the constitutional status of
the institutions, the BOB controls only the total state appropriation
to an institution. The legislature audits expenditures in relation to
the legislative fiscal agency tracking summary, but there are no formal controls over these budget categories. The governor has line-
item veto authority, but cannot reduce lines.

TEXAS (1973-75 Biennium)

Formulation of higher education operating budgets in Texas is
characterized by: (1) the use for over 15 years of designated formulas

FIGURE B.5

Texas: Higher Education Operating Budget Flow Chart, 1973/74 Budget

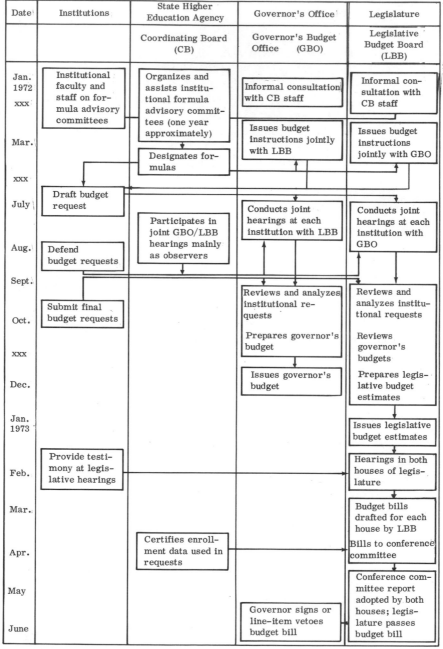

Date	Institutions	State Higher Education Agency	Governor's Office	Legislature
		Coordinating Board (CB)	Governor's Budget Office (GBO)	Legislative Budget Board (LBB)
Jan. 1972 xxx	Institutional faculty and staff on formula advisory committees	Organizes and assists institutional formula advisory committees (one year approximately)	Informal consultation with CB staff	Informal consultation with CB staff
Mar.			Issues budget instructions jointly with LBB	Issues budget instructions jointly with GBO
xxx		Designates formulas		
July	Draft budget request		Conducts joint hearings at each institution with LBB	Conducts joint hearings at each institution with GBO
Aug.	Defend budget requests	Participates in joint GBO/LBB hearings mainly as observers		
Sept.			Reviews and analyzes institutional requests	Reviews and analyzes institutional requests
Oct.	Submit final budget requests		Prepares governor's budget	Reviews governor's budgets
xxx				Prepares legislative budget estimates
Dec.			Issues governor's budget	
Jan. 1973				Issues legislative budget estimates
Feb.	Provide testimony at legislative hearings			Hearings in both houses of legislature
Mar.				Budget bills drafted for each house by LBB
Apr.		Certifies enrollment data used in requests		Bills to conference committee
May				Conference committee report adopted by both houses; legislature passes budget bill
June			Governor signs or line-item vetoes budget bill	

Source: Compiled by the author.

222

that generate about 85 percent of the budget requests of the senior institutions; (2) very close personal and professional relationships among the staffs of the three state agencies with primary budget responsibility; (3) joint executive and legislative staff hearings at institutions on initial requests; and (4) an apparently equal balance of power between the executive and legislative branches. Texas has a biennial budget with a fiscal year beginning September 1 of even-numbered years (see Figure B.5). The responsible state agencies are as follows.

Executive Branch

The Governor's Budget Office (GBO) has a staff of ten, two of whom are responsible for higher education operating budgets.

Legislative Branch

The Legislative Budget Board (LBB) has a staff of 18, three of whom are responsible for higher education operating budgets. The LBB has a Program Evaluation Unit created in 1974, staffed by 11 professionals who are engaged in performance audits, some in the area of higher education.

State Higher Education Agency

The Coordinating Board, Texas College and University System (CB) has a staff of 60, three of whom are responsible for higher education operating budgets.

Higher Education Coordination and Governance

The CB is a coordinating agency with specific and limited budget authority. It is responsible for the designation of detailed and comprehensive formulas by which institutional budget requests are generated. After designation of such formulas, however, it has no formal or structured role in the budget review process. It is responsible for the coordination of 34 four-year colleges and universities and two-year centers (either lower or upper division), governed by 16 governing boards. The University of Texas and Texas A&M multi-campus systems plan a major role in budget formulation at the state-wide level. The CB also coordinates 47 two-year college districts, which receive approximately 60 percent of their support from the state, based on historically derived cost rates for 18 academic programs.

Major Elements of the Budget Process

Presubmission Activity

Budget instructions are issued jointly by the GBO and the LBB in March and include the formulas previously designed by the CB in January. Formulas are developed by some 15 advisory formula study committees, made up of some 115 to 200 institutional representatives and lay citizens, with CB staff liaison. Recommendations of the advisory committees and the CB staff are reviewed and formulas designated at a formal Coordinating Board meeting.

Budget Requests

Campuses submit separate requests, and the identity of each campus remains clear throughout the budget process. First drafts of requests are submitted in July and final requests in October. Requests are submitted to the GBO, LBB, and CB as well, although the CB does not have a formal budget review role following formula designation. Formula computations generate the largest part of the institutional requests, but Special Items usually add needs that fall outside the designated formulas.

GBO and LBB Joint Staff Hearings

Following the submission of first drafts of institutional requests, the GBO and LBB conduct joint hearings at the institutions from July through September. Hearings vary in length, generally lasting a day for major institutions. Hearings focus on the needs of the institutions. Members of the CB staff attend these hearings as observers.

Review and Analysis

The CB staff limits its formal review and analysis to formula study committee recommendations. Although the CB uses institutional role and scope determinations in the review of new academic programs, there is no formal or structured relationship between program approval and operating budget formulation. Programs not approved by the CB cannot be funded. The GBO and LBB rely on the role and scope determinations in analyzing budget requests. The staffs generally use institutional comparisons to revise factors in the designated formulas, and rely on information furnished by the CB staff. The CB is developing an Educational Information Center, based on the extensive data collected for formula use.

Governor's Budget

The governor's budget is submitted in December, prior to legislative hearings. It is functional in form, aggregating institutional requests according to the 11 designated formulas, and separately stating the special items. The governor does not submit a budget bill.

Legislative Hearings

After receiving the governor's budget, the LBB issues Legislative Budget Estimates. Informal consultation with the CB staff may take place during the preparation of these estimates. Beginning in February, institutional budget requests are heard separately by both houses, each institution having approximately 30 minutes to present its request. Hearings focus on the needs of the institutions; special items may be requested for projects not included within the formula structure.

Budget Bill

After hearings, the LBB staff drafts separate budget bills for each house. After passage of bills in each house, differences are resolved by a conference committee, resulting in a single bill for all state services. Institutional appropriations are in functional format, with additional lines for specific objects of expenditure and organizational units.

Control and Veto

Legislative intent and restrictions on transfer are stated in the appropriation bill. Transfers among such items as faculty salaries, libraries, and special items are controlled. The governor has line-item veto authority but cannot reduce appropriations within lines.

NOTES

1. Both previous classifications and the difficulty of classification are discussed by Robert O. Berdahl, Statewide Coordination of Higher Education (Washington, D.C.: American Council on Education, 1971), particularly pp. 23-26.
2. Council of State Governments, Budgeting by the States (Lexington, Ky.: Council of State Governments, 1967), pp. 14-16.
3. Berdahl, Statewide Coordination of Higher Education, p. 72.

4. Allen Schick, Budget Innovation in the States (Washington, D.C.: Brookings Institution, 1971).

5. Robert D. Lee, Jr., and Ronald W. Johnson, Public Budgeting Systems (Baltimore, Md.: University Park Press, 1973), p. 82.

6. Western Interstate Commission on Higher Education/National Center for Higher Education Management Systems, Program Classification System.

BIBLIOGRAPHY

U.S. AND GENERAL COMPARATIVE SOURCES

Altbach, Philip G., ed. 1976. Comparative Higher Education Abroad. New York: International Council for Educational Development.

American Council on Education. 1975. "The Labor Market for College Graduates." Policy Analysis Service Reports 1 (June). Report of a seminar held September 12, 1974.

Bailey, Stephen K. 1975. "Education and the State." In Education and the State, edited by John F. Hughes. Washington, D.C.: American Council on Education.

Bartley, David M. 1975. "The Legislative Organization from a Speaker's Perspective." Public Administration Review, no. 5 (September-October).

Berdahl, Robert O. 1971. Statewide Coordination of Higher Education. Washington, D.C.: American Council on Education.

_____, and George Altomare. 1972. Comparative Higher Education: Sources of Information. New York: International Council for Educational Development, Occasional Paper no. 4.

_____, and Ladislav Cerych. 1975. "Comparative Research on Higher Education in Western Europe: A Selective Report." Draft report for the International Council for Educational Development. Mimeographed.

Bowen, F. M., and L. A. Glenny. 1976. State Fiscal Stringency and Public Higher Education. State Budgeting for Higher Education. Berkeley: Center for Research and Development in Higher Education.

Burn, Barbara. 1971. Higher Education in Nine Countries. New York: McGraw-Hill. Sponsored by the International Council for Educational Development and the Carnegie Commission on Higher Education.

_____. 1973. The Emerging System of Higher Education in Italy. Report of a seminar, International Council for Educational Development, Conference Report no. 1. New York.

Callan, Patrick M. 1975. "Evaluating Planning by Statewide Boards." In Evaluating Statewide Boards, edited by Robert O. Berdahl. San Francisco: Jossey-Bass.

Carnegie Commission on Higher Education. 1971. The Capitol and the Campus. New York: McGraw-Hill.

Center for Research and Development in Higher Education, Berkeley. State Budgeting for Higher Education series.

  1975. Data Digest. By L. A. Glenny, F. M. Bowen, R. J. Meisinger, Jr., Anthony Morgan, R. A. Purves, and F. A. Schmidtlein.

  1976. Information Systems and Technical Analyses. By R. A. Purves and L. A. Glenny.

  1976. Interagency Conflict and Consensus. By L. A. Glenny.

  1976. State Fiscal Stringency and Public Higher Education. By F. M. Bowen and L. A. Glenny.

  1976. The Uses of Formulas. By R. J. Meisinger, Jr.

  1977. The Political Economy of the Budget Process. By F. A. Schmidtlein and L. A. Glenny.

Cerych, Ladislav. 1974. Comparative Higher Education: Relevance for Policy Making. New York: International Council for Educational Development, Occasional Paper no. 10.

_____. 1975. Access and Structure of Postsecondary Education. Paris: European Cultural Foundation Occasional Papers.

Clark, Burton R. 1976. "The Benefits of Disorder." Change 8 (October).

_____. 1977. "Problems of Access in the Context of Academic Structures." Yale Higher Education Program Working Paper YHEP-16, Institution for Social and Policy Studies. New Haven, Conn.: Yale University.

_____. 1978. "The Changing Relations between Higher Education and Government: Some Perspectives from Abroad." Yale

Higher Education Research Group Working Paper YHERG-21,
Institution for Social and Policy Studies. New Haven, Conn.:
Yale University.

Classification of Educational Systems in OECD Member Countries.
1972. Paris: Organization for Economic Cooperation and Development.

Cross, Patricia K. 1971. Beyond the Open Door. San Francisco:
Jossey-Bass.

Downs, Anthony. 1967. Inside Bureaucracy. Boston: Little, Brown.

The Economic Research Institute of the State Planning Committee of
the U.S.S.R. Council of Ministers. 1972. Soviet Planning:
Principles and Techniques. Translated by Leo Lempert. Moscow: Progress.

Entwistle, Noel. 1976. Strategies for Research and Development in
Higher Education. Proceedings of an educational research
symposium at Goteborg, Sweden, September 7-12, 1975. Am-
sterdam: Swets and Zeitlinger.

European Center for Higher Education, ed. 1976. Statistical Study
on Higher Education in Europe 1971-72 and 1972-73. Bucha-
rest: UNESCO-CEPES.

Glenny, L. A. 1976. Interagency Conflict and Consensus. State
Budgeting for Higher Education. Berkeley: Center for Research and Development in Higher Education.

_____, Robert O. Berdahl, Ernest G. Palola, and James G. Paltridge.
1971. Coordinating Higher Education for the '70s. Berkeley:
Center for Research and Development in Higher Education.

_____, F. M. Bowen, R. J. Meisinger, Jr., Anthony Morgan, R. A.
Purves, and F. A. Schmidtlein. 1975. Data Digest. State
Budgeting for Higher Education. Berkeley: Center for Research
and Development in Higher Education.

_____, and Thomas K. Dalglish. 1973. Public Universities, State
Agencies, and the Law. Berkeley: Center for Research and
Development in Higher Education.

Gordon, Margaret S., ed. 1974. Higher Education and the Labor Market. Published for the Carnegie Commission on Higher Education. New York: McGraw-Hill.

Hecquet, Ignace, Christiane Verniers, and Ladislav Cerych. 1976. Recent Student Flows in Higher Education. New York: International Council for Educational Development.

Heidenheimer, Arnold J. 1976. "Major Reforms of the Swedish Education System 1950-1975." Draft report submitted to the World Bank. Mimeographed.

International Studies in Six European Countries: United Kingdom, France, Federal Republic of Germany, the Netherlands, Sweden, Italy. 1976. Report to the Ford Foundation. New York: Ford Foundation.

Landau, M. 1969. "Redundancy, Rationality, and the Problem of Duplication and Overlap." Public Administration Review 29 (July-August).

Lee, Eugene C., and Frank M. Bowen. 1975. Managing Multicampus Systems. San Francisco: Jossey-Bass.

Lee, Robert D., and Ronald W. Johnson. 1973. Public Budgeting Systems. Baltimore: University Park Press.

McConnell, T. R. 1962. A General Pattern for American Public Higher Education. San Francisco: McGraw-Hill.

McGurn, George W. 1974. "A United States View." In Comparative Higher Education, edited by Ladislav Cerych and George W. McGurn. New York: International Council for Education Development, Occasional Paper no. 10.

Meisinger, R. J., Jr. 1976. The Uses of Formulas. State Budgeting for Higher Education. Berkeley: Center for Research and Development in Higher Education.

Millard, Richard M. 1976. State Boards of Higher Education. ERIC/Higher Education Research Report no. 4. Washington, D.C.: American Association for Higher Education.

Najman, Dragoljub. 1974. Le Monde Sans Frontieres. Paris: Fayard.

National Center for Education Statistics. 1977. The Condition of Education 1977, vol. 3, pt. 1. Washington, D.C.: U.S. Government Printing Office.

Noah, Harold, and Max Eckstein. 1969. Towards a Science of Comparative Education. New York: Macmillan.

Paltridge, James G. 1966. California's Coordinating Council for Higher Education: A Study of Organizational Growth and Change. Berkeley: Center for Research and Development in Higher Education, University of California.

_____. 1968. Conflict and Coordination in Higher Education: The Wisconsin Experience. Berkeley: Center for Research and Development in Higher Education, University of California.

Petri, Gunnar. 1976. Functions of the Swedish Ministry of Finance. Stockholm: Ministry of Finance.

Purves, R. A., and L. A. Glenny. 1976. Information Systems and Technical Analyses. State Budgeting for Higher Education. Berkeley: Center for Research and Development in Higher Education.

Richards, Graham. 1977. "America's Contribution to Science." New Scientist, vol. 72.

Ruyle, Janet, and Lyman Glenny. 1976. "State Budgeting for Higher Education: Trends in State Revenue Appropriations, 1968-1975." Berkeley: Center for Research and Development in Higher Education, University of California.

Schick, Alan. 1971. Budget Innovation in the States. Washington, D.C.: The Brookings Institution.

Schlesinger, J. A. 1965. "The Politics of the Executive." In Politice in the American States: A Comparative Analysis, edited by R. Jacob and K. N. Vines. Boston: Little, Brown.

Schmidtlein, F. A., and L. A. Glenny. 1977. The Political Economy of the Budget Process. State Budgeting for Higher Education. Berkeley: Center for Research and Development in Higher Education.

Scott, Peter. 1978. "Britain to 'Rationalize' Its System of Higher Education." The Chronicle of Higher Education, vol. 15 (January 9).

Sharkansky, Ira. 1968. "Agency Requests, Gubernatorial Support, and Budget Success in State Legislatures." American Political Science Review, December.

_____. 1970. The Routines of Politics. New York: Van Nostrand-Reinhold.

Wildavsky, Aaron. 1974. The Politics of the Budgetary Process. 2d ed. Boston: Little, Brown.

U.S. Department of Commerce, Bureau of the Census. 1974. "Social and Economic Characteristics of Students, October 1972." Current Population Reports, Series P-20, no. 260, February.

_____. 1976. "Major Field of Study of College Students, October 1974." Current Population Reports, Series P-20, no. 289, February.

_____. 1978. "Population Estimates by Race, for States: July 1, 1973 and 1975." Current Population Reports, Series P-23, no. 67, February.

_____. 1978. "School Enrollment—Social and Economic Characteristics of Students, October 1976." Current Population Reports, Series P-20, no. 319, February.

Zhamin, V. 1973. Education in the USSR: Its Economy and Structure. Moscow: Novosti Press Agency.

FRANCE

Assemblée Nationale. 1976. Avis présenté Tome VIII Universités, by M. Le Pensec, Deputy. Annex to the verbal discussion of the session of October 12, 1976, no. 2530. Criticisms of the budget of the secretary of state for the universities.

Bienaymé, Alain. 1975. "Le Financement des Universités." La Documentation Française, Paris.

Le Financement des Universités. n.d. Report of the commission that was charged to propose a better system of allocation of funds for the state universities. Paris: Secretariat d'Etat aux Universités.

"Les Difficultés Financières des Universités." 1977. Le Monde, January 26, p. 16.

"L'Université Abandonée." 1976. Le Monde de l'Education, no. 21 (October).

Geiger, Roger L. 1975. "Reform and Restraint in Higher Education: The French Experience, 1965-1974." Yale Higher Education Program Working Paper YHEP-2, Institution for Social and Policy Studies. New Haven, Conn.: Yale University.

_____. 1977. "A Retrospective View of the Second-Cycle Reform in France." Yale Higher Education Research Group Working Paper YHERG-18, Institution for Social and Policy Studies. New Haven, Conn.: Yale University.

Millot, Benoit, and François Orivel. 1976. "L'Allocation des Resources dans l'Enseignement Supérieur." Ph.D. dissertation, Research Institute on the Economics of Education, University of Dijon.

Ministère de l'Education. 1976. Le Compte Economique de l'Education et des Formations. Etudes and Documents no. 34. An annual publication for both basic and higher education.

_____, Department of Computer and Statistical Studies. 1975. "Evolution des Effectifs dans l'Enseignement Supérieur depuis 1960." Etudes and Documents no. 31. Paris: Secrétariat d'Etat aux Universités.

Ministère de l'Education Nationale, Institut National de Recherche et de Documentation Pedagogiques. 1974. Les Etapes de la Recherche.

"Open Admissions—Oui ou Non." 1977. Change, March 1977.

Projet de loi de Finances pour 1977. 1976. Supplementary document, Scientific Research and Technique in France in 1976. Paris: Imprimerie Nationale.

GREECE

Ministry of National Education and Religious Affairs. 1976. Study of Costs of Higher Education. Athens.

National Statistical Service of Greece. Statistical Yearbook, Greece, 1955-76. Athens: Ministry of Education.

ITALY

Chiarante, Giuseppe. 1976. "Communists for the Start of University Reform." A Communist party position paper. Mimeographed.

Clark, Burton R. 1976. "The Structure of Academic Governance in Italy." Yale Higher Education Program Working Paper YHEP-7, Institution for Social and Policy Studies. New Haven, Conn.: Yale University.

Consiglio Nazionale delle Ricerche. 1975. Bilancio di Previsione dell'Esercizio Finanziario 1976. Rome.

_____. 1976. "Relazione del Presidente del C.N.R. Sullo Stato della Ricerca Scientifica e Technologica in Italia per I1 1976." Rome, September.

Francesco, Corrado de. 1977. "The Growth and Crisis of Italian Higher Education during the 1960s and 1970s." Istituto di Sociologia, Università di Milano. Mimeographed.

Istituto Centrale di Statistica (ISTAT). 1976. Annuario Statistico Italiano. Rome: ISTAT.

SWEDEN

Berg, Barbro, and Bertil Ostergren. 1977. Innovations and Innovation Processes in Higher Education. Stockholm: National Board of Universities and Colleges.

Bergendal, Gunnar. 1977. Higher Education and Manpower Planning in Sweden. Contribution to a joint ILO-UNESCO project. Stockholm: National Swedish Board of Universities and Colleges.

Bjorkland, Eskil. 1975. "Research into Higher Education, a Review of Current Swedish Projects (preliminary version). Research Project Group, Stockholm, Office of the Chancellor of the Swedish Universities, June. Mimeographed, 61 pp.

Fredriksson B., and J.-E. Lane. 1978. The Swedish System of Higher Education 1945-1977: An Organizational Approach. Sweden: Liber.

Fredricksson, Bert. 1976. "Regional Boards of Higher Education in Sweden." Umeå University, Department of Political Science. Mimeographed, 10 pp.

Heidenheimer, Arnold J. 1976. Major Reforms of the Swedish Education System 1950-1975. Draft for comment, World Bank. Mimeographed, 102 pp.

Lane, Jan-Erik. 1977. "University Autonomy, a New Analysis." Working Paper no. 6, Center for Administrative Studies. Umeå: Umeå University.

The National Swedish Board of Universities and Colleges. 1976, 1977. R&D for Higher Education. A monthly information series on research and development in postsecondary education. Stockholm.

Ostergren, Bertil. 1975. Planning for Change in Higher Education. Stockholm: Office of the Chancellor of the Swedish Universities.

"Sweden Tests the Future." 1977. Change, August 1977.

"Sweden's Strange New 'Conservatism.'" 1978. U.S. News & World Report, February 20, p. 53.

Swedish Ministry of Education and Cultural Affairs. n.d. "The Reform of Higher Education 1975." Mimeographed, 14 pp.

ABOUT THE EDITOR
AND CONTRIBUTORS

LYMAN A. GLENNY, a political scientist, is professor of education at the University of California, Berkeley; formerly director of that university's Center for Research and Development in Higher Education; formerly Executive Director of the Illinois Board of Higher Education; and a professor of political science. His research and writing encompass the major problems of planning, coordination, and financing of colleges and universities by state and national governments. He has written or contributed to many books and articles on these subjects, the last being <u>Budgeting Higher Education in the States: Interagency Conflict and Consensus</u>. He has consulted for 22 of the state governments in the United States on higher education organization and planning and has offered seminars in five European countries and Australia.

ROSSETOS E. FAKIOLAS, an economist, heads the Population and Labour Force Division, Center of Planning and Economic Research in Athens, Greece. He has written extensively on Greek and other European economic and labor problems through journal articles and four books. He has lectured at several universities in the United Kingdom and conducted research for the Organization for Economic and Cultural Development in Paris.

ALDO GANDIGLIO holds a <u>Laureato</u> in Science Economics and Commerce and is a fellow at GREIS, the Higher Education Research Group of the University of Rome. His research interests focus on the financing and economics of education. He has worked with the Ministry of Public Instruction on several studies on the efficiency of the Italian educational system.

PIERRE CLAUDE GOLDBERG since 1975 has been a consultant to the Division of Higher Education and Research, Secretariat of State for the Universities, Paris, France. He received his master's degree in Applied Economics and is currently working on a doctorate on "Planning of French Higher Education" under the direction of Professors Alain Bienaymé and Jacques Delors, at the University of Paris, Dauphine.

JAN-ERIK LANE is assistant professor of political science, University of Umea, Sweden. He heads the research group at the

Center for Administrative Studies at Umeå. His scholarly work includes research and publications in public administration, comparative politics, and political theory. His current research is on Swedish university organization and his most recent book is University
Autonomy: A New Analysis (1977).

ALBERTO MONCADA is a teacher and researcher at the University of Madrid and Scientific Director of the Moncada-Kajon Foundation. He holds a doctorate in Sociology of Education and Educational Administration. He has held many consultancies with the
Spanish and Peruvian governments and with UNESCO and OECD.
The most recent of his four books is Education and Employment Di-
versification in Postsecondary Education (1977). He has been a visit-
ing scholar at Stanford University and the University of California,
Berkeley.